NEW WAYS OF LIVING THE GOSPEL
Spiritual Traditions in Catholic Education

Edited by
Jim and Therese D'Orsa

THE BROKEN BAY INSTITUTE
MISSION AND EDUCATION SERIES

Published in Australia by
Vaughan Publishing
32 Glenvale Crescent
Mulgrave VIC 3170

Vaughan Publishing
A joint imprint of The Broken Bay Institute and Garratt Publishing

© 2015 Copyright James D'Orsa and Therese D'Orsa
All rights reserved. Except as provided by Australian copyright law,
no part of this publication may be reproduced in any manner
without prior permission in writing from the publisher.

Designed by Cristina Neri, Canary Graphic Design
Cover image – Thinkstock.com

Printed in Australia by McPhersons Printing

Nihil Obstat: Monsignor Gerard Diamond MA (Oxon), LSS, D.Theol
                Diocesan Censor

Imprimatur: Monsignor Greg Bennet
                Vicar General

Date: 10 February 2015

The Nihil Obstat and Imprimatur are official declarations that a book or pamphlet is free of doctrinal or moral error. No implication is contained therein that those who have granted the Nihil Obstat and Imprimatur agree with the contents, opinions or statements expressed. They do not necessarily signify that the work is approved as a basic text for catechetical instruction.

National Library of Australia Cataloguing-in-Publication entry

>   Title: New ways of living the Gospel: spiritual traditions in
>   Catholic education / Jim D'Orsa,
>   Therese D'Orsa, editors.
>
>   ISBN: 9780987306050 (paperback)
>
>   Subjects: Catholic Church--Education--Australia.
>   Catholic schools--Australia.
>   Religious education--Australia.
>   Catholic Church--Doctrines.
>
>   Other Creators/Contributors:
>   D'Orsa, Jim, editor.
>   D'Orsa, Therese, editor.

Dewey Number: 371.071294

COMMENDATION

The way in which we locate ourselves in history has changed. In fact, several writers speak of a change of epoch:

> *The defining aspect of this change of epoch is that things are no longer in their place. Our previous ways of explaining this world and its relationships, good and bad, no longer appears to work. Things we thought would never happen, or that we thought we would never see, we are experiencing now, and we dare not even imagine the future. That which appeared normal to us will probably no longer seem that way. We cannot simply wait for what we are experiencing to pass, under the illusion that things will return to being how they were before.*
> (Pope Francis to priests of Rome, 2013)

In *New Ways of Living the Gospel: Spiritual Traditions in Catholic Education*, the authors have boldly gone to the frontier of this time of liminality, placed a searchlight on our Australian story of charismatic leaders in the past, and probed the present with searching questions. Their searchlight shows how we are building on the spiritual traditions that are a vital element of our Catholic heritage. Various contributors from a sample of religious congregations provide evidence that this is not a self-indulgent nostalgia trip, but a revelation of the ways those charismatic leaders and their religious families rose to the challenges of earlier times, providing Catholic education and particularly in reaching out to those made poor. Theirs is a 'story to enter, a language to speak, a group to belong, a way to pray, a work to undertake and a face of God to see'.

Their probing questions are about the significant endeavours to rebuild the spiritual capital needed to sustain identifiably Catholic school communities. That spiritual capital now resides largely in the lay leaders and teachers who staff our schools. The lived experience of early formation and continuing formation of religious was the key to the influence of these religious. The question posed by one contributor, Bishop David Walker, is do we have a critical mass of mature lay Catholic education leaders? Are we building spiritual leadership density? We could similarly ask are we investing as much energy into formation as we are to buildings and curriculum and school improvement? It is pleasing to see chapters dealing with recent initiatives to energise lay staff in our schools, both at the school level and system level. As the authors observe, such initiatives in a sense chart what God's Spirit has done and point to the possibilities of what God's Spirit can accomplish. The other probing question raised by the authors is that just as leaders in Catholic schools over the past two decades have learned to move their thinking from the operational to the strategic, the challenge of the next decade will be to move from the strategic to the missional.

This text worthily follows earlier texts in this Mission and Education series. Many readers will easily identify with the spiritual traditions they have inherited. The mapping of these and the present 'disturbing' questions will exercise the waking hours of all committed to sustaining and enhancing our spiritual capital in this liminal time.

Tony Whelan,
cfc AM Adjunct Professor Australian Catholic University

DEDICATION

This book honours those pioneering priests who, during the First Era of Catholic Education (1820 to approximately 1870), founded schools for Catholic children across the colonies.

It also celebrates leaders in the Fourth Era of Catholic Education (from approximately 2000 to the present) who are creatively refounding Catholic Education in tumultuous times. It celebrates in particular the dedicated and creative work of Terry Feely (1955-2011), Foundation Principal of St Peter's College Cranbourne.

ACKNOWLEDGEMENTS

Financial Support

Since the inception of the program, the Mission and Education series has received financial support from a number of Catholic Education authorities. Their assistance with research and publication costs is gratefully acknowledged:
- *Queensland* – The Catholic Education Offices of Brisbane, Cairns, Rockhampton, Toowoomba, and Townsville.
- *New South Wales* – The Catholic Education Offices of: Armidale, Broken Bay, Maitland-Newcastle, Parramatta, Sydney, Wagga, Wollongong.
- *Australian Capital Territory* – Catholic Education Office of Canberra-Goulburn.
- *Victoria* – The Catholic Education Offices of Ballarat, Sale and Sandhurst.
- *South Australia* – Catholic Education South Australia (Archdiocese of Adelaide and Diocese of Port Pirie).
- *Tasmania* – The Catholic Education Office Hobart.
- *Northern Territory* – Catholic Education Office Darwin.
- *Religious Congregations* – Good Samaritan Sisters, Marist Brothers (Sydney Province), Marist Brothers National, Edmund Rice Education Australia, De La Salle Brothers.

Advice on aspects of the text

The authors are grateful to the following for their expert advice on aspects of the text: Jim Quillinan, Tony Whelan cfc, Mary Coloe pbvm, Monsignor Tom Doyle. Any errors remain the responsibility of the authors.

Editorial

Ms Kate Ahearne for patiently assisting the authors in finalising the text.

Scripture

Biblical quotations are from the New Revised Standard Version, with the exception of the chapter by Bishop David Walker, in which the Jerusalem Bible is used.

THE BROKEN BAY INSTITUTE MISSION AND EDUCATION SERIES

The Mission and Education publishing project is divided into two series. The *Exploratory Series* seeks to serve leaders in Catholic education. It explores aspects of contemporary Catholic education in the light of the Church's official teaching on mission, and of the experience of those who attempt to embrace this mission in their personal and professional lives. The *Educator's Guide Series* is being prepared specifically for teachers in Catholic schools.

The richness of the resources now at the disposal of those who seek to explore education theologically can come as a surprise. Because the faith held by the Catholic community is a living faith, Catholic Church teaching on mission has developed, and continues to develop, in the light of contemporary societal and cultural changes. Similarly, Scripture continues to yield its treasures. Only now, for example, is the Bible being widely recognised as a witness to God's purpose or mission in the created universe, and as an account of human response to the unfolding of that mission.

We live in a period of rapid cultural change driven by global dynamics. This has its impact on how we understand what knowledge is, how it is acquired, and how schools are best led and organised so as to maximise student learning and the economic and social benefits that are presumed to flow from sound educational policies. Very often the emphasis in such developments shifts from 'the learning student' to the more abstract concept of 'student learning'. This sits uneasily with the concept of a Catholic education.

The consequence of rapid societal change is that, in our time, new areas of mission present themselves with real urgency. It is now clearly necessary to include within the mission agenda both the processes of knowledge construction and meaning-making, and the modes of Christian participation in the new public space created by both globalisation and the communications media. These new areas of mission take their place alongside those fields already familiar to the faith community.

The Mission and Education Series seeks to bring together, in the one conversation, the light that human experience, culture and faith throw on particular topics now central to the future development of Catholic education. It also seeks to honour the significant efforts that Catholic educators make, on behalf of young people, to address the contemporary mission agendas within the total process of education. It provides a forum designed to stimulate further conversation about the 'what' and the 'how' of Catholic education as a work of the Gospel in our complex society and culture.

It is the hope of the Mission and Education Editorial Board that Catholic educators, both in Australia and beyond, will view the series as an invitation to contribute their own creativity to this vital conversation.

Therese D'Orsa
Commissioning Editor
The Broken Bay Institute

Also in this series
Explorers, Guides and Meaning-makers: Mission Theology for Catholic Educators
Catholic Curriculum: A Mission to the Heart of Young People
Leading for Mission: Integrating Life, Culture and Faith in Catholic Education

CONTENTS

1 Scope of the Study   1

PART ONE
HISTORICAL PERSPECTIVES
Introduction to Part 1 9

2 The Message from Tradition   13
3 The Place of the Schools in the Australian Catholic
   Spiritual Journey   23

PART TWO
MISSION AND DISCIPLESHIP IN
THE GOSPEL OF JOHN
Introduction to Part 2 35

4 Mission and the Gospel of John: Reflections on a Unique
   Spiritual Tradition   39

PART THREE
LEADERSHIP BY RELIGIOUS CONGREGATIONS
AND THE LAY MOVEMENTS THEY INSPIRE
Introduction to Part 3 61

5 The Sisters of the Good Samaritan: A Spiritual Tradition
   is Sustained   67
6 The Spiritual Tradition of the Australian Sisters of St Joseph
   in Education in South Australia   81
7 The History, Pedagogy and Spirituality of St Don Bosco –
   Re-imagining and Responding in a New Era   95
8 Spiritual Traditioning: The Mercy of God through the Actions
   of Catherine McAuley   109

9	Educating for Liberation and Possibility – The Edmund Rice Vision for Education Alive Today	121
10	Looking for New Wineskins: The Marist Experience	135
11	The Coming of the Teaching Brothers	149
12	Charism and Mission in the Ignatian Spiritual Tradition	165

PART FOUR
LEADERSHIP – DIOCESAN AND LOCAL
Introduction to Part 4   177

13	Parish Schools Embracing Ignatian Spirituality	183
14	Christian Meditation – A Prayer for our Times	193
15	Cultivating and Sustaining Missionary Discipleship as a Defining Spiritual Element in Broken Bay Catholic Schools	207
16	The Charism of St Peter's – What's in a Name?	221
17	Epilogue: Rebuilding Spiritual Capital	237

1
SCOPE OF THE STUDY

Our Christian understanding is that God is not distant, but rather that God has taken on our human condition and is actively involved in it. This heritage has its origins in the experience of our ancestors in the faith, the Hebrew people, who were sustained by a deep awareness of God's involvement in their history. The heritage was enriched and grounded definitively in God's entering human history in the person of Jesus of Nazareth. Jesus' mission and closeness continues through the mysterious action of God's inspiring and sustaining Spirit at home among Jesus' disciples across time, and also guiding all people of good will, furthering God's purpose in the created universe, including life on this planet.

We are used to thinking about the action of the Holy Spirit within the Church, teaching and guiding. In more recent times, however, Catholic theologians have broadened their understanding and now accept, for example, that God's goodness is reflected in what is good and worthy in all human communities and cultures. God's action is both indirect and direct, hidden as well as discernible.

SPIRITUAL TRADITIONS

'Spirituality' is the word most commonly used to describe the human experience of the transcendent, which is an important component of all cultures and is interpreted within a variety of frameworks. Spiritual traditions are coherent sets of beliefs and practices which have evolved over time as communities make sense of the transcendent and orient individuals, and sometimes whole communities, towards God. There is a rich array of Christian and Catholic spiritual traditions carried by sponsoring faith communities, and recognised by the Church as important resources in assisting people to engage in the spiritual quest or journey that gives meaning and purpose to human life. These traditions have played a role in the emergence of all Catholic cultures.

Spiritual traditions which endure can often be traced back to the ability of charismatic individuals to interpret and articulate their experience of God in a way that is appreciated by and meaningful to their followers. The traditions have served a purpose beyond expressing and explaining personal and communal experience because invariably God calls people to action in the context of human need. Catholic spiritualities have been important in sustaining people in works of mission, often to a heroic degree. The litmus test for any authentic Christian spirituality is the extent to which it carries forward the mission of Jesus to create 'Kingdom spaces' within human contexts.[1] A spiritual tradition will be organised in a way suited to particular cultural or historical settings, and have its characteristic pedagogical expressions, practices and devotions, but to be authentic, it must also be rooted in the Christian faith community and its mission in the world.

In Catholic education, as in other aspects of the Church's ministry, spiritual traditions have developed as a response to the 'signs of the times'. As many of the chapters in this book well illustrate, those that endure are re-shaped and re-expressed as contexts change. The traditions are carried in the stories of particular communities.

The focus of this book is a sample of those spiritual traditions, old and new, that have salience within Catholic schools, and the contribution these make to the fulfilment of Jesus' mission in the twenty-first century cultural tapestry which constitutes the way of life of contemporary Australians. These traditions play an important role in helping to sustain the Catholic identity of the schools by keeping before leaders, and the entire school community, that the enterprise is committed to a spiritual quest that transcends the secular. They serve to shape the mission of the school and the patterns of relationship within and beyond it.

New Ways of Living the Gospel: Creating and Sustaining Spiritual Traditions in Catholic Education represents a snapshot in time of how individual schools and groups of schools go about the task of affirming God's action alive in the life of the school, giving it a unique identity and mission.

---

1   See for example discussion in Jim and Therese D'Orsa, *Leading for Mission: Integrating Life, Culture and Faith in Catholic Education* (Mulgrave: Garratt Publications, 2013), 246-7.

IDENTIFYING AND EXPLORING SPIRITUAL TRADITIONS IN SCHOOLS

The presence of spiritual traditions within Catholic schools raises a number of questions:
- Which traditions have genuine salience for Catholic education today?
- Why have these grown in importance in recent years?
- What is the present form of the tradition?

While space has been a constraint in addressing these questions, we believe the sample of traditions covered in this book illustrates the growing role spiritual traditions play in stabilising the Catholic identity of the schools.

To be meaningful, spiritual traditions have to be consciously articulated and so become cultural expressions. As such, they can be analysed in cultural terms. Such an analysis raises a number of questions:
- What is the narrative of the tradition?
- What mythic elements does the narrative emphasise?
- What values does the tradition honour?
- Have these changed over time, and if so, how and why?
- What are the tradition's main forms of expression among young people today?

Because spiritual traditions shape how Christian life is understood and lived, they are circumscribed by the context in which they emerged. They helped, and in many cases inspired, people to see the Gospel calling them to service in a new way, a way matched to the evident needs of particular contexts. Many of the traditions that developed in the eighteenth and nineteenth centuries, for instance, responded to the needs of unemployed, socially marginalised youth living in degrading conditions in industrial towns, often without aspiration and without hope.

To understand the genesis and trajectory of a tradition, it is important to ask:
- What social context gave rise to the tradition in its original form?
- What aspects of the Gospel message give the tradition its coherence?
- How has the tradition evolved as social conditions have changed?
- How has the sponsoring community changed and what impact has this had on the development of the tradition?

THE ROLE OF RELIGIOUS CONGREGATIONS

Many, but certainly not all, of the spiritual traditions explored in this book have a religious congregation as their sponsoring body. Such groups interpret their spiritual tradition within a theological and ecclesial framework in which the core concept is 'the charism of the founder'. Founders develop a particular emphasis on how they understand God, and what this understanding calls them to do in response to the needs of the time. This is perhaps simply illustrated by Ignatius of Loyola in the spirituality which calls on people 'to see God in all things'. The Holy Spirit is regarded as playing an active role in helping founders see the world with an enthusiasm and vision that attracts followers and enables a community to form which is capable of addressing the mission needs of an era. 'Charism' is a gift to the Church and to the wider society that the community who carry the gift is called upon to serve. It is therefore important, in respect to congregational traditions, to ask:

- How does the congregation understand, articulate and seek to communicate the charism of the group?
- How has this understanding evolved as times and contexts change?
- What forms of witness has the charism given rise to, and what dialogue partners are now seen as essential in sustaining the tradition?

OTHER SPIRITUAL TRADITIONS EMERGE

While spiritual traditions have been largely sponsored by religious congregations, the Holy Spirit is by no means constrained by this historical fact. As the membership of congregations has contracted, as schools have amalgamated, and as new schools with no connections to congregations have been founded, the Spirit continues to act to sustain the spiritual quest for God that is the privilege of every human life and every human community. In some cases this has resulted in schools calling on the richness of multiple spiritual traditions, and in other cases embarking confidently on creating their own tradition, as one of the chapters in the book illustrates. Such a project is not without its pitfalls and there is much to be learned from the experiences of those engaged in them. What is clear in each case is that the adoption of a spiritual tradition, either through historical connection or conscious choice, provides a means to help leaders evangelise not only the students, but also the school's culture. A spiritual tradition provides school leaders with a coherent way to proclaim the Gospel that brings together the three components of authentic mission – word, witness and dialogue.

When it comes to mission, a school does not act on its own in today's world; it requires dialogue partners to be effective. So it is necessary to ask:
- Who do school leaders recognise as necessary dialogue partners in achieving the school's mission?

- How does it seek to engage them?
- What do the dialogue partners bring to the table?
- What does the school leadership learn from its dialogue partners, and what do they, in turn, learn from the school leadership?

Spiritual traditions have a theological content that is used to make sense of the human experience of God at work in the lives of individuals and groups. They also have a unique way of expressing this understanding in practices and devotions. Some spiritual traditions are understood principally in terms of these.

To understand the tradition, it is necessary to ask:
- What religious practices/devotions are integral to the tradition?
- How have these evolved over time?
- What have been the principal drivers of this change?

Finally, spiritual traditions provide an important means in evangelising students and school cultures. If the Holy Spirit is active in the life of the school, which is what our faith tells us, then there must be some evidence of this, which raises a final set of questions:
- What are some of the important impacts that the school's spiritual tradition has on students? teachers? parents?
- What positive impact does the spiritual tradition have on school culture?

THE MANDATE ACCEPTED BY THE CONTRIBUTORS TO THIS STUDY

The various contributors to this 'snapshot in time' were asked to explore what is happening in their school or system of schools in light of the questions raised above. The experiences set out in the chapters that follow provide examples, options, and some warning signals. They chart a willingness to explore the Gospel in our time, and a willingness to discern where in the context of human need and human aspiration 'Kingdom spaces' can be created.

STRUCTURE OF THE BOOK

The book is set out in four parts.

Following the Introduction, Part 1 focuses on matters historical. Bishop Walker outlines aspects of the historical development of Christian spirituality, so setting a context for the discussions that follow. Jim and Therese D'Orsa provide, in broad brush strokes, elements of the narrative of spiritual traditions as these have emerged in Catholic education in Australia.

They do this from the perspective of participant-observers.

In Part II the emphasis is scriptural. Discipleship is a major theme in all Christian spirituality, and this finds a much-loved articulation and theological warrant in the Gospel of John. Therese D'Orsa explores this Gospel as a gift capable of sustaining mission.

Part III looks at how spiritual traditions operate in a sample of congregational schools. This sample illustrates the way in which spiritual traditions help anchor the leadership, mission and Catholic identity of these schools. The congregational traditions featured in Part III are those of the Good Samaritan Sisters, Sisters of St Joseph, Salesians, Mercy Sisters, Christian Brothers, Marist Brothers, De La Salle Brothers and Jesuits.

Part IV provides examples of where three diocesan school systems and a regional Catholic college have set out to sponsor a spiritual tradition appropriate to their needs. In the case of the Diocese of Broken Bay, the spirituality centres on the notion of discipleship with the school system working within a framework developed with the Bishop for the Diocese as a whole. In the second, the Diocese of Townsville's Catholic school system has adopted a spiritual tradition of meditation based on the work of the Benedictine, John Main. The school system in the Diocese of Lismore has adopted the spirituality pioneered by St Ignatius of Loyola in pursuing its development of teachers for the Catholic schools of the diocese. Finally, St Peter's College Cranbourne has developed, since its inauguration under the founding principal, Terry Feely, a spirituality based on the person of St Peter, as we know him from the Gospels.

Because spiritual traditions help people make sense of their experience of God, both as individuals and as communities, they operate within the ambit of mystery, and an element of ambiguity. It is not uncommon to hear critics of the promotion of particular spiritual traditions claim that teachers and students seem to know more about Marcellin Champagnat, Mary MacKillop or Edmund Rice, than they do about Jesus. The fact is, however, that at a certain point in a young person's religious development, such heroic figures play an important role in mediating what being a follower of Jesus can mean, and the relevance and shape of participation in God's mission. The Holy Spirit is especially active in shaping human aspiration. This is a fundamental tenet of Ignatian spirituality and a theme in other traditions. Heroic figures mediate Jesus and his mission to young people and are an important resource in living a full Christian life.

The founders of congregations, in their own way, embarked on a mission to the marginalised, inspired by their reading of the Gospel. In doing so they often redefined the patterns of Christian life, revitalising the Church and creating hope for the people they worked with. This combination of spirituality, vision and action drew other people to them, companions who shared their aspiration and eventually their mission. This is a dynamic of the Spirit, and there is no reason to believe that the Spirit is not as much at work in the world today as when these heroes of the past were inspired. The forms that the work of the Holy Spirit takes, as Part IV illustrates, may be different from the past, but Catholic educational leaders and sponsors can be confident that the Holy Spirit is still active. Developing and sustaining spiritual traditions remains a major challenge for those leading and sponsoring Catholic schools. From Gospel times until now, such traditions have been most effective vehicles of God's mission.

Part One
HISTORICAL PERSPECTIVES

Charism...
a story to enter,
a language to speak,
a group to which to belong,
a way to pray,
a work to undertake,
a face of God to see.

(CLAUDE MARÉCHAL)

David Walker

Ordained Bishop for the Catholic Diocese of Broken Bay in 1996, Bishop Emeritus David Walker served as chief pastor until his retirement in November 2013. He remains deeply committed to the promotion of a truly Australian spirituality and to furthering serious theological study and adult faith formation. During his time as priest and bishop, David founded the Catholic Correspondence Centre, the Centre for Christian Spirituality and The Broken Bay Institute. He is distinguished as a speaker and writer in areas of faith renewal, spirituality, mysticism, formation of clergy and Church leadership. Bishop David most recently served as Chair of the Australian Catholic Bishops' Commission for Church Ministry. His promotion of *lectio divina* through new media has taken the Word of God into the hearts and homes of people in Australia and beyond.

2

THE MESSAGE FROM TRADITION

David Walker

Tradition is an important source of our understanding of the journey to God. The Scriptures offer us the basic mystery of our faith, but each age dialogues with the Scriptures, reflects on them and draws new insights and inspirations from them. Tradition is the sum total of that reflection on, and dialogue with, the Scriptures carried out over the centuries of the life of the Church. In every age, Christian life is to be lived in terms of what it has received from the Scriptures and the Church's reflection on them and the issues of the particular age. This is not an intellectual process but a life process. We can look back and see this taking place in our history, and learn about the process which is just as essential for us today as it was then.

The proclamation of our faith requires faithfulness to the tradition, to the message given to us, and faithfulness to the present, to the people to whom we preach it. This openness to past and present is the appropriate and necessary attitude that we must bring to the journey to God and the ministries associated with it. It can be easy to be faithful to the message, but contain it within past formulations that are not meaningful to the present age. In all of the Church's reaching out to the needs of the times, the same mistake can take place. On the other hand, the needs of the age can perhaps cause us to distort our message to meet those needs. This too is a mistake that we can make in every age. *What is important is the balance of past and present, of tradition and today, of the message and the need.*

When pressure of work caused the Apostles to appoint deacons to do some of the work, they did so in order that they could devote themselves to 'prayer and the preaching of the Word' (Acts 6:4). This comment offers an insight into the lives of the apostle: their role is not just to preach the word, but to lead a life of prayer. There is a bond here between the external actions that they perform and their interior lives of prayer. They need to make their own in their hearts what they are proclaiming to others.

From the beginning, the Church reached out in many ways to the needs of the times. But it was meant to be done from a life of prayer. Throughout our tradition, this same inseparable bond between external action and interior life is borne out. It is not the purpose of this article to explore in detail the tradition. The task is to point to the *close connection between Christian action and the heart from which it flows,* and particularly the connection between Catholic education and the interior life from which it proceeds.

In the century following Jesus, it was the various ministers of the Church who provided formation in the faith. Their roles were not yet clearly defined, but teaching seems to have been a role shared by many of them. Gradually the bishop came to be seen as the key teacher. Controversy occurred as the understanding of fundamental beliefs was hammered out. The School of Alexandria emerged as the first formal centre of learning and was distinguished by such teachers as Clement of Alexandria and Origen. Origen transformed the traditional learning style which was centred round the classics, by substituting for them the Scriptures. In his writing, he developed an understanding of the inner life, which was an important part of his teaching. The great bishops who followed him, Athanasius, Basil, Gregory of Nazianzus, Gregory of Nyssa, and Augustine, developed further an understanding of the inner life.

It was the Desert Fathers of Egypt, and those influenced by them, who developed further the Catholic teaching on the inner life. From them emerged the great monastic tradition which was founded on a commitment to the inner life: to shape the heart of the monk after the teaching of the Gospels and embrace Christ as the example for their lives. The monastic movement played a large part in the development of knowledge, both human and supernatural. Much learning took place within the monasteries of both men and women. There was no real distinction between what was human and what was divine. The interior life of the monks brought together all of knowledge within the framework of God.

The cathedral schools that emerged also played a part as education went beyond the monasteries, but the same perspective of the divine pervaded what was being done. When universities emerged there began to be a split between the human and the divine, but there were many Catholic universities where the common vision remained. In the thirteenth century, the Friars emerged as wandering preachers, but soon became involved in education, and the Dominicans and the Augustinians particularly were involved in scholarly pursuits. The motto of St Dominic's followers, 'handing on to others the fruit of our contemplation' (*Contemplata aliis tradere*), brings to mind what was said of the apostles and captures the spirit not only of his followers, but of those who went before him.

An important movement emerged in the fourteenth–fifteenth century to confront the immoral living of the popes, cardinals, bishops, priests and religious. It was the Devotio Moderna (Modern Devotion), an intentionally lay movement. It is probably the most influential lay movement in the history of the Church; it exercised a significant influence in the European Church in the century prior to the Protestant reformation. Its practitioners drew the attention of John Gerson, one of the most important spiritual and educational figures of that age. Gerson and the Modern Devotion came together around an emphasis on two things: the interior life and education.

In the sixteenth century, there began the formation of the religious congregations of men and women who would take up more explicitly the education of young people. The founders of these congregations were great Christians and demanded of their followers a deep interior life. These congregations have carried on their mission to our present day, in education and other needs of the world around them. As religious congregations, prayer was an important part of their life and ministry.

As we look back at our tradition, it is clear that education was normally carried out within a context of deep faith, by people deeply committed to God. Many of these figures have been canonised, and even those not canonised are held in great respect for their holiness. We remember them not just as educators, but as models of how to live our faith and how to perform the ministries that flow from it. Education has been carried out by those who saw the important relationship between faith and their ministry. The environment of education was determined by the faith of those who carried it out. I believe these people were driven rather than drawn: driven by their love of God rather than just by the need of the day. They saw Jesus coming to them in the person of those in need. The way the Church reaches out to the needs of a present age will change, but the grounding of its ministry in the inner life will not change.

The interior life, then, has been closely associated with education within our Catholic tradition. However, what does this expression 'Interior Life' mean? It will be helpful first to consider the exterior aspect of our Christian life in order to appreciate its interior aspect. This exterior aspect embraces many things. It includes the visible, observable elements of our Christian life: keeping the Ten Commandments, observing the laws of the Church, celebrating the Liturgy of the Church, devotional practices, the fulfilment of our duties in life, apostolic activity, acts of mercy and charity. For religious it can be observing the rules and constitution of their congregation; for clergy the fulfilment of their duties as bishops, priests, or deacons. We often make judgements about believers by these external signs of their faith, their Christian *appearance*. However, we see only the exterior, but God sees the interior: the intention and motivations of these actions. These external actions do not always give us the real picture.

There are some who do not progress in the Christian life beyond the externals. They sometimes are not only unaware of the interior life, but also can be unsympathetic to it. Sometimes those with little faith may have human skills that are important to the Christian community. They assume an important role and exercise a significant influence and can therefore influence the community to focus more on external things, than on its interior aspect.

St Paul bears witness to the interior struggle which lies at the core of the interior life. He bears witness to an experience that all human beings must be aware of: an interior conflict in which we must engage to live as we choose to live.

> *The Law, of course, as we all know, is spiritual; but I am unspiritual: I have been sold as a slave to sin. I cannot understand my own behaviour. I fail to carry out the things I want to do, and I find myself doing the very things I hate… for though the will to do what is good is in me, the performance is not, with the result that instead of doing the good things I want to do, I carry out the sinful things I do not want. … In fact, this seems to be the rule, that every single time I want to do good it is something evil that comes to hand. In my inmost self I dearly love God's Law, but I can see that my body follows a different law that battles against the law which my reason dictates.*[2]

Many authors in our tradition have reflected on the interior life. Let us consider a few definitions or descriptions of it, and then draw some conclusions. Dom Jean-Baptiste Chautard OCSO defines the interior life as 'the state of activity of a soul which strives against its natural inclinations in order to REGULATE them, and endeavours to acquire the HABIT of judging and directing its movements IN ALL THINGS according to the light of the Gospel and the example of Our Lord' (author's emphasis).[3] In another place he says, 'The life of action ought to flow from the contemplative life, to interpret it and extend it, outside oneself, though at the same time being detached from it as little as possible.'[4]

He points to the close relationship of the two aspects of our lives, though it is clearly the transformation of the heart that gives meaning to the actions that we perform. He makes it clear that the interior life is not the enemy of the active life, so that one avoids the latter. Rather, it is an essential

---

2 Rom 7:14-25
3 Jean-Baptiste Chautard, *The Soul of the Apostolate* (Illinois: Tan Books, 1974), 13.
4 Ibid, 52.

expression which the interior life is meant to have. The purpose of the endeavour is to centre one's life around Jesus and live as he lived.

A similar insight comes from Fr Louis Lallemont S.J. 'The interior life consists in two sorts of acts, viz., in thoughts and affections… Our thoughts, says St Bernard, ought to be ever following after truth, and our affection ever abiding in the fervour of charity. In this manner, our mind and heart being closely applied to God, being fully possessed by God, in the very midst of exterior occupations we never lose sight of him, and are always engaged in the exercise of his love… The essence of the spiritual and interior life consists in two things: on the one hand, in the operations of God in the soul, in the lights that illumine the understanding, and the inspirations that affect the will; on the other, in the cooperation of the soul with lights and movements of grace.'[5]

This teaching is taken up in the *Catechism of the Catholic Church*. 'Great is the mystery of our faith. The Church professes this mystery in the Apostles Creed (part 1) and celebrates it in the sacramental liturgy (part 2), so that the life of the faithful may be conformed to Christ in the Holy Spirit to the glory of God the Father (part 3). This mystery, then, requires that the faithful believe in it, that they celebrate it, and that they live from it in a vital and personal relationship with the living and true God. This relationship is prayer (part 4)'.[6] It is the interior life of prayer that is the key to the appreciation of the external aspect of our Christian life.

The fruit of working with our interior life is that our thoughts are centred on God and our affections are free of temporary desires and focused on the desire to do all for the glory of God. In the midst of external actions one can still be aware of God, and direct one's actions to the glory of God. We need to respond to God's grace by working with our thoughts and affections to ensure they cooperate with the grace of God which inspires them. The *Imitation of Christ* sums it up well by saying that our intention must be only to please God, and that our affection must be purified of all things. 'By two wings is a man lifted above earthly things, viz., by simplicity and purity. Simplicity must be in the intention. Purity in the affection.'[7]

Our tradition makes a distinction between the natural and the supernatural. One person can be motivated by human intentions, responding to the revelation of God in creation. Another can be motivated by faith in Jesus, which is a response to God's revelation in the Incarnation. It is the latter that we find in the great social reformers and educators of our tradition. Many founded religious orders to carry on this work at the supernatural level. Some did not found religious orders, but demanded of their followers

---

5 Allan G. McDougall (ed.), *The Spiritual Doctrine of Father Louis Lallemant of the Society of Jesus* (Maryland: The Newman Press, 1955), 180-181.
6 *Catechism of the Catholic Church* (Homebush: St Pauls, 1994), #2558, 613.
7 Thomas à Kempis, *Imitation of Christ* (Leeds: Laverty and Sons, 1951), Book 2 Ch 4, 110-111.

a maturity of faith that could preserve what they had begun. It was not just a good human work that was being passed on, but a deep faith response to recognising in these people the presence of the Lord. Their social or educational ministry was exercised within the context of a deep faith.

The natural needs to be infused with divine charity, and this brings about a transformation that affects all that is done. When the supernatural is lacking, good things can be done, but they do not necessarily focus on the faith of the enterprise. People acting from natural motives may focus on the quality of education, the physical means necessary for it, and raising money to achieve it. But the supernatural elements can be lost. It may be the best educational establishment in the society, but it is not necessarily a faith school. That requires something completely different – an environment that fosters a commitment to Jesus, one set by those who have such a deep commitment.

It is people who create the ethos of the school, and if it is to be a Catholic ethos, then it is mature Catholic believers who set the tone. An institution is really Catholic when there is a critical mass of staff who are mature in their faith. By a critical mass I mean enough to ensure that the faith dimension is the focus of the whole endeavour. These are the key persons in the institutions. It is not to play down the need for other aspects necessary to achieve educational goals, but to say that these easily take over, because they are so obviously necessary. An educational enterprise can reach levels of excellence without faith, but we learn from our tradition that it is the mature faith context that is the key to Catholic education. Nothing else can substitute for this requirement.

Over the past few decades a significant change has taken place in Catholic education. It has been the movement from educational institutes conducted by religious congregations, with the whole staff, or most of them, being religious, to educational institutes that are staffed exclusively by the lay faithful. When religious staffed the schools, every member of the staff was a person committed to living their life in a way that was directed to deep union with the Lord. It would be an exaggeration to say that every religious lived up to this, because not all responded to the spiritual environment that was meant to achieve this goal. However, I am sure that the majority exercised their ministry within the framework of a deep love of God. In our present situation, it is often the case that there would be fewer rather than more staff dedicated to this deep union. This is not to say that lay teachers cannot reach the deep union with Jesus that religious bore witness to. However, to do that they have to develop their faith life using the means that are necessary to achieve it. Often lay teachers are people of faith, though in many cases it is a faith that is not practised. Even when faith is practised on an external level, the depth of interior life, which requires a deep commitment of one's whole life, is often not present.

There is no doubt that a deeply committed lay person, strongly committed to close union with the Lord and perseveringly working to meet the challenges that are necessary to achieve it, can take up the ministries of a similarly committed religious and carry them out as effectively. However the issue here is not whether the person is lay or religious, but *rather the nature of their commitment* and how they have met and are meeting the challenges necessary to pursue it. *The call to holiness is for all believers and can be achieved in any Christian way of life.* However, the way of life is merely the framework within which the person needs to do what is necessary to plumb the depths of this holiness. The interior journey is the same for all believers. It is the choice to transform the heart that makes the difference. Baptism offers us this potential, but we have to realise it by working with grace to transform ourselves to be worthy and intimate disciples of Jesus.

The Church *presumed* that the core of the religious and clerical calling was the interior life, but did not extend that presumption to the lay faithful. As a consequence the latter were not challenged sufficiently to develop a deep interior life, and indeed were not offered the sort of assistance given to priests and religious. The Church demanded of religious and clergy a long period of preparation and a definite lifestyle. It did not do as much for the lay faithful. This affected their image of themselves as disciples of Jesus. I recall working with a parish pastoral council where none could identify with the word 'holiness' and could only attribute it to the religious or clergy. This does not mean that some lay faithful did not come to a maturity of faith. However, they did it more on their own initiative rather than with strong support of the Church. How could we have thought that the lay faithful, whose mission is to be the face of the Church to the world, did not need a deep intimate union with Jesus?

I once heard a story that stemmed from fourth century Egypt when many thousands of believers went there to live their Christian lives in a way similar to the early church. It was an early stage of the later monastic living. One monk wanted to know who was the humblest, and therefore the most holy, person in Egypt. He asked the Lord, who told him that the next person to knock on his door was the humblest, holiest person in Egypt. When the knock came he rushed to the door to find out which monk it was, only to find it was the man from the village delivering the bread. It was not a monk at all. The message to the monks was that holiness was not just the preserve of the monks. This was not a lesson that the Church learned easily because for almost up to our times the lay faithful were not associated with holiness, at least in their own minds. It was Vatican Council II that definitively declared that holiness is for all. This message has still not been widely spread among the lay faithful. There is an urgent need for the Church to address this.

I believe the challenge for today is to make the lay faithful aware of their call to deep holiness and to provide them with the means to help them. The Second Vatican Council, in its declaration that holiness was for all, ended any doubts that the lay faithful are called to holiness.[8] But there are still many who live the *limited Christianity* that was preached to them in the past. Much renewal today centres around deeper study: diplomas and degrees in religious subjects. However, this intellectual emphasis, while important, will not achieve the required goal. It is the heart of the faithful that needs to be targeted, their will to deepen their relationship with Jesus. This requires a different methodology, at a time when many of our leaders may not have been equipped to relate to the lay faithful in this way.

Knowledge has an important part to play in the development of the interior life. However, we need to make a distinction between knowledge that comes through study and a knowledge that we come to through experience. It is one thing to study the nature and essential issues of marriage; another to be married and know what it is at first hand. It is one thing to study the Scripture and another to experience it through *lectio divina*. It is one thing to study the nature of the Christian life, and another to live it. In our current situation there is plenty of opportunity to study the realities of our faith. There is less opportunity to form the lay faithful in the experience of those realities, through the development of their interior life. We need to focus more on their will than their intellect.

The great need for Catholic education, and other Catholic activities, is to deepen the interior life of those who are involved in these ministries. This is said to be the age of the lay faithful. The lay faithful will not be able to bear the burden placed on them unless they are challenged to lead a deep interior life and given the support necessary for them to do so.

---

8 *Lumen Gentium* Ch 5. 'The Universal Call to Holiness in the Church'.

Therese D'Orsa

Therese D'Orsa is a Catholic missiologist and educational leader who has taught in primary, secondary and tertiary settings. She has exercised a wide range of leadership roles in Catholic education systems, including that of Director of Catholic Education (Sale) and Director of Religious Education (Sydney). Therese has taught in several tertiary institutions and is currently Conjoint Professor of the University of Newcastle and The Broken Bay Institute, a research associate of the Melbourne University of Divinity, and an honorary fellow of Australian Catholic University. Therese has published widely across her career and, with her husband Jim, has co-authored several books focused at the interface of missiology and education.

Jim D'Orsa

Dr Jim D'Orsa's contributions to Catholic education include teaching and senior leadership in Catholic schools and systems. He pioneered the preparation of lay leaders to take responsibility for the vision and mission of colleges, and has extensive experience in reviewing large systems and in pastoral planning. Jim is currently senior lecturer at The Broken Bay Institute and a research associate of the Melbourne University of Divinity. His community involvements include governance responsibilities on the Board of the Yarra Institute for Religion and Social Policy. Recent publications include four books integrating missiology and education (with his wife Therese), and with Bishop Hilton Deakin a book on the Catholic Church and the recent struggles of the East Timorese people.

3

THE PLACE OF THE SCHOOLS IN THE AUSTRALIAN CATHOLIC SPIRITUAL JOURNEY

Jim and Therese D'Orsa

Catholic schools in Australia today represent a particular blessing to the Church and to the wider society. At a time when Catholics have lost a good deal of faith in institutional Church leadership, Church teaching, and the parish system, they have retained faith in the Catholic school, where numbers continue to grow. While the Church, as a community of faith, will 'bounce back' from present crises, which pale into insignificance when judged against the scale of others faced in the history of Catholicism, those leading Catholic schools have to deal with the constraints and opportunities embedded in the contemporary situation, and frame the mission of the schools in response to it. This often requires a new way of thinking about the mission and place of the school within the Catholic community. How leaders do this will determine in large part how quickly, and in what direction, any 'rebound' will take.

IDENTITY OF CATHOLIC INSTITUTIONS

At the present time, within Catholic institutions, much attention is being focused on their identity as 'Catholic'. This is certainly not a new situation in Catholic school education. Similar identity crises occurred in the 1870s and the 1970s. The first saw the emergence of Catholic schools as we came to know them for almost a century, while the second occurred as lay people increasingly replaced religious, first as teachers in Catholic schools, and later as school leaders.

In Australia we are fortunate that the conversation about 'Catholic identity' is still an active one and a source of real energy. In many parts of the developed world the secularisation process has proceeded to the point where Catholic schools have simply been absorbed into the public system (as in parts of Europe) or struggle to survive financially (as in the US).

Australian Catholic schools are, as the NSW Catholic Bishops pointed out in 2007, 'at a crossroads'[1] – a place where choices with fairly dramatic consequences have to be made, and where consensus has to be built rather than assumed. The NSW Bishops clearly indicated that the narrative of Catholic education in this country has reached the end of one chapter and the beginning of another. Catholic educators would seem to proceed at their peril if they lose sight of earlier chapters in the narrative of Catholic schooling, and the way these have reflected changes occurring in Australian society, particularly over the past five or six decades. Many of the contributors to this book have lived through these changes and have come to see the developments within the broader context of the *Australian Catholic spiritual journey*. To discuss the issue of identity without taking note of this journey is simply to fish in a dry pond.

While important aspects of the narrative of Catholic education have been taken up elsewhere in the Mission and Education series,[2] it is worth detailing something of the spiritual journey that underpins this story and its impact on how Catholics see the world at the present time. This changing worldview determines the importance people place on Catholic schooling. Put another way, it will be helpful to contextualise the various contributions that follow, since these represent a snapshot in time of what Catholic school leaders are attempting to achieve in reinforcing the spiritual dimension of Catholic education in the face of rapidly advancing secularisation, de-traditionalisation[3] and aggressive secularism.[4]

---

1 Bishops of New South Wales and ACT, *Catholic Schools at a Crossroads*, 2007, http://www.cecnsw.catholic.edu.au/db_uploads/catholic-schools-at-a-crossroads.pdf
2 Jim and Therese D'Orsa, *Leading for Mission* (Melbourne: Vaughan Publishing, 2013).
3 'De-traditionalising' is an attitude that discounts the relevance in past experience. De-traditionalised people live only in the present.
4 Secularism is a view of the world which holds that religion is a phenomenon associated with an earlier period of human development and should now have no place in how society organises itself. It can assume a variety of forms from benign to bitterly anti-religious. 'Secularism' is to be distinguished from secularisation that denotes the gradual assumption by government of service areas once delegated to the churches. The process does not seek to exclude the role churches play in public life, but places limits on their participation, for example through controlling the financial support offered them and the legal constraints imposed on their participation. A second and very positive aspect of secularisation is the creation of a freely accessed public 'space' where people of goodwill who hold a variety of religious or ideological views can interact in a respectful manner in contributing to the building up of the social fabric.

CONTEXTUALISING THE PRESENT CHALLENGES

If we journey back within the memory of the present authors, we arrive at the Church of the late 1940s and 1950s where there was a nexus between Catholic families, the parish, the presbytery, the convent/monastery, and the school. The level of integration was such that it was possible for a young person to grow up in a predominantly Catholic environment. In this historical context the Catholic school was integral to the functioning of the Catholic cultural system, a largely closed world in which Catholics mainly associated with and married other Catholics. It was a world in which the clergy had a highly respected place as teachers and sources of moral wisdom. The spirituality of the era saw an extraordinary emphasis placed on rules and on doing one's duty. The spirituality of ordinary Catholics is summed up in the often-quoted maxim – 'the proper role of lay Catholics was to pray, pay and obey'. The era was far from a golden age of faith, as it is sometimes depicted, as most Catholics were treated as spiritual children.

Catholic schools reinforced the prevailing Catholic worldview and its associated notion of what 'being Catholic' meant. However, the schools also served another purpose, helping young Catholics break out of the social ghetto into which they had been trapped by poverty in the pre-World War II years. Catholic schools were valued not least because they created life chances. This project was much encouraged by Church leaders such as the dominant and highly influential Archbishop of Melbourne, Daniel Mannix. Mannix helped create a Catholic political elite centred in the trade union movement and a Catholic academic elite based in Melbourne University. He was also instrumental in the development of Catholic secondary schooling in Melbourne as were other bishops elsewhere. Archbishops Mannix of Melbourne and James Carroll of Sydney both figured significantly on the country's political stage, albeit in different ways and using different strategies. Mannix's political agenda was not overtly focused on education, but it had implications in terms of impact. Carroll's agenda was more direct in terms of education, but for both of them, as for their fellow bishops, Catholic schools were worth working and fighting for.

Across Australia in the 1960s and 1970s, the children of migrants and poor Catholics gradually moved up the social scale when, as a result of their education, significant numbers were employed in the police force and the public service. At the time, as in earlier decades, Catholics found it difficult to make progress in other sectors of public life where Masonic influence was still strong.

Throughout this era, the spiritual journey of Australian Catholics is best characterised as highly devotional and Church-centred. The focus was on what Bishop David Walker in the previous chapter calls the 'exterior' dimension of Christian life. This found expression in particular practices such as saying the family rosary, benediction, parish missions, Eucharistic festivals, rosary crusades, and so on. The devotional life of the parish complemented its social life and was sustained by various sodalities such as the Children of Mary, the Legion of Mary, the Catholic Young Men's Society (CYMS) and the Young Christian Workers (YCW). Catholic drama clubs and walking clubs were also quite common. In Catholic schools, the 1950s and 1960s was the heyday of the Young Christian Students' movement (YCS). For the majority of Catholics, the Mass was understood as a faithfully-attended devotion, and Sunday Mass attendance was the principal marker of their Catholic identity. In this era the 'inner dimension' of Christian life was viewed as the preserve of clergy and religious and the result of extended 'formation' programs. The religious life of ordinary Catholics centred around duty and obligation and little emphasis was given to the experience of God in their lives.

Australian Catholics' understanding of what 'being Catholic' meant owed a good deal to the worldview of Church leaders who were Irish, or strongly influenced by developments in the Church there. Catholics did indeed have 'a story to belong to', and it was one with Irish overtones. As Catholics advanced up the social ladder in this country, a new story emerged, and the older story became less and less relevant to the prevailing experience. Australian Catholics began to question a way of 'being Catholic' that seemed locked into an Anglo-Irish narrative.

This model of Church also came under threat in the 1950s and 1960s with the arrival of significant numbers of Catholics from southern Europe, and in the 1970s from Eastern Europe and the Middle East These brought with them a different 'story to belong to' and, associated with this, their own way of 'being Catholic'. Many found the Anglo-Irish model of Church rather like 'soup without salt'.[5] The new arrivals, sensing that education was the path to opportunity, sent their children to Catholic schools in large numbers. This created something of a spiritual schizophrenia at the time, since the new arrivals did not follow the Anglo-Irish model of being Church and gave their own cultural forms to 'being Catholic'. This also challenged the predominant spiritual model – many migrants, for example, treating the practice of attending Mass every Sunday as optional.

---

5 This is the title of a monograph written by the Scalabrinian priest, Fr Adrian Pittarello. It was probably the first attempt in Australia to explore the need for Church leaders to take into account the multi-cultural nature of the Church, and challenged some of the assumptions underpinning the Anglo-Irish model of 'being Catholic'. Adrian Pittarello, *Soup Without Salt: The Australian Catholic Church and the Italian Migrant* (Sydney: CMS, 1980).

In the 1960s the arrival of migrants in large numbers in Catholic schools created a management crisis in secondary education, one which amplified an existing crisis in the development of education more broadly as Australia shifted economic gears. Catholics who had been viewed as a minority suddenly became a very influential political grouping who complained about the injustice of funding two school systems – the public system to which they were not sending their children was being funded through their taxes, and the Catholic system to which they were sending their children was being funded predominantly through the payment of school fees and the contributed services of religious. The political mobilisation of Catholics, more than the justice of their claim, became a matter of concern for previously 'deaf' politicians at both state and federal levels. The spiritual quest took on a new and characteristically Australian dimension when Catholics demanded a 'fair go' or else the consequences would be deeply felt at the ballot box! This period saw the more vigorous participation of Catholics in political life in all major parties. Along with other developments such as the mobilisation of Catholics to oppose the growth of communism in the union movement in the context of the Cold War, it also challenged any purely passive role for lay people in the life and mission of the Church.

In Catholic schools a further dynamic was being played out as the religious congregations who staffed them became over extended. Across the first half of the twentieth century, religious congregations had become highly institutionalised. This suited a form of spirituality that placed a high value on rules and conformity. One consequence was that in the staffing of schools and other institutions, many round pegs were forced into square holes to prop them up – eventually with devastating effects. Congregational leaders often ignored danger signs associated with this practice because, in the optimism of the times, young women and men were joining teaching congregations in large numbers.

Up until the 1970s congregational schools operated more or less as religious franchises. People knew the difference between the brands. For boys there were the Christian Brothers, Marist Brothers, Jesuits, Salesians and De La Salle Brothers; for girls there were the Mercy Sisters, Josephite Sisters and the Good Samaritan Sisters – to name only those who feature in this book.

Catholic education as an enterprise began to shudder to a halt in the late 1960s and early 1970s as religious reached a point of spiritual exhaustion caused by a combination of under-training and overwork. Two developments saved the day in Australia.

The first was the advent of Government funding for Catholic schools, and the second was the call for 'the renewal of religious life' issued at the Second Vatican Council (Vatican II). Government funding to Catholic schools had an immediate impact at two levels. It enabled existing schools to hire lay teachers, and so take the strain off the overworked religious.[6] Many of these were working very full days and then after hours seeking to advance their qualifications through part-time university study so that the Catholic system could expand to meet the demands of Catholics for places in Catholic schools.

Fifty years on it is hard to assess the immediate impact of the Second Vatican Council on the Australian spiritual journey as this is now masked by subsequent developments. The most obvious impact was on the liturgy, changes to the Mass being the most significant and obvious liturgical change. The place of the Mass in Christian life moved from being an external devotion to a ritual that invited intelligent and informed participation. It became possible for the broader Catholic population to build a spirituality around such participation. The notion of the Mass as a core element in the inner lives of Catholics appeared novel to a population unaccustomed to active participation. The liturgical renewal of the late 1960s and 1970s had a profound impact on how Catholics interpreted what 'being Catholic' meant. Attending Mass was transformed from being a weekly ritual which was a badge of membership, to being the springboard of a deeper spiritual life for all – a defining aspect of Christian spirituality. Many Catholics were unable to make this transition and began to look back with nostalgia to earlier formulations of what being Catholic meant, and the cultural world that supported this view. As one by one the props supporting this cultural world gave way, they found themselves spiritually lost This was an unintended consequence of the changes initiated by the Vatican Council.

RENEWAL IN RELIGIOUS LIFE

The call for the renewal of religious life was something of a 'sleeper' issue for the Catholic Church in Australia initially, and its significance was at first only dimly grasped. In the early 1970s a number of religious congregations sent some of their most capable people to Europe to study the shifts in perspective that marked the Second Vatican Council. On returning two or three years later they became key personnel in driving the renewal movement in their respective groups. Renewal soon developed two major thrusts: the first was *general* and was to make members more aware of what had happened at the Second Vatican Council, and its significance for Catholic educators. The second was *specific* – to help define what 'renewal' meant in the context of their own congregation. The latter thrust soon

---

[6] In the 1960s and 1970s congregations struggled to provide adequately educated religious to teach senior classes. The only option open to them was for teachers to teach all day and then to attend university on a part time basis.

came to centre on 'living out of the charism of the founder' but in a way transposed into the prevailing mission context. Religious congregations, thanks to government funding, were able to free up members to attend national, and in some cases international, formation programs not only to come to terms with the change in mindset and outlook represented by the Vatican Council, but also with the implications of re-appropriating the charism of their own congregation. The spiritual quest implicitly embedded in Catholic education was strongly influenced by this development, one that operated at a number of levels.

For most congregations, the exploration of charism took the form of critical analysis in which the narrative of the founder was stripped of mythological and historical accretions so that the purposes of the founder and his or her motivation could be clearly understood. In most cases, founders of congregations engaged in what in their era were known as 'works of charity'. The unique way in which they undertook these reflected a faithful living of the Gospel that in many cases was innovative. In the theology of the Second Vatican Council, charism is recognised as both a new way of living the Gospel and a gift to the Church at large. The charism of a founder cannot be separated from the founder's spirituality or inner life as this informed that person's understanding of mission. In almost all these narratives there is a period of struggle in which the inner and outer aspects of Christian life become integrated. The classic example is Ignatius of Loyola where this process went on over a number of years and involved a good deal of trial and error.[7]

Across the 1980s, religious congregations faced three significant challenges. The first was to articulate the charism of the founder. The second was to explore its implications for the ministries they were engaged in. The third was to share these developing understandings with their rapidly growing band of lay collaborators. In some cases, this exercise led to numbers of religious opting out of teaching to work on other forms of ministry more aligned with what the group had been originally founded to do.

THE SITUATION OF THE CLERGY

The renewal movement occurring in religious congregations could not be paralleled by similar developments among the clergy, where there was more limited scope to free people to study. Thus something of a chasm soon opened up about the meaning and significance of the Vatican Council between the understanding of religious and their co-workers in schools

---

[7] A useful account of the life of Ignatius and the Jesuit spiritual tradition is found in James Martin's highly readable *A Jesuit Guide to (almost) Everything: A Spirituality for Real Life* (New York: Harper One, 2010).

and the clergy and lay people in parishes. The nexus between parish and convent/monastery, so much a part of the development of Catholicism in Australia, was first stretched, and then it broke. The internal changes within Catholicism brought about by the Council, the changing demographic of the clergy themselves, and the broader societal and cultural changes affecting all social institutions including the family, meant that schools could no longer serve their former role of cultural reproduction within Catholicism, nor could they play the same role as previously in ensuring young people attended Sunday Mass and participated in the parish. Increasingly, many clergy began to become disengaged from schools as a consequence.

The spiritual journey integral to Catholic life in Australia also lost momentum as dioceses began to incorporate the understandings of the Second Vatican Council into catechetical programs. This often happened in the face of serious opposition from certain members of the clergy and some bishops who took the theological understandings and practices of the counter-Reformation as definitive of Catholic teaching. From their perspective, and that of their lay supporters, the development of doctrine implicitly and explicitly agreed to by the assembled Bishops at the Council was at best misguided, and at worst wrong. Subsequently, a number of bishops opted for an intermediate stance, claiming that the Council's teachings were being 'misinterpreted' by 'left-wing' Catholics. Confusion at the official level about the goals of catechetical programs produced even greater confusion at the school level.

Nowhere in Australia was this battle for the soul of the Council fought out more vigorously than in Victoria, where the political elite responsible for defeating communism in the trade union movement threw in their lot with conservative bishops to challenge the 'orthodoxy' of the 'new catechetics'.[8] This intervention was to prove disastrous for the Australian Catholic spiritual journey as it added to the growing confusion about what 'being Catholic' now meant. In many cases the confusion sapped the confidence of lay teachers, many of whom were drafted into teaching Religious Education in Catholic schools by default. In consequence, in the eyes of many teachers, Religious Education lost its standing as a serious element in the curriculum. In the confusion of the time, many school leaders found it difficult to articulate what the mission of the Catholic school was when bishops were squabbling among themselves about the issue.

---

8 For Mgr Tom Doyle, efforts to develop curricula and resources to support Catholic teachers at this time were the result of what he termed a 'people's movement' in which, for the first time, lay educators, assisted by religious, were given appropriate responsibility for a role that was properly their own. Monsignor Doyle held the roles of Director of Religious Education, and later that of Director of Catholic Education in the Catholic Education Office Melbourne. This point was made in personal conversation with Jim and Therese D'Orsa.

Leaders of religious congregations began to seriously question the effectiveness – in the language of the day, 'the apostolic effectiveness' – of the Catholic schools they ran. They sensed the need to consolidate the Catholic identity of the school around something they had confidence in – the charism of their founder and the mission calling that was implicit in his or her way of reading the Gospel. This quickly became the touchstone of authenticity in their schools. Charism became part of the spiritual journey of the Catholics, parents, teachers and students who were associated with the schools. Renewal in religious life was seen as integral to renewal in the schools. This development often happened outside the purview of parishes and parish life, adding to the sense of disconnection between parish and school and making many priests wary of 'charism', seeing it in political rather than ecclesial terms.

FROM INSTITUTION TO COMMUNITY – THE MISSION OF SCHOOLS

One of the little-considered side effects of the renewal movement in religious life was the de-institutionalising of the Catholic bodies for which they were responsible. Nowhere was this more evident than in Catholic schools, a matter highlighted in the first document on Catholic education published after the Council in 1977.[9] In the 1980s and 1990s, schools began to seriously consider themselves as 'educational communities' made up of teachers, students, parents, clergy, etc., with a unique identity and mission. Developments in religious congregations fed neatly into this change in the basic identity of the schools, and it was the religious congregations in the 1980s who first took up the challenge of articulating the mission of the schools and so putting their Catholic identity again on a sound footing. They were followed by Catholic Education Offices who benefitted from the experience of the religious congregations. As a consequence, by the mid 1990s, there were very few Catholic schools in Australia that did not have a mission statement setting out, in quite explicit terms, the 'lived Christian values' to which the school stood as witness, and the goals that it sought to achieve.

The processes used to arrive at these understandings were various, but most had a strongly spiritual dimension aimed at discerning God's action both in the life of the school community and in the witness the school offered to the wider Church and society. Schools began to take Catholic social teaching as a serious part of their agenda, particularly its expressed concern for the marginalised. God's action in school life became recognised by a detailed

---

9 Congregation of Christian Education, *The Catholic School* (Homebush: Paulist Press, 2007), #22. The document uses the term 'community' over 30 times to drive home its message.

exploration of the school's narrative. Furthermore, 'charism' became seen not as the prerogative only of schools associated with religious congregations, but as something implicit in all Catholic school communities who were attempting to chart their course in openness to the Holy Spirit in their own story. One can see why this was so by looking at the most common understanding of charism discussed in later chapters: viz., 'a story to enter, a language to speak, a group to belong to, a way to pray, a work to undertake, and a face of God to see'.[10] This understanding brings into balance the inner and outer dimensions of Christian life highlighted in the previous chapter.

In the Anglo-Irish tradition, Catholic schools took on a name associated with the parish. This might honour an important feast, a well-known saint, and in a number of cases, obscure Irish saints. When some of these school communities have sought in recent years to re-affirm their identity as Catholic, they have done so, not in terms of the school's name (although that is clearly a possibility), but with reference to the religious congregation that founded the school and the presence of its charism in the 'lived values' that mark its corporate history and life. Other school leaders have chosen to 'adopt' the charism of a congregation as a way of engaging more fully with the spiritual journey that is part of Catholic life.

The challenge facing the leaders of new schools is to create a mythology from which its charism can eventually crystallise. The name of the school and its symbol system are important resources when used by skilful leaders seeking to ensure that what happens in the school carries some spiritual depth. The final chapter illustrates how this can be done.

The developments noted above have been important in stabilising the identity of Catholic schools. They stand as a counter to other movements that compromise that identity, and so produce a tension between mission and identity. Nowhere does this tension become more evident than in the area of 'school improvement'. Here secular demands run headlong into the best aspirations of mission. The secular constraints on mission come not only from Government; today they also come from within the school community itself, from parents and teachers. Shaping expectations of teachers and educating parents have become important aspects of the school's mission without which it is impossible to ameliorate the impact of secularisation. Shaping the expectations of clergy about what schools can achieve given the contemporary mission context is also important.

Schools cannot by themselves arrest or reverse the changes that have occurred in the Australian Catholic community any more than parishes

---

10   Fr Claude Maréchal, 'Toward an effective partnership between religious and laity in fulfilment of charism and responsibility for mission'. Charism and spirituality. Proceedings of the 56th Conference of the Unione Superiore Generali, Rome.

can. What we are dealing with is a new mission context, and Catholic schools have a constructive role to play in that context. In doing so, as the various chapters in the book highlight, they are not starting from scratch. While much remains to be learned, much has already been learned, and the authors of subsequent chapters encapsulate this learned wisdom. They explore an unfolding narrative and attempt to balance the interior and exterior dimensions of Christian life, so that people come to see the face of God through their service of the other and through prayer.

Consolidating the identity and mission of Catholic schools is not an operational or strategic issue; *it is, and always has been, a mission issue.* Just as leaders in Catholic schools over the past two decades have learned to move their thinking from the operational to the strategic, the challenge now and across the next decade will be to move it from the strategic to the missional.[11]

Pope Francis has brought the sense of hope to the Church that was very much a part of Catholic life in the immediate post-Vatican II years but which has since dissipated. The present is again a time of hope under the leadership of the first Jesuit pope. The Ignatian charism is often expressed as 'seeing God in all things' and the present Pope has made it clear in what he says and does that he finds God in places where many others have not looked, or have ceased to look. Where this approach leads remains to be seen, but his actions do illustrate the power of charism in pursuing mission.

It is perhaps not too much to hope that, just as renewal in religious congregations led to renewal in Catholic schools, the renewal of the latter can feed into renewal in the Australian Church more broadly. This will happen if the spiritual journey of Catholics is better balanced, focusing not only on the exterior (which has clearly failed), nor exclusively on the interior. One outcome of the latter focus is people who claim to be spiritual but not religious, and so are located in isolation from any community that can help them sustain an inner life. In giving young people 'a story to enter, a language to speak, a group to belong to, a way to pray, a work to undertake, and a face of God to see', schools can have a major impact, *but this requires leadership.*

As Bishop Walker has rightly pointed out, developing the critical mass of 'mature Catholics' to provide such leadership is the great mission challenge of our age. In this context the following chapters represent something of a 'report card' on how religious congregations, Catholic schools systems, and the new movements of lay educators are approaching this task, as well as the ways in which they endeavour to bring a new balance to the Australian Catholic spiritual journey.

---

11 See Jim and Therese D'Orsa, *Leading for Mission* (Mulgrave: Garratt Publishing, 2013), 244-255.

Part Two
MISSION AND DISCIPLESHIP IN THE GOSPEL OF JOHN

The Gospel of John emerged from a community living in a particular time and cultural context which had its own social dynamics, and which shaped the content and style of the Gospel.

No evangelist places more emphasis on the inner life of the Christian than the writer of John. John's Gospel is also important because of the stress it places on the equality of all Christians, and so on all being called as equals to discipleship and to mission. However, the Gospel of John is highly symbolic, more so than the synoptics, and this can tend to mask its mission dimension unless the reader is aware of the way the writer approached his task.

The Johannine writings collectively recognise the role and function of the 'Paraclete' in the life of the Christian community. The role of the Paraclete is presented as that of teacher and empowering Spirit. The notion of charism is explained in later chapters of this book as the work of this Spirit in action through people and communities across human history.

In Part II of this book, Therese D'Orsa re-balances the emphasis on discipleship and the inner life of the Christian as traditionally associated with the Gospel of John, with the Gospel's deep and sophisticated treatment of mission, a loving and enriching gift for Christ's disciples engaging with the contemporary context.

Therese D'Orsa

Therese D'Orsa is a Catholic missiologist and educational leader who has taught in primary, secondary and tertiary settings. She has exercised a wide range of leadership roles in Catholic education systems, including that of Director of Catholic Education (Sale) and Director of Religious Education (Sydney). Therese has taught in several tertiary institutions and is currently Conjoint Professor of the University of Newcastle and The Broken Bay Institute, a research associate of the Melbourne University of Divinity, and an honorary fellow of Australian Catholic University. Therese has published widely across her career and, with her husband Jim, has co-authored several books focused at the interface of missiology and education.

4

MISSION AND THE GOSPEL OF JOHN: REFLECTIONS ON A UNIQUE SPIRITUAL TRADITION

Therese D'Orsa

'I've never thought of John's Gospel in that way,' said a friend recently when I mentioned that I was preparing a reflection on John's Gospel and mission. Many Christians, even those who know the Gospel well, might, I suspect, say much the same thing should the subject arise. They are not used to thinking of John's Gospel as a missional document. However, 'mission' is as broad as God's intentions in the created world and the Gospel of John is a missional document par excellence.

The following reflections on aspects of mission and the Gospel of John are offered as a 'work in progress' and in the hope that they will encourage others in their own exploration. For missional leaders[1], praying the scriptures and working with them in leadership situations is 'of the essence' of who they are and of their role in the Church community. Missional leadership, particularly in the education sector, has been my ministry for several decades, and hence has come to shape and provide coherence to my approach to Scripture. Exploration into mission in the Bible began for me many years ago when I realised how woefully inadequate my formation in Biblical theology and spirituality had been up to that time. If I was to pursue the path opening up to me, it was clearly going to be necessary to rectify that deficiency.

To be sure, like most practising Catholics, I had heard many homilies on the 'great mission command' at the end of Matthew's Gospel (Matt 28:18–20), usually delivered in connection with the Mission Sunday

---

[1] The term 'missional' is used because it does not carry the specific connotations of the adjective 'missionary' which in Christian circles in recent centuries, has tended to have cross-cultural connotations, developed particularly during the missionary endeavours which paralleled the colonisation of South America, Asia and Africa from the sixteenth to the nineteenth centuries.

appeal.[2] I knew much more than that, of course, but not in a connected or wholistic way. I was at the stage where I approached Scripture piecemeal, as selected uncontextualised texts which, whilst these may have included much loved passages, did not necessarily ever add up to a meaningful whole. At the time, Scripture scholarship was gathering pace in Catholic circles, and the riches on offer seemed somewhat overwhelming. Where to start, and how to become confident? My aim was never to become a 'scripture scholar' in the technical sense. What I clearly realised that I needed was a general competence, and there were plenty of mainstream high quality resources to help with that.[3] As well, and much more important, was prayerful familiarity and spiritual enrichment – an intelligent cultivation of a Biblical heart and imagination. Mine was to be a long and delightful journey, and it continues.

In the early days of my journey, and confident in my grasp of Matt 28:18–20, I barely noticed the existence of the other mission commissions given by Jesus in the post-resurrection sections of the Gospels of Mark, Luke and John.[4] Had I done so, I would have seen that a post-resurrection mission commission exists in each of the four canonical Gospels, those in Mark, Luke and John being different from, but not contradictory to, that in Matthew, the themes and settings reflecting the mission theology of the particular Gospel. There are overlapping themes and an obvious complementarity between the four post-resurrection commissions. This is because each reflects significant elements of the memory of Jesus carried in separate post-Resurrection, post-Pentecostal Christian communities. For example, the commission in John (including reference to the setting) usually reads as follows:

> When it was evening on that day, the first of the week, and the doors of the house where the disciples had met were locked for fear of the Jews, Jesus came and stood among them and said, 'Peace be with you.' After he said this, he showed them his hands and his side. Then the disciples rejoiced when they saw the Lord. Jesus said to them again, 'Peace be with you. As the Father has sent me, so I send you.' When he had said this he breathed on them and said to them, 'Receive the Holy Spirit.

---

2 Prior to the first and second expansions of Europe into the Americas, Africa and Asia (15th to 19th centuries), this text did not hold such a dominant place in Christian considerations of mission as it did subsequently. For many centuries the parable of the great feast (Luke 14:15–24) held pride of place as a mission text.

3 For example in growing in familiarity with the Gospel of John, I have been resourced by such well-known scholars as Raymond Brown, Francis Moloney, and Senior and Stuhlmueller. For example Raymond Brown (edited by Francis Moloney), *An Introduction to the Gospel of John* (New York: Doubleday, 2003); Donald Senior and Carroll Stuhlmueller, *The Biblical Foundations for Mission* (London: SCM Press, 1983).

4 These are to be found in Mk 16:15–16; Lk: 24:46–49 (and Acts 1:8–9); John 20:19–23.

If you forgive the sins of any, they are forgiven them; if you retain the sins of any, they are retained' (Jn: 20:19–23).

An eminent Biblical scholar, Sandra Schneiders, has drawn attention to the need to consider the translation of the last sentence in this commission. Schneiders points out that in the second part of this sentence there is actually no mention of sin. However, the phrase is usually translated in the light of Matthew 16:19 which speaks of binding and loosing in relation to Peter's authority. The sentence is, in her view, better understood as a mission of forgiving sin and of holding firm to one another in community. Schneiders states, 'Translated literally it says:

Of whomever you forgive the sins, they are forgiven to them; whomever you hold are held fast' (Jn 20:23).[5]

John's missional mandate explicitly emphasises peace, reconciliation, community care and cohesion, and the sending forth of disciples – aspects of mission with a most contemporary ring. It is delivered in conjunction with the giving of the Holy Spirit. Study of John's Gospel itself reveals even more dimensions of mission. Clearly mission is multi-faceted.

In due course, I have come to see the Bible, in its entirety, as a mission document par excellence. Its various books, themes and traditions shed light on God's purpose in the created universe as revealed to faithful people across many generations. They also record human responsiveness in particular times and contexts, many of which, like our own, have demanded great trust in God's constant love.

CLARIFYING MISSION

The word 'mission' comes from the Latin 'mittere', to send. In the discussion which follows, 'mission' is used in the general sense of what one is sent (literally or metaphorically) to do, and so means one's purpose or one's work. In contemporary usage it has come to include the specifics of what a person or group does to carry out their purpose. Hence a mission statement often includes not only the broad direction to be taken by an individual, or more likely a group, but also some of the plans and timeframes within which it is intended that mission is to be carried out.

In its religious usage, the word 'mission' parallels general usage. The community of disciples (the Church) has the purpose or mission of

---

5 See Sandra M. Schneiders, 'The Resurrection (of the Body) in the Fourth Gospel', in John R. Donahue, *Life in Abundance: Studies of John's Gospel in Tribute to Raymond E. Brown* (Collegeville: Liturgical Press, 2005), 186–87.

continuing the work of Jesus in the world. The disciple and the community of disciples are 'sent' to accomplish that mission. It is worthy of note that in the Gospel of John, Jesus speaks of his mission in terms of 'the work' the Father has sent him to do. For example: *But Jesus answered them, 'My Father is still working, and I also am working'* (Jn 5:17); '*We must work the works of him who sent me while it is day; night is coming when no one can work*' (Jn 9:4); '*I glorified you on earth by finishing the work you gave me to do*' (Jn 17:4).

The terms 'mission' and 'evangelisation' are closely connected. The mission of the community of disciples (the Church) is to evangelise, which means to speak and enact good news. Evangelisation involves bringing the Gospel to life in human lives, communities and contexts.[6]

MISSION IN CONTEXT

In the twenty-first century, mission has a global context. The world is rapidly becoming interconnected and interdependent in many respects, even as human communities seek to strengthen their local identities in reaction to this process. There is resulting tension, conflict and dislocation. We humans struggle with issues of justice, peace and reconciliation. Societies, including our own, are becoming increasingly pluralistic and much more complex. As pluralism advances, especially demanding of the Christian disciple is the responsibility, emanating from Baptism, to proclaim the Gospel in a way that is meaningful to people in terms of their own way of life (culture). At the same time there is recognition that the Gospel can and should enrich and heal cultures which, as human constructs, are entities where the wheat and the weeds grow together (Matt 13:24–30). Even when people have a sufficiency or perhaps a surplus of this world's goods, many seem lost and lack meaning in their lives. Like so many humans, mother earth herself is subject to degradation and selfish exploitation. All of these scenarios fall within the scope of Christian mission. The Gospel of John, whose focus is very directly on life and love, has much to offer contemporary societies and cultures. The Christian community exists to carry on the work entrusted by God the Father to Jesus, who became human at a particular time and place and in a particular context, so as to enable humanity to flourish in every time, place and context. The fullness of human flourishing occurs when individuals and communities are open and responsive to God's invitation to become children of God, and committed to God's loving purpose in the world, as exemplified by Jesus – '*But to all who received him, who*

---

6 See Stephen Bevans, 'The Mission has a Church: An Invitation to the Dance', *Australian e-Journal of Theology* (Vol 14, no 1, 2009). This excellent article explores the theme of the Church as instrument of God's mission.

believed in his name, he gave power to become children of God' (Jn 1:12).

Discussion of mission in today's world takes us to the very raison d'etre of the Christian community. In a rapidly changing context, experienced by many as chaotic, discouraging, and even downright inimical to the Gospel, we find it necessary to return to our Christian roots in the life, death and resurrection of Jesus as given to us in the New Testament, especially in the Gospels. It is good to remind ourselves that in the Gospel of John we see Jesus being rejected by some of his own people, the Jews, and more widely by 'the world'. At one point some of his own disciples choose to walk away. *When many of his disciples heard it, they said, 'This teaching is difficult; who can accept it?' … Because of this many of his disciples turned back and no longer went about with him* (Jn 6:60, 66). Although quite clearly some Jews and some gentiles become believers, the majority do not.[7] Two thousand years later, Jesus' disciples share a commonality of experience with the Johannine community.

MISSIONAL TRADITION IN JOHN'S GOSPEL

Reflection on mission in each of the canonical Gospels is equally rewarding for the missional leader. John's Gospel has been chosen as the focus of this reflection because in recent centuries its provenance as a missional tradition has been downplayed, and the Christian Church has been the poorer for that. Once one actually looks closely at the Gospel, it seems particularly surprising that Christians fail so often to recognise it as a missional document.[8] It is, after all, a Gospel, that is, a rendition of Jesus' good news, and its writer has been known throughout the life of the Church as an evangelist.[9]

To a profound degree, John's Gospel probes God's purpose (mission) in the created universe and provides a mission theology and spirituality par excellence, setting disciples of every age on a sound missional path. At this stage it is timely to paint in very broad brushstrokes some of the main mission themes which form the warp and woof of the Gospel, and which attest to its obvious mission credentials.

---

7 It is important that readers of the Gospel of John understand that the writer is using 'the Jews' in a specific rather than a general way to describe those who were excluding the Johannine community from the synagogues, and in a sense rendering them non-Jews. Most members of the Johannine community were Jews, so obviously the writer was not using the term of all Jews.
8 Donald Senior and Carroll Stuhlmueller, *The Biblical Foundations for Mission* (Orbis: Maryknoll N.Y., 1983), 280. This classic work remains an indispensable reference for the study of mission in the Bible.
9 Lucien Legrand, *Unity and Plurality: Mission in the Bible* (Maryknoll N.Y: Orbis, 1990), 131.

From the very beginning, and in a majestic introduction strikingly similar to the opening of the Book of Genesis,[10] the reader is caught up in the sweep of mission emanating from the life of our Creator God, with a loving movement into the world in the person and mission of Jesus of Nazareth. We see Jesus calling people to discipleship (Jn 1:35–51) which is not an individual call only, but an invitation to membership of a community of faith. In fact, discipleship in John is a three-year apprenticeship of simply being with Jesus, and the disciples are sent out on mission only after the resurrection. Empowered through their relationship with Jesus, and after his death re-enlivened by the Holy Spirit, these disciples are enabled to carry on the mission of Jesus following his return to the Father. We learn that all disciples in Jesus' community are equal – female and male are depicted as equally strong disciples in the Gospel of John.[11] We learn that faith means trust. We see that faith grows in stages as people are invited by Jesus' words and his witness to the truth to respond to his invitation to participate in mission.[12] The hard lesson that commitment to mission means sharing Jesus' suffering and passion is laid out starkly and at length in John.[13] We see how great and unselfish love leads to the cross, and we learn that through the cross, all can be drawn to Jesus and new life. This paradigm of mission's nature, purpose and goals, set out so clearly in the Gospel, is being lived out in Christian communities in many parts of the world today where followers of Jesus continue to pay a high price for their discipleship, even to laying down their lives.

Perhaps one of the reasons Christians have in recent centuries failed to recognise the mission theology and spirituality which are such integral features of John's Gospel is the historical dominance of the Gospel of Matthew as a source for instruction in the faith, including mission. Matthew's organisation of his Gospel into five great 'sermons' or discourses dealing with aspects of Christian life,[14] has commended it in a special way to teachers and preachers of the Christian faith, and so until recent decades it was generally the best known of the Gospels. The historical dominance of the 'great mission command' at the end of Matthew's Gospel (Matt 28:18–20) has already been referred to and reflects the pre-eminence of Matthew in the instruction of the faithful.

---

10   Mary Coloe, *A Friendly Guide to John's Gospel* (Mulgrave: Garratt Publishing, 2012), 5. This helpful and creative introduction to the Gospel is highly recommended to all who wish to deepen their understanding and appreciation of John's Gospel.
11   Mary the Mother of Jesus is paralleled by the Beloved Disciple; Martha and Mary by Lazarus; the woman at the well becomes a fearless missionary just as the royal official brings his whole household to faith.
12   For example, the man born blind is depicted as passing from no faith to full faith in Chapter 9. A similar journey is made by the Samaritan woman in Chapter 4.
13   Chapters 12 to 19.
14   These are the Sermon on the Mount (Matt 5–7); the Mission Discourse (Matt 10); the Parables of the Kingdom Discourse (Matt 13); Discourse on Life in the Community (Matt18); and the Eschatalogical Discourse (Matt 23–25).

BACKGROUND TO THE GOSPEL OF JOHN

The writer of John's Gospel was a Christian who wrote under the authority and in the tradition and spirit of the Beloved Disciple who features in the Gospel as a heroic figure, one who had been close to Jesus during his earthly ministry.[15] Although there is no agreement on the exact date when the Gospel of John reached its final form, many scholars date it towards the end of the first century. The evangelist used the narrative mode for his rendition of the Good News, a mode which had been similarly adopted to great effect in the synoptic Gospels (Mark, Matthew and Luke), although John's Gospel draws predominantly on different sources from the Synoptics.[16]

The retellings of Jesus' life and teachings in what we know today as the canonical Gospels occurred, in the understanding of Christian believers, under the inspiration of the Holy Spirit. Consequently, each has its unique wisdom for Christian life and mission. By the time the Gospels came to be written, the communities were encountering, in their various contexts, the joys and sorrows of living the Christian life in times and places very different from those in which Jesus pursued his mission. Each community was confronted with a unique range of issues which gave a particular character to how its members remembered and expressed the story of Jesus for a new generation.

A huge sorrow affecting the community and hence influencing the writing of the Gospel was the rift with fellow Jews who did not accept Jesus as Messiah. The trauma of the Roman destruction of the temple shocked and disoriented the entire Jewish community, and exacerbated the divisions already existing. All were suffering great trauma and dislocation resulting from the catastrophic destruction in 70 A.D. of what had been the centre of their religious, and also their social and economic life. Already the Johannine community, struggling to live the Christian life faithfully in depressingly uncertain times, is beginning to emerge as a group of people whose experience of missional involvement resonates with our own at the beginning of the twenty-first century. Like them, we also experience the unravelling of an old and familiar religious culture, together with unparalleled social changes, in our time resulting from the impact of globalisation, and the economic consequences of financial arrangements which often work cruelly against the poor.

---

15 Mary Coloe, *A Friendly Guide to John's Gospel*, 5.
16 The writer most likely adopted certain pre-existing material, for example the Prologue (John 1:1–14) is believed to be based on a pre-existing hymn, and an already extant Book of Signs is also widely believed to have been adopted and adapted to the theological purpose of the writer.

As Jewish lay leaders sought to rebuild their faith community, the issue of who was to be included in the renewed community became a real one. By the time John's Gospel was written, the exclusion of Jesus' followers from the synagogues was clearly an issue for this community.[17] The polemic between Jewish Christians and those Jews who did not accept Jesus as the Messiah forms a backdrop to the narrative of John's Gospel. We see this intruding overtly into the narrative itself, for example in the account of the man born blind, where the reality of Jesus' followers being expelled from the synagogue is expressed (Jn 9:22; also 12:42). On the eve of his Passion, Jesus warns his disciples, *They will put you out of the synagogues* (Jn 16:2).

The Johannine community appears to have been composed mainly of Jewish followers of Jesus. We can assume this because throughout the Gospel there is much attention given to aspects of Jewish life and practices, for example, the Jewish feasts.[18] Yet, there are other groups depicted as within or close to the community. For example, the Samaritans feature in one of the Gospel's remarkable and detailed accounts, an encounter which resonates with our contemporary mission situation in a remarkable way (Jn 4:4–42). It features a profound dialogue between Jesus and a Samaritan woman. This is a cross-cultural encounter, one which also bridges a religious divide. The woman is pictured in John's Gospel as becoming a remarkable carrier of the Good News to her fellow Samaritans. It is a passage of the Gospel which provides inspiration and guidance to those engaged in mission today for whom mission involves dialogue with the followers of other religions, with the social and culturally marginalised, and with genuine truth-seekers of many philosophical and ideological backgrounds.[19]

Besides the general Jewish population and the Samaritans, also named specifically in the Gospel are the Greeks, who are probably Gentiles (e.g. Jn 7:35; 12:20) and the followers of John the Baptist (Jews). The use of widely-recognisable symbols such as light and darkness, bread and oil, that are recognised and appreciated beyond one culture, would suggest that the Gospel is consciously directed to a range of people in the wider Romanised world. Note the inscription on the cross which John points out as being in three languages – Hebrew, Latin, and Greek – (Jn 19:20) symbolising that Jesus' death has significance far beyond the Jewish people, indeed for the whole known world of the time.[20]

---

17 Scholars are not clear as to whether the expulsion was widespread beyond John's community.
18 Mary Coloe, *A Friendly Guide to the Gospel of John* is a helpful resource on many aspects of the Gospel's background and structure.
19 For example, Thomas Ascheman, 'Mission from the Heart of the Church: Water, Worship and Harvest (John 4:1–42)' in Thomas Malipurathu and L. Stanislaus, *The Church in Mission: Universal Mandate and Local Concerns* (Gujurat Sahitya Prakash: 2002), 1–26.
20 Legrand, 131–2 (drawing on the work of Cothenet).

Cutting across the nature of individual social groups interacting with the community positively or negatively, there is the issue of people from whatever background proceeding on their journey of faith in Jesus. Faith in Jesus and a relationship with Jesus is seen in this Gospel as the goal of the community's mission. The account of the man born blind (John 9:1–34) is most instructive, since he is depicted as coming to faith in stages. Other figures are shown to have perfect faith, for example the mother of Jesus (Jn 2:1–11) and the royal official (Jn 4:46–54); some, such as Nicodemus (Jn 3:1–21) have only partial or weak faith, while some are depicted as having no faith in Jesus, such as the Jewish leaders (Jn 2:13–25). Some figures are seen to move through the stages from no faith to perfect faith, for example the Samaritan woman. All of these are paradigmatic of those, from whatever cultural or social group, who are privileged in each era to hear the Gospel.

INTERPRETING THE STORY OF JESUS – A RESPONSIBILITY OF MISSIONAL LEADERS

Taking time to probe the issues and questions which faced the community out of which the Gospel came, is to be 'in on the ground' as the community's leader went about the vital task of retelling the story of Jesus in very difficult times, and so establishing a spiritual tradition in regard to mission which has had much to offer Christians across two millennia. His task was much more than the assembling of facts. It was a matter not only of recording important elements of the life of Jesus, but also of *interpreting* Jesus' life and teaching, death and resurrection in the light of issues and questions facing his community several decades after Jesus' death. He was composing a narrative, that is a *consciously interpreted story,* and in so doing, weaving a theology of God and God's mission in the world carried out through the agencies of Christ and the Holy Spirit. Missional leaders in every age have the similar challenge of retelling the story of Jesus against the background of their current context. It is a task of faithful reinterpretation and a key aspect of mission.

MEANING-MAKING POST RESURRECTION AND POST PENTECOST

This interpretation first occurred through the double lenses, as it were, of both the resurrection of Jesus and the coming of the Holy Spirit at Pentecost. These lenses enabled the significance of much that Jesus said and did to become clearer, and enabled a deeper appreciation of who Jesus was to grow within the community.

Several times in the Gospel of John the writer states very explicitly that the disciples remembered the words of Jesus after the resurrection:

> *After he was raised from the dead, his disciples remembered that he had said this; and they believed the scripture and the word that Jesus had spoken* (Jn 2:22).

Similarly, after the triumphal entry into Jerusalem:

> *His disciples did not understand these things at first; but when Jesus was glorified, then they remembered that these things had been written of him and had been done to him* (Jn 12:16).

An important issue is that the disciples were remembering, or putting things together, making sense of things, not only *at a later time* (post-resurrection), but *in the light of* their experiences of the risen Jesus, and of having received the gift of the Holy Spirit.

There are two layers of meaning-making occurring here. The original disciples of Jesus, characters in John's 're-enactment' of the Jesus story, are depicted as making sense of things in the light of the Resurrection. In the second layer, the members of John's community, who are later disciples, are also making sense of their own lives and circumstances several decades after Jesus' death. They are doing so in the light of the earlier theological interpretations made by Jesus' original disciples, and in the light of issues and questions raised by what was then happening to themselves, particularly as the result of the destruction of the Temple and of being disbarred from the synagogues.

In a way, each of the four canonical Gospels is an example of this kind of sustained and profound theological reflection undertaken in the light of the mission experience of a particular community and shaped by the effects of that missional engagement on the internal life of that community. Just as is the case of all Christian communities across time, the early communities existed to continue the mission of Jesus, and missional engagement created its own pastoral needs in terms of community life. Later disciples like ourselves continue that process. As already indicated, *one of the key skills for missional leaders is to be able to continue the meaning-making process encountered in the Gospels, in their own time and place.* This process is called theological reflection for mission.

As becomes clear through study of the Gospels, theological reflection is a process which cuts through any artificial divide between the pastoral and missional aspects of a faith community's life. In the Gospels each of these dimensions exists in relation to the other. Sadly, in the life of the Church in recent centuries, these have become separated into two distinct arms with little to do with each other. This division in Catholic Church life has become embedded in the Church's culture, and is very hard to change. In its organisation, theological education tends to reflect this, to the serious detriment of the Church community's wellbeing and its mission.

In the balance of this brief reflection, I want to highlight certain themes from John's Gospel which I have found particularly important in theological reflection on mission today.

TO WHOM CAN WE GO? (JN 6:68) – THE PERSON OF JESUS AS CENTREPIECE

If each of the Gospels has its own distinct mission theology, how is mission portrayed in John's Gospel? The centrepiece of mission theology in John's Gospel is not the teachings of Jesus, for example Jesus' teaching on the Kingdom of God which is the centrepiece of mission in the synoptics; rather it is Jesus himself. He is the incarnation of God's reign amongst us. Jesus' mission is one of invitation to faith and discipleship. Through the faithful community of disciples, God's salvific purpose will be continued, and light and life will flow to the world, so that all might become children of God.

> For God so loved the world that he gave his only Son, so that everyone who believes in him may not perish, but may have eternal life. Indeed, God did not send the Son into the world to condemn the world, but in order that the world might be saved through him (Jn 3:16–17).

John Paul II, in a famous passage in his encyclical on mission (*Redemptoris Missio* 1990), reminded Catholics of the fact that the ultimate goal of mission is a relationship with God, and from this flow the works of God. He was drawing attention to the fact that Christianity involves more than the practice of a set of values, an ethic, important as this is. In his discussion of the Kingdom of God, John Paul II addressed the propensity in some circles to reduce Christianity solely to an ethic, even granted that the ethic generates involvements which are integral to Christian life and which demonstrate the validity and strength of a disciple's relationship with Jesus. John Paul II was reminding Catholics that more foundational than works of charity and justice is the relationship with a Person, and from this flows the capacity to engage in and sustain the Christian's involvement in charity and in social justice which is the manifestation of charity in social situations.

> The kingdom of God is not a concept, a doctrine, or a program subject to free interpretation, but it is before all else a person with the face and name of Jesus of Nazareth, the image of the invisible God (*Redemptoris Missio* #8).

The Gospel of John has the person, Jesus, as its focus and the clear expression and vehicle of the Father's mission in regard to humankind. The phrase, 'kingdom of God' (Mark and Luke) or, 'kingdom of heaven' (Matthew) was used by Jesus in the synoptic Gospels to describe his mission. It was particularly meaningful to the Jews, given their hopes and expectations of political deliverance, and their concept of God as King found especially in the Psalms. Yet in John's Gospel, the phrase, 'the Kingdom of God' occurs only twice, in Jesus' discussion with Nicodemus (Jn 3:3,5). While the phrase is not common in John, the symbolism of Jesus as King is a strong theme in the Passion. Pilate asks if Jesus is a king (Jn 18:33–38), and then he is crowned and dressed in purple, and presented to the people as a king (Jn 19:1–5). John's theology takes the issue of the Kingdom of God to another level. The Kingdom is focused on the *person of Jesus*, the incarnate Word of God. The theme is established from the very beginning of the Prologue where Jesus is depicted as sharing God's creating and salvific mission for all eternity. The word used throughout the New Testament for the message of the Gospel – 'logos' – is here personified. Jesus is the Logos, the message of the Gospel.[21]

PROCLAMATION BY WITNESS – THE BOOK OF SIGNS

Following the Prologue (Jn 1:1–18), the main body of John's Gospel consists of two sections often called the Book of Signs (Jn 1:19–12:43) and the Book of Glory (Jn 13–20). Each section contains important mission themes and contributes to the development of the mission theology and spirituality of the Gospel. Most powerfully, both the Book of Signs and the Book of Glory place the emphasis on witness, the testimony of deeds done and choices made which speaks most strongly of the central message of the Gospel, the love of God for humankind.

The Book of Signs, bookended by the Prologue and an Epilogue which recapitulates the intent of the Book of Signs (Jn 12:44–50), is so called because the emphasis is very much on seven 'signs', which are termed miracles in the Synoptic gospels. John names them as 'signs' because the emphasis is on their symbolic power, and what they reveal about the person and mission of Jesus.[22] The word 'sign' is the leitmotif of the Book of Signs.

---

21 Legrand points out many passages where 'logos' (lower case) is used in John e.g. 12:48; 14:24; 15:3 (logos as what Jesus says); 2:22, 4:50 (the message which is believed in; 5:24,8:43 (the message which is heard), 6:51, 52, 53; 14:23; 15:20; 17:6) and many others. It is also the message of the Gospel transmitted by those who receive it (4:41, 17:20). Legrand,132.
22 The signs chosen are: the changing of water into wine at the wedding feast of Cana (Jn 2:1–11); the curing of the royal official's son also at Cana (Jn 4:43–54); the healing of the cripple on the Sabbath (Jn 5:1–15); the feeding of the multitude (Jn 6,1–14); the crossing of the sea (Jn 6:16–21); the cure of the man born blind (Jn 9:1–41); and the raising of Lazarus (Jn 11:1–57).

The word does not re-occur until the end of the Gospel, when the writer refers to many other signs of Jesus not recorded in the Gospel.[23] In the Book of Signs we read that some do not believe despite the signs, and some achieve only imperfect or limited faith through fear or some other reason, for example Nicodemus. We also learn that faith may grow gradually and in stages. The dramatic story of the man born blind in Chapter 9 operates at both the immediate physical level of a cure from blindness since birth, and the parallel allegorical level, dealing with a person initially without faith coming to faith by stages. It is a most heartening 'sign' for those whose mission is education either of youth or adults.

In John's Gospel we find discourses, some of which are lengthy, explaining the significance of certain signs. Examples can be found following the cure of the paralysed man in Chapter 5 and following the miracle of the loaves in Chapter 6. Missional leaders today might well reflect that it remains a serious responsibility for Christians that, at appropriate times and places, they are able to speak about the connection between what has been accomplished because of commitment to the mission of Jesus, and its significance for the faith life of the community. Can leaders in various ministries – health, education, outreach, pastoral work – speak with conviction and credibility about the 'why' as well as the 'what' of their ministry?

Study of the Book of Signs reminds the missional leader of the dynamic of witness and word in the ongoing work of forming disciples of Jesus. Today, we are painfully aware that if people are to be attracted to the message of Jesus (and remember that, in John, Jesus *is* the message personified), they will respond only if the proclamation is made predominantly by means of witness.[24] Words, important as they are at the right time, are not and never can be a substitute for the Gospel in practice. Nowadays, we humans have so many means at our disposal for working 'miracles' in people's lives – we have resources which can be shared and applied, knowledge which can lead to 'miracles' for people in need. Witness to Jesus demands that we continue to make it possible for people to have faith in Jesus through the credibility of his community on earth. This includes the most demanding work of justice for those cast on society's margins. Justice for the most marginalised is the particular Gospel 'edge' to the many achievements of both the broader society and communities of faith.

Within our own ranks, there are the daily and unseen 'miracles' at the local level, 'signs' by which the Christian community's members improve the life and situation of others. They do so because of their commitment

---

23 Legrand's detailed study of this section of the Gospel is helpful, 134–138.
24 This point was famously made by Pope Paul VI in *Evangelii Nuntiandi* (1975). 'Modern man listens more willingly to witnesses than to teachers, and if he does listen to teachers, it is because they are witnesses'(#41).

to continue the mission of Jesus. Those who work in schools know the 'miracles' which can be worked to help families and children on the margin to take their place in the mainstream. They know too how often staff work minor miracles of the loaves and fishes kind, by the unobtrusive sharing perhaps of what has been put away 'for a rainy day', but parted with gladly when there is need. These 'signs' can similarly lead to faith when it becomes clear that what is done is not a 'one-off' good deed, but the habitual modus operandi of the community. This can and does cause people to wonder and to seek reasons and motivations.[25]

PROCLAMATION BY WITNESS – THE BOOK OF GLORY

For the writer of John's Gospel, the glory of God is the manifestation of the very depths of the divine being, and thus of the divine love.

In the Prologue and in the Book of Signs, the writer speaks of the glory of God:

> *And the word became flesh and lived among us, and we have seen his glory, the glory as of a father's only son, full of grace and truth* (Jn 1:14).

> *Jesus did this, the first of his signs in Cana of Galilee, and revealed his glory; and his disciples believed in him* (Jn 2:11; see also Jn 12:42–43).

In the second half of the Gospel, Jesus' glory is revealed as the glory of the cross. Three times in John, Jesus speaks of his death as a 'lifting up' (Jn 3:14; 8:28; 12:32) and this expression carries both the sense of being lifted up on a cross, and also of being exalted. The Passion in John is the ultimate revelation of Jesus' glory. On the eve of his departure Jesus' prayer to his Father resounds with the theme of 'glory'.

> *'Father, the hour has come; glorify your Son so that the Son may glorify you, since you have given him authority over all people, to give eternal life to all whom you have given him. And this is eternal life that they may know you, the only true God, and Jesus Christ whom you have sent. I glorified you on earth by finishing the work that you gave me to do. So now, Father, glorify me in your own presence with the glory*

---

25 Not surprisingly, 1 Peter 3:15 has become one of the great mission texts of our time as Christians devote themselves, sometimes in a life-long commitment, to the often thankless task of befriending, honouring and assisting those who can offer nothing material in return: – 'Always be ready to make your defence to anyone who demands from you an accounting for the hope that is within you; yet do it with gentleness and reverence'.

that I had in your presence before the world existed (Jn 17:1–5).

God the Father's glory, and the glory of God's only Son, is the glory of loving.[26] Whereas the motifs of light and life dominated in the first twelve chapters of the Gospel, in the Book of Glory these are muted; the dominant motif of the Book of Glory is love. Love gives definition to what light and life mean in John's Gospel.

There is a theme of judgement running through the Gospel of John paralleling the love theme. The world which God so loves (Jn 3:16) is also a world at present caught up in forces of evil, so much so that Satan is called the 'ruler of this world' (Jn 12:31) and this ruler is condemned. One of the tasks of the Spirit is to reveal both sin and righteousness for what they are, and in his final discourse Jesus speaks of this role of spiritual discernment, which will guide the disciples in the future.

> *Nevertheless I tell you the truth: it is to your advantage that I go away, for if I do not go away, the Advocate will not come to you; but if I go, I will send him to you. And when he comes, he will prove the world wrong about sin and righteousness and judgment: about sin, because they do not believe in me; about righteousness, because I am going to the Father and you will see me no longer; about judgment, because the ruler of this world has been condemned* (Jn 16: 7–11).

THE GOSPEL OF JOHN – LIVING THE TRADITION

A tradition is a body of beliefs, values and understandings about life treasured and handed down in a community. John's Gospel is such a treasure, embracing a tradition about Jesus and his mission. Given the complexity of the contemporary context, it is not surprising that the fundamentals of mission take a variety of forms depending on the needs of human communities and of the earth which supports them. The roots of these forms are to be found, implicitly or explicitly, within the Gospels themselves, since they respond to perennial human needs. We saw some of these forms named explicitly when we noted the mission commission found towards the end of the Gospel (Jn 20:22–23).

Although most of the current forms of evangelisation are not new, they manifest themselves in new and specific ways in the current context. There has always, for example, been the need to care for the individual members of the community, and to re-order human arrangements to take better care

---

26 I am here indebted to the excellent discussion of the Book of Glory in Legrand, 138–143.

of everyone, especially those thrown to the margins by communal or social dynamics. In our societal context we now call this form of evangelisation, social justice. Likewise, there has always been the need to help people to develop God's gifts in order to be their best selves as children of God (personal development), but in our time we recognise human gifts in a different way, one which may demand more of the community than in the past. Another form of evangelisation is the work of caring for mother earth, which has become so pressing in our time, but which was recognised in the Book of Genesis and re-echoed in the Prologue of John's Gospel. These are examples we readily recognise.

The following diagram maps the fundamental modes of mission (proclamation and dialogue) against a list of mission's contemporary forms.[27] It can be used to help us to map mission in John's Gospel, but also in our current context.

A few basic concepts need to be clarified before one embarks on such an exercise. Proclamation by both word and especially by witness, is the fundamental mode of mission in the Gospels. It must however always be coupled with dialogue, although this has been a recent insight of the Christian community.[28] Dialogue has come to the fore in our time in a special way as a result of insights provided by the social sciences which probe our way of life (culture) and our human modes of knowing and knowledge construction. We now see much more clearly that truth must always be searched for since no one can ever fully understand the Mystery Who is God. We undertake the search as individuals, and with others, and dialogue with fellow searchers of goodwill is integral to the quest However, in our pilgrimage to God, both individuals and communities gain insights only with humility, painstaking effort, and dependence on God and one another.

In mission studies, faith and culture are traditions of meaning which are each recognised as providing wisdom for human living, and for engagement in mission. When both faith and culture are brought together by the disciple in pursuing any of the various forms of evangelisation, the insight provided achieves a completeness not possible if either faith or culture is missing, or even downplayed. An example would be in the disciple's commitment to bring the Good News to bear on the sustainability of the planet as God's creation and the source of life for all God's creatures. In this work, both our faith tradition which recognises and respects God's creation and the physical sciences which provide necessary data as to its status, are sources of wisdom

---

27 Jim and Therese D'Orsa, *Leading for Mission: Integrating Life, Culture and Faith in Catholic Education* (Mulgrave: Garratt Publishing, 2013), 109.
28 For example Congregation for the Evangelisation of Peoples, 1991 *Proclamation and Dialogue* www.vatican.va/roman_curia/pontifical_councils/interelg/documents/rc_pc_interelg_doc_19051991_dialogue-and-proclamatio_en.html

for the task in hand. A further example might be taken from the work of justice as a key form of mission. In the work for justice, the disciple must source the best of human analysis on the subject, for example homelessness or affordable housing, as well as the spiritual insight and motivation that those for whom one is working are God's beloved children. Finally, in encouraging prayer and worship, the human sciences can assist in finding approaches and expressions appropriate to the particular human needs of the worshippers, to be utilised in conjunction with the insights of scripture and the spiritual traditions of the faith community.

Such integration of faith and culture always involves dialogue, and dialogue requires two parties. The partner to the dialogue may not be immediately obvious. Dialogue partners may be found in either the Christian communities or in the broader society. The importance of the question: 'Who are our dialogue partners?' can scarcely be overestimated, and must always be considered no matter what form of missional engagement we are called upon to undertake.

In the section which follows, some references and brief commentary will be provided on each form of mission in the light of the Gospel of John. The reader is invited to take the exploration beyond the limits imposed by this short reflection.

		Fundamental Modes of Mission		
		Proclamation		Dialogue
		By Witness	By Word	
Forms of Mission	Prayer & Worship			
	Pastoral Ministry & Sacraments			
	Liberation – Personal and Communal			
	Reconciliation – Peoples & Cultures			
	Justice & Peace			
	Care for the Earth			
	Inculturation			
	Inter-religious Dialogue			
	Evangelisation of cultures			
	(Forms yet to be articulated)			

Mission Matrix[29]

The foregoing discussion focused on the Gospel of John has furnished many examples of the forms of mission named in the matrix above. The following brief notes simply enhance that discussion.

PRAYER AND WORSHIP

Jesus' prayer to the Father in Chapter 17 is a prayer for the disciples present and future. It contains some of the themes we have already encountered in the post-resurrection mission commission (Jn 20:20–23). Reading this prayer you will notice the themes of sending, giving life, receiving and keeping God's word, the loving union between Father, Son and disciples, and the truth of God's word. In a very real way this great missional prayer and the post-resurrection mission commission given by Jesus echo each other.

---

29 Jim and Therese D'Orsa, *Leading for Mission*, 109.

PASTORAL MINISTRY AND SACRAMENTS

The 'signs' in the Book of Signs and their accompanying discourses are examples of Jesus' healing and teaching ministries directed to his own disciples and others in need. It is important to note that there is no institution of the Eucharist in John's depiction of the Last Supper. The sacraments of Eucharist and Baptism are dealt with in the midst of life's needs and struggles, for example, the feeding of the five thousand and the accompanying discourse (Chapter 6), and the discourse with Nicodemus and the accompanying instruction about being reborn of water and the Holy Spirit (Chapter 3).

LIBERATION – PERSONAL AND COMMUNAL

Then Jesus said to the Jews who had believed in him, 'If you continue in my word, you are truly my disciples; and you will know the truth, and the truth will make you free' (Jn 8:31). Contemporary disciples of Jesus who take on the role of educators of young people search for truth themselves and encourage and equip young people to do the same. Jesus promises them the freedom of the children of God.

The Jewish feasts figure prominently in John's Gospel. Jesus' passion, death and resurrection occur in the context of the Passover – the great Jewish feast of the people's liberation from slavery. For followers of Jesus, his Passover from death to life is also the foundation of their hope in ultimate liberation from the self-centredness which is sin, and from the human arrangements, political, economic and social, which oppress vulnerable people.

RECONCILIATION

In the mission command (Jn 20:20–23), Jesus speaks of the forgiveness of sins and of holding one another in community. Any relationship knows this experience. Living with love will call for the largeness of heart that can forgive the slights and hurts of another, and for holding as a precious gift the vulnerability and fragility of the other. Such love in action will bear witness to the boundless love of God – *By this everyone will know that you are my disciples, if you have love for one another* (Jn 13:35).

JUSTICE AND PEACE

Much of the world's lack of peace can be sourced to injustice in that, in a world of plenty, many are denied reasonable access to the world's goods, even to the bare necessities. Whilst social justice is a modern historical term, the virtue which is its foundation, love, is the major theme of this Gospel. Social justice is simply love applied to human arrangements such as economics, politics, and social institutions and decisions. Right ordering of these, according to the principle of love especially for the most needy, is an element of mission to which this Gospel calls Jesus' contemporary disciples.

Peace, according to John, is the first gift of the resurrection (Jn 20:20), and in peace, empowered by the Holy Spirit, disciples are sent on mission to the world – *Peace be with you. As the Father has sent me, so I send you.* When he had said this, he breathed on them and said to them, *Receive the Holy Spirit* (Jn 20:21–22).

CARE FOR THE EARTH

From the beginning of this Gospel, God is depicted as Creator (Prologue). As the disciples are invited into, and respond to, Jesus' mission to carry on the work of the Father, they become co-creators and co-carers of God's creation.

INTER-RELIGIOUS DIALOGUE

This particular example of dialogue as it applies amongst peoples of different religious faiths has been referred to in the discussion of Jesus and the Samaritan woman in Chapter 4. It is one of the most reflected upon, and loved, passages in regard to the mission challenges of our time.

EVANGELISATION OF CULTURES

'Culture' is a modern term. However, the reality of people's way of life (culture) is timeless and the subject of all the Gospels. By means of his words, actions, choices and relationships, Jesus challenged what was not in accord with his Father's will in all human arrangements – political, economic and social. His claim to be *the way, the truth and the life* (Jn 14:6) concretised the principles by which people can bring their way of life into alignment with God's will.

IN CONCLUSION – WITH THE HOLY SPIRIT

The disciple of the twenty-first century is called to mission in ecclesial and societal contexts which are complex – vastly different from, yet bearing some uncanny similarities to, the contexts in which the Johannine community lived. Making the translation across from their situation to ours demands of the missional leader openness and a humble dependence on the strength and insight which comes from the Holy Spirit, who in John, as in Luke–Acts, is depicted as a major actor in the Gospel. Just as the Holy Spirit accompanied Jesus from the start of his public mission (Jn 1:33) to the moment when 'the work' was completed on the cross (Jn 19:30), so too, post-Resurrection, Jesus ensures the Holy Spirit continues to accompany the community of believers across time – *Jesus, breathed on them and said to them, 'Receive the Holy Spirit'* (Jn 20:23). The disciple is able to proceed with humble confidence because, despite the darkness and seeming failure which often accompany the most earnest of efforts, God's Spirit is constantly at work in the world, which remains the object of God's love and loving purpose (mission).

Part Three
LEADERSHIP BY RELIGIOUS CONGREGATIONS AND THE LAY MOVEMENTS THEY INSPIRE

This section outlines the understandings and leadership initiatives currently being taken by a sample of religious congregations and the lay movements which they inspire and foster. The purpose of these initiatives is to rebalance the internal and external elements in the Christian life so as better to sustain the thrust of mission. The chapters make it clear that various congregations conceptualise and articulate the challenge in different ways, and actualise it with widely differing resources. In general, those congregations with extensive international connections are able to direct much more 'firepower' to the task. So, too, are those who actually maintain some ownership as well as operational responsibility for schools. A different kind of challenge faces those like the Sisters of St Joseph who are finding ways to support school leaders of diocesan schools who are presently seeking to reclaim the spiritual mantle of St Mary MacKillop long after organisational connection with the congregation has ceased.

Spiritual traditions do not exist in the abstract but in particular contexts, and they are valued precisely because they enable people living in those contexts to balance the inner and outer dimensions of Christian life, and in the process sustain a clearly articulated mission. This mission might find its focus within the Church community or be directed outwards to meet wider needs.

The traditions explored in this section exist today because they are publicly recognised and honoured ways of living Christian life. They are recognised by the wider Church and especially honoured within the communities in which they originated and have subsequently developed. The founders of these sponsoring communities encapsulate, each in his or her own life, the essence of what will become the tradition. The founder takes on a symbolic value as the tradition becomes grounded in the narrative of his or her life and then in the unfolding narrative of the group.

The eight traditions explored in this section are sponsored by religious congregations whose members understand and articulate their respective spiritual traditions within the somewhat broader concept of 'charism'. 'Charism' is a gift of the Holy Spirit given to a group for the benefit of the Church in order to empower its life and serve its mission. It is a fulfilment of Jesus' promise that He would send the Holy Spirit to be with the disciples after his work had been done (e.g. Jn 16:7).

As the subsequent pages show, congregations understand this concept, and invite others to share it, in different ways. A number call on the articulation provided by Claude Maréchal for whom charism represents 'a story to enter; a language to speak, a group to which to belong, a way to pray, a work to undertake and a face of God to see'.[1] The balance between the interior and exterior dimensions of Christian life implied in this articulation of charism seems self-evident.

Each of the eight groups featured in this section has a unique spiritual tradition because of the way each engages with and embodies the six defining elements outlined above. Across the past twenty years, as recruitment to religious congregations has fallen away, and as members previously working in schools have been re-deployed to other assignments in Australia or overseas, there has been a significant change in the way congregational leaders have come to understand and promote their charism (and the spiritual tradition in which it is embedded). All have moved to share it with lay people. This invitation, initially extended to their co-workers in the schools, has now been extended to, and accepted by, other groups, both those wishing to appropriate the tradition in order to sustain the spiritual life of their members, and those seeking to re-appropriate the tradition where the connection with the congregation has been broken. These have been significant movements within the life of the Australian Church and demonstrate the function of charism as 'gift to the Church'.

A complementary development has been that congregational *identity* has been extended to lay movements. While this has long been true for some groups such as the Franciscans, its extension to other congregations has been a more recent development. A particular formal recognition of

---

1 Fr Maréchal was superior general of the Assumpionist Augustinians from 1987 to 1999. He first articulated this understanding of charism at a Union of Superiors General Meeting in Rome in 1987.

authenticity by the Church is the granting of canonical standing to some of these groups. This is a contemporary development in 'the story to enter'.

As the subsequent chapters show, the task of keeping a spiritual tradition alive is far from easy, and groups differ widely in the way they understand the task and how they pursue it. The chapters reflect both different understandings and different stages of development.

While the founder responsible for a spiritual tradition holds a revered place within the tradition, charism is not confined to, nor limited by, the outlook of the founder, important as this is. As a gift to the Church at large, charism (and its embedded spiritual tradition) has a dynamic quality since all six of its defining elements will continue to evolve as contexts and people change, and as the direction of mission evolves in response to human need, particularly among the marginalised in our societies. All eight case studies chart such developments.

While founders are rightly seen as heroes of the faith, who lived the Christian life in their particular time, each in his or her own way has developed a faith map[2] with Jesus at its centre. All eight accounts stress the mediating role of the founder in pointing beyond themselves to the person of Jesus and his mission to enable the Kingdom of God to be recognised and grow within human history. They point up the reality that this is the good news sustained through the action of God's Spirit.

The chapters that follow fall into two broad categories: those whose spiritual traditions flow from the charism of congregations founded in Australia and which operate predominantly within Australia, albeit with some commitments elsewhere; and those movements that are more international in character and whose leaders can call on and mobilise a wider range of experience and expertise. The Good Samaritan Sisters (Chapter Five) and the Sisters of St Joseph (Chapter Six) fall into the first category. The Salesians (Chapter Seven), the Mercy Sisters (Chapter Eight), the Christian Brothers (Chapter Nine), the Marist Brothers (Chapter Ten), the De La Salle Brothers (Chapter Eleven) and the Jesuits (Chapter Twelve) fall into the second group.

These eight chapters highlight the degree of pluralism that exists within the broader Catholic spiritual tradition; the way the tradition grows as people process the experience of the divine at work in their lives; the ways in which the tradition helps people depth their relationship with God; and the important place active engagement in a community and its mission plays in Christian life.

---

[2] See Michael Paul Gallagher, *Faith Maps: Ten Religious Explorers from Newman to Ratzinger* (New York: Paulist Press, 2010).

The contention of this book is that these traditions have come to be valued by lay people because they intuitively sense that unless they can hold in balance and sustain the inner and outer dimensions of Christian life, any mission that flows from it will prove highly problematic. From an organisational perspective, a spiritual tradition alive in a school is capable of sustaining its Catholic identity where it is shared by a critical mass of leaders and teachers. Creating such a critical mass is an important mission objective that all groups featured in this section now aspire to achieve.

Monica Dutton

Monica Dutton has been involved in Catholic education for 40 years, including 12 years in Good Samaritan schools. She is currently the Immersion and Resources Coordinator for the Good Samaritan Education Mission Team. During her career as an educator, Monica has worked in primary, secondary and adult educational settings. She has held the positions of Teacher Consultant in the Parramatta Diocese and Religious Education Coordinator in a number of diocesan and congregational schools. Monica has a particular interest in developing, implementing, and evaluating formation and immersion programs and resources for staff and students in Good Samaritan schools.

5

THE SISTERS OF THE GOOD SAMARITAN: A SPIRITUAL TRADITION IS SUSTAINED

Monica Dutton

GENESIS

The spiritual tradition of the Sisters of the Good Samaritan of the Order of St Benedict has its genesis in a story Jesus told about a man travelling along a winding, dusty road from Jerusalem towards Jericho. The Parable of the Good Samaritan, found only in the Gospel of Luke (Luke 10:25–37), is one of the most widely recognised of the parables, and the enduring message is one of compassion and love.

The Good Samaritan tradition emerged from the parable. Its spirituality was nourished by the wisdom of the Rule of St Benedict, brought to Australia by John Bede Polding OSB and sustained in Catholic educational communities in urban, rural and remote areas of Australia and across the Asia-Pacific region since 1857.

The Sisters of the Good Samaritan were the first religious congregation established in Australia. They were co-founded by Archbishop John Bede Polding – an English Benedictine monk – and Mother Scholastica Gibbons – an Irish Sister of Charity. The 'Good Sams' have had a significant role in the life of Catholic education in Australia since their foundation. Their directive from Polding was to be 'ready to teach in schools… and to apply themselves to every other charitable work'.[1] From their earliest days, the sisters committed themselves to assisting destitute women and educating young children in the fledgling penal colony of Sydney. The work of the congregation in schools and refuges has continued to this day – fulfilling Polding's vision for them as missionary Benedictines in the Great South Land of the Holy Spirit. The narrative of the Parable of the

---

1   Rules of Polding, *Scope and Character of the Institute* #1. Trustees of the Sisters of the Good Samaritan, 1982.

Good Samaritan has informed the ministry of the sisters and, historically, they have responded to the call to be neighbour in different ways, times and places across three centuries.

THE CHARISM OF THE SISTERS OF THE GOOD SAMARITAN

The word 'charism' itself stems from the Greek 'charisma', meaning 'gift', 'favour' or 'extraordinary power'. It is 'a pure gift of God for the good of the Church. Charism attracts people to engage in an overall task together, providing a constancy of orientation while allowing for internal growth and change'.[2] The charism of the Sisters of the Good Samaritan is clearly expressed. In 2011 when the congregation gathered in chapter, the sisters endorsed their vision statement (2011–2017), giving shape and direction to their life of prayer and service:

> *As Sisters of the Good Samaritan*
> *we seek God*
> *who impels us to be neighbour.*
> *We commit ourselves to:*
> *– the Work of God;*
> *– partnership;*
> *– creation.*

There are many ways to view charism. Augustinian Claude Maréchal describes it as giving 'structure, being and action, and involves a story to enter, a language to speak, a group to which to belong, a way to pray, a work to undertake, a face of God to see'.[3] Maréchal's concept of charism frames formation for mission in the Good Samaritan context.

'A story to enter' involves engagement with the key elements of the tradition – The Parable of the Good Samaritan, Benedictine spirituality and the history, mission and ministry of the sisters. 'A language to speak' refers to an awareness of the explicit values which are common to all Benedictine educational institutions. The values of love of Christ and neighbour, prayer, stability, conversatio,[4] obedience, discipline, humility,

---

2 Pope Paul VI, *Evangelica Testificatio* #11, 1971.
3 Fr Claude Maréchal, *Toward an effective partnership between religious and laity in fulfilment of charism and responsibility for mission. Charism and spirituality*. Proceedings of the 56th Conference of the Unione Superiore Generali, Rome.
4 *Conversatio* is a commitment to engage in practices that over a lifetime bring about conversion into the likeness of Christ and, in particular, Christ's giving of self for others. (Association of Benedictine Colleges & Universities Statement [The Ten Hallmarks of Benedictine Education]: Education within the Benedictine Wisdom Tradition rev 27 August 2007. http://www.abcu.info)

stewardship, hospitality, community, justice and peace underpin policies, practices and procedures in Good Samaritan schools.

'A group to which to belong' invites participants into the wider Good Samaritan community to form partnerships with members of other Good Samaritan Education schools, and raises global awareness of the connectedness to the Benedictine network of schools throughout the world. 'A work to undertake' provides insight into the mission of the Sisters in the early years and the diversity of contemporary ministries in which they are involved. Significantly, the educational dimension which was traditionally the core work of the Sisters is now sustained in partnership with their lay colleagues.

'A way to pray' and 'a face of God to see' invite a personal response to the expression of the Good Samaritan Benedictine charism through traditional and communal prayer, *lectio divina*,[5] and personal reflection.

HISTORICAL PERSPECTIVES

To vision the future we must understand the past. The diversity of congregationally founded schools in Australia is largely a product of its unique historical context. The belief that authentic Catholic education is an integrated process was clearly articulated by Polding in 1859.

> His idea of a Catholic School was a holistic one. At its centre was 'the living teacher, the living pupil' interacting within a fully Catholic atmosphere where Religion was not just one subject amongst others, but the coordinating principle of the entire school.[6]

With this as the blueprint for Catholic education in Australia, the introduction of various Acts of Parliament in the colonies inaugurating the removal of government funding from denominational schools across the country[7] provided the impetus for bishops to seek additional congregations to establish, administer and staff Catholic schools, particularly in remote areas. The hierarchical nature and frugal needs of the congregations enabled Catholic schools to expand rapidly and flourish throughout the colony. Along with other religious orders, many from Ireland and Europe, the

---

5 Prayerful reading of Scripture.
6 Margaret Walsh, *The Good Sams: Sisters of the Good Samaritan 1857–1969* (Mulgrave: John Garratt Publishing, 2001).
7 These Acts established public school systems. The 1872 Victorian Act most clearly established public education as 'free, compulsory, and secular'. In other colonies there were a variety of Acts over several decades cumulating into the overall situation which caused the Australian Catholic Bishops to see the necessity for assuming responsibility for providing Catholic education for Catholic children in this country. See Craig Campbell, *Free, Compulsory and Secular: Education Acts Australia, 1850–1910*. dehanz.net.au/entries/free-compulsory-secular-education-acts/

Sisters of the Good Samaritan ministered primarily in education for the next hundred years. Throughout the nineteenth and twentieth centuries, the Sisters responded generously to the invitation of bishops to establish schools throughout Australia, particularly in the eastern states.

Less than a hundred years after being founded, the congregation answered a request for help from overseas for the first time when in 1948 five sisters went to Japan. Bishop Yamaguchi of Nagasaki had written to ask for assistance in reconstructing his diocese, which had been devastated by the atomic bomb. He needed a community of Sisters to set up a clinic and establish schools. The Sisters of the Good Samaritan responded with overwhelming generosity to the bishop's call, and Our Lady of the Cherry Blossom Kindergarten and Seiwa High School in Sasebo were established in 1952–53, and remain thriving school communities today. A community of sisters continues to live in Nara – one of the oldest cities in Japan.

In the 1980s, the church in Japan expressed a strong desire for solidarity with the poor in Asia. After sending two sisters to study in Manila, and following a significant period of discernment, the Good Samaritan sisters in Japan decided to establish a community in the Philippines. In 1990, sisters from Japan and Australia took up residence in Bacolod. The Good Samaritan Kinder School opened its doors in 2004, and the sisters are today involved in a broad range of ministries including spiritual direction, teaching at the seminary, a long term commitment to Concepcion Parish, and ministry to the urban poor in nearby slums.

In 1988 the sisters responded to an invitation from the Bishop of Kiribati to assist with the education of young people. Again, the congregation answered the call to be neighbour with generosity and compassion through ministries in education at the Kiribati Pastoral Institute and Religious Education. The sisters now have two communities, run a preschool and offer pastoral care in villages and centres for people with disabilities. Closer to home, after the atrocities of the Indonesian occupation of Timor-Leste, the Sisters of the Good Samaritan responded to the call for assistance and have had an active presence in education since 2001.

In exploring the question 'Who is my neighbour?' (Luke 10:29), and its imperative 'Go and do likewise' (Luke 10:37), the work of the congregation has expanded well beyond urban, rural and remote Australian communities, as the sisters have responded to the needs of our neighbours in the Asia Pacific region, both near and far.

CONTEMPORARY PERSPECTIVES

From approximately the 1870s–1880s until the mid–1960s, Catholic schools in Australia were the domain of members of religious congregations.[8] Their particular ethos and charism were transmitted through the lived example of the sisters, brothers and priests who were highly visible and influential members of school communities. Their presence was also instrumental in attracting vocations, which ensured perpetuity of the order.

After the Second Vatican Council (1962–65), there was a rapid and marked decline in the numbers of religious in Catholic schools. In the spirit of aggiornamento, many congregations reviewed their position in Catholic schools in the light of their founding charism and moved into ministries of justice with the poor and marginalised. After the upheaval in the Church during those years, a significant number left religious life altogether. Across Australia, this decline in numbers of religious in Catholic schools has been rapid and has had an enormous impact on the leadership and staffing of Catholic schools.

While religious maintained a high profile in schools, the transmission of their spiritual traditions occurred quite naturally. In the immediate 'post-religious' phase, it was thought by many that the process would continue almost by osmosis. The reality, however, was quite different. Within a short period of time and with many schools being subsumed into diocesan systems, the particular heritage, traditions and spirituality of some congregational schools became diluted to the point of being indistinguishable.

It became clear that religious orders needed to work in collaboration with their lay counterparts to ensure the life of their spiritual traditions in educational settings. The Second Vatican Council challenged all involved in Catholic education to adapt their worldview in line with contemporary thinking.[9] It also commended the rightful position of lay people and their 'proper and indispensable role in the mission of the Church'.[10] As the Sisters of the Good Samaritan clearly recognise that the Holy Spirit confers spiritual traditions not only on religious congregations, but also on the 'faithful of every rank',[11] they continued to develop strong and visionary partnerships with their lay colleagues.

---

8 For the first fifty years from approximately 1820 to 1870, most of the education provided to Catholics was the work of dedicated lay women and men often in close partnership with local priests. A few schools were conducted by religious during this period.
9 Congregation for Catholic Education, *The Catholic School* #17.
10 *Gaudium et Spes* #4.
11 *Lumen Gentium* #12.

NEW MODELS OF GOVERNANCE

For the first hundred years, the Sisters of the Good Samaritan were responsible for the administration of their schools – often within parish communities and in partnership with the laity. In the latter stages of the twentieth century, the congregation acknowledged the need for a new model of governance for their schools. They engaged in a long process of discernment, conversation and negotiation to determine the most appropriate way forward to take their schools into the future. By 1993 each of the ten remaining Good Samaritan schools was incorporated as a company limited by guarantee and governed according to a constitution.[12]

In the early 2000s, with gradually declining numbers, an ageing population and with many involved in ministries outside education, the Sisters of the Good Samaritan again recognised the need to review their governance structures to ensure the sustainability of their spiritual tradition in the educational setting. Between 2009 and 2011 a process of consultation was undertaken to discern the most appropriate model of governance to meet the current and future needs of the ten Australian Good Samaritan schools. Central to the process was the understanding that 'at all times the Church carries the responsibility of reading the signs of the times and of interpreting them in the light of the Gospel if it is to carry out its task'.[13] After hearing from the entire community[14], and much deliberation, it emerged that a diocesan collegial public juridic person (PJP) was the most appropriate governance structure for the future life of the ten schools.[15] The PJP is a model adopted by a number of religious congregations in recent times. It is 'established by ecclesial authority with an apostolic purpose; it is perpetual in nature; it has canonical rights and obligations and has its own internal statutes'.[16]

With the agreement of the Archbishops of Melbourne and Brisbane and the Bishops of Wollongong and Broken Bay, Good Samaritan Education (GSE) was constituted by the Archbishop of Sydney, Cardinal George Pell, in July 2011. Good Samaritan Education 'assumed the rights and obligations pertaining to the ministry of Catholic education'.[17] A fitting synergy exists in that the sisters were founded by the first Archbishop of Sydney, John Bede Polding, and the PJP Good Samaritan Education was constituted by the Archbishop of Sydney at the time, Cardinal George Pell.

---

12 *Good Samaritan Education: A History* (hereafter cited as *GSE: A History*), (Sydney: Good Samaritan Education, 2011), 7.
13 *Gaudium et Spes* #4.
14 *Rule of Benedict* #3.
15 *GSE: A History*, 7.
16 John Date, *Implications of Canon Law for Church Organisations Operating in Australia* (Masters Research thesis, Law, the University of Melbourne, 2008), 27–28.
17 *GSE: A History*, 7.

The new ecclesial entity, Good Samaritan Education, involves ten schools across three states in five dioceses: St Scholastica's College and Rosebank College in the Sydney Archdiocese; Mount St Benedict College and Stella Maris College in the Broken Bay Diocese; St Patrick's College, St Mary Star of the Sea College and Mater Dei School in the Wollongong Diocese; Mater Christi College and Santa Maria College in the Melbourne Archdiocese and Lourdes Hill College in the Brisbane Archdiocese.

As a collegial PJP, Good Samaritan Education is committed to communio (the building of an authentic community), and to discernment as fundamental to life. As a community of faith, established to participate in the ministry of Catholic education, Good Samaritan Education is enriched by its heritage, now taking on new form and new expression according to its Statement of Charism[18]:

> The charism of Good Samaritan Education is centred on the person of Jesus Christ in the communal seeking of God, believing that it is together – not as isolated individuals – that we go to God (RB 72:12), our hearts overflowing with the inexpressible delight of love (RB Prologue 49).
>
> Enriched and inspired by the Parable of the Good Samaritan, the Rule of Benedict and the Sisters of the Good Samaritan, the mission of Good Samaritan Education is to sustain and nurture communities of learning in the Catholic tradition.
>
> Such communities of learning are formed by essential values drawn from the Rule of Benedict: love of neighbour, prayer, stability, conversatio, obedience, discipline, humility, stewardship, hospitality, community and justice'.[19]

The sisters were clear and purposeful in their desire to pass on their tradition in ways that are meaningful and relevant to people in a post-modern context. The congregation instigated the changes of governance models and are very aware that 'a particular charism provides a story to enter but it must, first of all, be a story that attracts and is an intuitive fit for the person involved. It must inspire a response to the Gospel call to action'.[20] The responsibilities of Good Samaritan Education include oversight of the expression of the ethos, the care of temporal goods and achieving the objects of the companies.[21]

---

18   *GSE: A History*, 7.
19   Ibid., 7.
20   *GSE: A Handbook*, 4.
21   Ibid., 10.

SUSTAINING THE SPIRITUAL TRADITION OF THE SISTERS OF THE GOOD SAMARITAN

Catholic Identity and Mission

Good Samaritan Education schools are firmly grounded in a rich Catholic heritage and culture. Catholic schools are Christocentric and aim to promote a worldview based on the teachings of Jesus. They are both educational communities and Christian communities.[22] Central to the culture of a Catholic school is its call to be a living expression of the mission of the Church. The Catholic School 'participates in the evangelising mission of the Church and is the privileged environment in which Christian education is carried out'.[23] The authentic Catholic school is determined by the extent to which the Church is present in the school and the school is present in the Church. Christian ideals and values which sustain the mission of the Church are nurtured through formation and immersion in a particular spiritual tradition.

The focus of mission in the ecclesial sense has shifted in recent years. Post-Vatican II, mission is viewed as being for the reign of God, to the world, by the community of believers. This approach to mission calls for a greater focus on dialogue and demands genuine collaboration with non-ordained members of the Church. This more contemporary view is expressed by Stephen Bevans, one which does not deny that the Church has a mission, but which points to a more fundamental reality, viz., that it is not so much that God's Church has a mission, but rather, that God's mission has a Church.[24] The Catholic school is part of the Catholic Church, and as such is an agent of this mission.[25]

For a spiritual tradition to be a dynamic part of a school community it must be shared by all stakeholders. The Catholic school is unique because it provides a religious community within a learning community. All members of the community are called to follow Jesus and to commit to be and to build Church. Provision of opportunities for all members to engage with the history, traditions, values and spirituality of the charism needs to be strategically planned. Within the Good Samaritan context, formation and immersion programs are 'presented within a climate of mutual respect and support and involving individual and shared reflection'.[26]

---

22 *Lay Catholics in Schools: Witnesses to Faith* #22
23 Congregation for Catholic Education, *The Catholic School on the Threshold of the Third Millennium* #11
24 Stephen Bevans, *The Mission has a Church: An Invitation to the Dance* (Melbourne: Yarra Theological Union, 2009).
25 Congregation for Catholic Education, *The Catholic School* #9
26 GSE: A Handbook, 9.

Good Samaritan Education

Since the inception of the new PJP, Good Samaritan Education, there has been a shift in responsibility and accountability for the ongoing transmission of the charism from the congregation to this new ecclesial entity. To that end, the *Good Samaritan Education Formation for Mission Framework*[27], along with the supporting document, *Good Samaritan Education Formation for Mission – A Handbook,* have been developed. These documents outline the progressive nature of programs for all members of Good Samaritan Education school communities, and their associated responsibilities. The expectation is clear: 'All who accept the invitation to join Good Samaritan Education will participate in formation experiences to assist them to grow in understanding of their ministry as part of the mission of the Catholic Church'.[28]

Responsibility for oversight of the expression of the Good Samaritan spiritual tradition within the schools now lies with Good Samaritan Education. Within its structure, the Good Samaritan Education Mission Team provides a range of formation and immersion opportunities for participants to 'become inspired by the charism to respond to the Gospel call to bring about the reign of God'.[29] The Good Samaritan Education Mission Team Charter Statement outlines its purpose:

> *The Good Samaritan Education Mission Team shares the story and stewards the spirit of the Good Samaritan Benedictine tradition with our school communities. Forming in the spirit, immersing in the story, developing resources and building partnerships are at the heart of all our programs.*[30]

Formation Programs

The effectiveness of formation programs may ultimately determine the effectiveness and credibility of Catholic schools with respect to their mission. Staff formation is acknowledged as a priority area for professional learning and is argued to be the ultimate basis by which teachers are empowered to pursue the mission of Catholic education.[31]

The Second Vatican Council is also clear in its statement pertaining to educators in Catholic schools in that they need to be 'willing to offer a

---

27 *Good Samaritan Education Formation for Mission Framework* (Sydney: Good Samaritan Education, 2011).
28 *GSE: A Handbook*, 6.
29 Ibid., 2.
30 Good Samaritan Education, *Mission Team Charter Statement* (Sydney: Good Samaritan Education, 2011).
31 *Lay Catholics in Schools: Witnesses to Faith* #22

permanent commitment to formation and self-formation regarding a choice of cultural and life values to be made present in the educational community'.[32] Spiritual formation of staff in Catholic schools has consistently been acknowledged by ecclesial authorities as vital to the effective mission of Catholic schools.[33] The formation and immersion programs offered by Good Samaritan Education are positioned within a spiritual formation framework and seek to be explicit in their expression of the particular educational mission of the Catholic school. They are designed to be developmental, ecclesial and vocationally contextualised.[34]

Formation in the spiritual tradition of the congregation is therefore central to all members of Good Samaritan Education school communities. A range of opportunities is provided for all to 'enter the story' in ways that are meaningful, and to offer points at which they are able to access and make a personal contribution to that story.

Formation for assembly members, directors, principals and senior management takes the form of conferences, retreats, targeted formation days and formation components in meetings. Leadership teams and staff members are provided with induction programs, refresher days, conferences, retreats and immersion opportunities. Students engage in programs directed towards leadership, service, retreat and immersion, and information sessions are offered to the parent community. All Good Samaritan Education programs are underpinned by resources and frameworks for education, and are designed to support structures for formation and immersion operating in individual schools.

A recent development in Good Samaritan Education schools is the formation of Mission Teams. The teams report to the principal and are responsible for the implementation of programs and initiatives which animate the mission life of the school. Typically, the team is led by the assistant principal/Dean of Mission and includes the Religious Education coordinator and the college chaplain. Staff involved in music, dance and drama are often consulted with respect to liturgical celebrations.

---

32 *Educating Together in Catholic Schools: A Shared Mission Between Consecrated Persons and the Lay Faithful* #5
33 Congregation for Catholic Education, *Lay Catholics in Schools: Witnesses to Faith* #24
34 *GSE: A Handbook*, 9

SUSTAINING THE GOOD SAMARITAN SPIRITUAL TRADITION THROUGH PARTNERSHIP

At the same time as congregations are working in partnership with their lay colleagues to sustain their spiritual traditions, many lay people themselves are being drawn to particular charisms to deepen their own spirituality. This phenomenon in turn regenerates and rejuvenates the charism and those who hold it.

The Congregation for Catholic Education insists that the 'transmission of charism depends on the effectiveness of the essential dialogue between religious and their lay successors', and makes reference to the term, 'charismatic circularity'.[35] This implies that a spiritual tradition will be enriched to the extent that those handing on the tradition are open to receiving from those who have encountered, or are encountering it.[36]

The challenge of sustaining the Good Samaritan spiritual tradition in educational communities into the twenty-first century has been met with vision, foresight and wisdom. Great respect for those who have carried the tradition in the past and for those who take it into the future is evident. Listening and discernment have been central to the initiatives that have emerged. The Sisters of the Good Samaritan recognise clearly that 'the spiritual tradition takes on a new life and energy and shape in the lives of those who embrace it. These people make meaning in a new time, coming into discipleship with Jesus and becoming a community of mission'.[37]

---

[35] *Decree on the Apostolate of the Laity* #3
[36] John Lydon, 'Transmission of the Charism: A Major Challenge for Catholic Education' *International Studies in Catholic Education*, 1 (1), 42–58.
[37] GSE: A Handbook, 4.

Catherine Clark rsj

Catherine Clark is a South Australian Sister of St Joseph. She spent many years as teacher and principal in Catholic and government schools. Catherine has served as Provincial leader of her congregation and Chair of the Education Committee of the Conference of Congregational leaders of Australia. For many years she chaired the South Australian Commission for Catholic Schools, and also served on the National Catholic Education Commission. Her community involvements embrace governance in social service settings. Catherine currently spends much time on the formation of Catholic school staffs. In 2003 she was awarded the Order of Australia medal for her contribution to education and social welfare.

6

THE SPIRITUAL TRADITION OF THE AUSTRALIAN SISTERS OF ST JOSEPH IN EDUCATION IN SOUTH AUSTRALIA

Catherine Clark rsj

The spiritual tradition of the Australian Sisters of St Joseph was the basis for many of the diocesan systems of Catholic education in Australia. The first formal diocesan system of Catholic schools, as distinct from individual schools for Catholics, in Australia was established in South Australia in response to the Education Act passed by the Legislative Council of South Australia in 1851, and promulgated in 1852. This Act was set in a time of Christian interdenominational conflict and its requirements in relation to the handing on of the Catholic faith tradition were not acceptable to the Australian Catholic bishops. This was to be the case with similar Acts passed later in the other Australian Colonies.

Bishop Murphy, the first Bishop of South Australia, arrived in 1844. He recognised the poverty of the South Australian Catholic population and that this poverty meant that the diocese could not attract the support of any teaching religious orders. He addressed this need by enabling the lay-conducted Catholic schools of the times to live within the requirements of the Act, by accepting the Government's financial and religious conditions during school hours and teaching the Catholic faith tradition outside the times required by the school day.

In 1859 Bishop Geoghegan arrived as the second Bishop to South Australia. He found the arrangement established by Bishop Murphy unacceptable. He addressed this in two ways: firstly, by reminding Catholics of their duty to make provision for Catholic schools. He did this by a series of what he termed 'missions', whereby he moved throughout the colony reminding Catholics of their obligations. Secondly, he demanded

Government assistance to fund the Catholic Schools. In 1860, he issued a pastoral letter on the issue, which concluded with the words:

> Wherever there is a Pastor and a Flock, we implore you to make a commencement of a Catholic School. Let each do what he can.[1]

At Penola, in the south-east of South Australia, the pastor Julian Tenison Woods was instrumental in establishing such a Catholic school. In 1866, with the retirement of the two women who taught there, Father Woods asked Mary MacKillop, a former governess in the area, to help him establish a special kind of school. Together they began a teaching religious order of women who:

> would live in some cottage in a bush settlement or lowly city area, in a religious community dedicated to prayer and observing the religious vows, prepared to forego the attendance at Mass and the sacraments for long periods, like the Catholics around them. They were to teach pupils in a Catholic context, supported by the local people, since their radical concept of poverty included having no property or other means of support.[2]

In the same year, Bishop Geoghegan was replaced by Bishop Sheil, who immediately appointed Father Woods as his secretary. He then created the position of Director of Catholic Education and appointed Woods to the role. Bishop Sheil visited Penola:

> to meet Mary MacKillop and her assistant teachers, addressed her as 'Sister Mary' and gave his approval to Father Woods' plan to bring them to Adelaide to help launch a system of schools to be organised and controlled by a central authority.[3]

Thus the Josephites became the basis for the extension of the first formal diocesan system of Catholic Education to be established in Australia. Various bishops in Australia and New Zealand then set up diocesan systems of schools, often staffed by the Sisters of St Joseph. As a consequence, a growing number of diocesan schools still claim the original spiritual tradition of the Josephites as the foundational spiritual tradition of the school. This has led to formal and informal associations of teachers and other staff to explore the relevance of the Josephite tradition in today's Catholic education systems. In this chapter, I would like to explore elements of their journey in South Australia.

---

1   Pastoral Letter, 1860 South Australian Archives, Archdiocese of Adelaide.
2   Margaret M. Press, *From our Broken Toil – South Australian Catholics 1836–1906* (Adelaide: Catholic Archdiocese, 1986), 157.
3   Ibid,158.

Unlike many other religious congregations, the Sisters of St Joseph have rarely independently owned the property and contents of the schools they have conducted. Hence, ongoing canonical governing structures have not been an issue in the future enlivening of their particular mission in education. Schools conducted by the Josephites were owned and canonically governed by individual parishes/diocese. As a consequence, the ongoing continuity of the what is at the heart of Josephite education is not so much an issue of canonical governance or ownership, but rather that of charism and spirituality. In South Australia, Mary MacKillop College is an exception to this.[4]

In the case where governance is in the hands of the Congregation, or where the Congregation sets up alternative governing structures, care must be taken to make sure that governance structures do not become mere administrative and financial operations. The following relationships need to be enshrined:

Relationship between GOVERNANCE and PURPOSE

GOVERNANCE is the *Famework*

which enables

CHARISM – which is the *Gift* – **the living Gospel**

to be expressed in the

MINISTRY – which is the *Medium*

to achieve the

MISSION OF GOD – which is the *Purpose*

Thus, in the many schools established in the Josephite tradition, but where the ultimate governing authority is the diocese, the local school board needs to recognise this relationship as a part of their responsibility for the ethos of the school.

ESTABLISHMENT OF STRUCTURE/S FOR THE DEVELOPMENT OF THE JOSEPHITE SPIRITUAL TRADITION IN EDUCATION

By 1960, Sister Maurice Roche had been appointed by the Congregation as Education Coordinator for Josephite Schools in South Australia. One aspect of her role was to assist the principals in inducting the growing number of

---

[4] This college grew out of the practice of providing secondary education within the primary setting for those who could not afford to attend the colleges. These students were gathered together and the Sisters of St Joseph established a secondary school which later came to be owned and operated by the congregation.

lay teachers in these schools in the Josephite tradition in education. This tradition was later articulated and explored through the formation of a Josephite Education Committee, first made up of the Josephites working in the ministry of education and, in the 1990s, incorporating the principals and senior leaders of schools which were established in the Josephite tradition. Through this structure, a more formal exploration of Josephite charism and spirituality in the ministry of education and its role in the mission of God began to be explored.

Discussion of 'charism' is often confused, even short-circuited, by incorrect and misleading impressions of what is being discussed. One example of this is the statement: '*In our school we focus on the Gospel rather than the charism.*' Another is '*To explore charism is to concentrate on the traditions of the past. We need to work in the context of today and not go back to the past.*' Such statements, which are occasionally heard, call for a clarification of what we mean by the words 'charism' and 'tradition'.

CHARISM

At the Second Vatican Council, during the drafting of the Dogmatic Constitution on the Church – *Lumen Gentium* – Cardinal Suenens pointed out that there is a tension between the institutional Church and the charismatic Church. He concluded that we need both dimensions – the institutional, with its structure and governance to coordinate direction, and the charismatic action of the Spirit of God, acting in humanity and creation, to prevent the institutional Church from becoming directionless.[5]

At a dialogue sponsored by the National Catholic Education Commission and the Australian Conference of Leaders of Religious Institutes, Sister Elizabeth Dodds, Sister of Charity, in speaking about charism, observed that despite the number of books and articles written on the subject, the concept remains elusive. She used the image of 'wind' to describe the visible face of the Spirit of God blowing amongst us.[6]

This Spirit of God working in humanity and all creation brings about the reign of God amongst us.

Charism is a particular action of the Spirit of God in our midst People gather around that charism, but it does not belong to them in any absolute way, because it is an action of the Holy Spirit. The Gospels record for us the mission of God in our midst in human form in the person of Jesus, and

---

5 Léon Joseph Suenens, 'The Charismatic Dimension of the Church' in Hans Kung, Yves Congar and Daniel O'Hanlon (eds) *Council Speeches of Vatican II* (London: Sheed and Ward, 1964).
6 Elizabeth Dodds, 'The Future of Charisms in Catholic Schools' Unpublished paper at the dialogue sponsored by NCEC and ACLRI in Caloundra, Queensland, 1998.

it was Jesus, 'God in our midst', who told us he must go, 'Because unless I go, the Advocate will not come to you' (John 16:7). Hence, our belief in God's mission continuing in our midst through the Spirit of God acting in particular times and places through particular people. Those who gather around that gifting of God's Spirit must continually identify what was at the heart of that manifestation of the mission of God in our midst, and bring it to life again in new times, new places and new ways.

We are reminded that:

> ...charisms are not given to Religious Institutes per se, nor are they owned by them. [Charisms are] about giving renewed vitality and efficacy to the Gospel of Jesus. They have given people a story to enter, a language to speak, a group to which to belong, a way to pray, a work to undertake, a face of God to see.[7]

In summary, a charism has been described as a distinctive way of incarnating the living Gospel, a particular igniting of the Gospel, or a bold revelation of God. Joan Chittister has a variety of poetic descriptions. One I recall and acknowledge from an address is her description of charism as the heart of a founding person aglow at one period of history, beating on in us, in another day and age. Charisms are a particular living of the Gospel that gives shape and vitality to spirituality and ministry.

TRADITION

Often 'tradition' is associated with something 'out of date', 'past' or 'old'. Working with groups of teachers and leaders, we have come to see it as captured in the following way:

> To take what is the strongest and the most vital part
> To carry it through into a new world
> And often,
> To express it in a new way.

Hence, tradition is not so much about the past, as about the *value* – the strongest and most vital part of something, or the principle that gives it meaning. It is a living, evolving concept, which carries what is at the heart of a people's meaning into the current lived situation and this will often require it to be expressed in a new way.

---

7 Michael Green fms, 'Charisms: Possibilities and Challenges', Marist Publishing, October 2000. Green is drawing on the work of C. Maréchal, 'Charism and Spirituality', *Proceedings of the 56th Conference of the Unione Superiore Generali*, Rome.

ARTICULATING THE GROUNDING OF THE GOSPEL IN THE LIFE AND ACTION OF MARY MACKILLOP

In order to identify and name particular aspects of the Gospel revealed in the life and work of Mary MacKillop, groups across schools in various geographical and social areas began by exploring the historical context in which Mary exercised her ministry. This was done by asking four questions:

- Who was the God that Mary knew and revealed through her words and actions and where did she meet that God in her life?
- Who were the people to whom she revealed that God? Did she have particular people as the object of her service?
- In what spirit did Mary conduct her service of the people to whom she was committed?
- Through what action did Mary serve people?

From the discernment of many groups over time, there developed the following particular expression of what was named the Spirit of Mary MacKillop:

> The SPIRIT OF MARY MACKILLOP is to
> Reveal the COMPASSIONATE GOD
> Present in the ORDINARY, LOCAL CIRCUMSTANCES OF LIFE
> To ALL PEOPLE
> Especially those who are POOR, or MARGINALISED or ISOLATED
> in a spirit of HUMILITY, SIMPLICITY AND PRACTICAL RESPONSE
> With a respect for each person's HUMAN DIGNITY
> In a manner that inspires CONFIDENCE AND EMPOWERMENT, and through the development of KNOWLEDGE AND SKILLS
> To be used for the LOVE AND SERVICE of others

Hence the charism has been expressed as:

> A passionate desire to respond to and reveal the Compassionate God
> - a God who is present in the ordinariness of life
> - a God who reaches out to all people
> - a God whose special love is for those who are poor, marginalised or isolated

- *a God to be revealed through a life of simplicity, humility, and practical response*
- *a God whose love for each calls for a respect for human dignity*
- *and an empowerment of each person by calling forth and developing confidence, knowledge and skills*
- *so that each may lead a life of love and service of others*

From the above it can be seen that in the exploration being undertaken the words 'charism' and 'spirit of Mary MacKillop' carry the same meaning.

It is at this stage of looking at the historical perspective that it is imperative that we enable a reflection that goes deeper and wider than the historical context. In answering the four questions posed above, it is important to recognise that we are exploring words and actions which took place in the context of different *human experiences* and a different *cultural context* from that of today. To use the same words and to do the same actions would mean that we are over a hundred years out of date. We need to see how the historical person, Mary MacKillop, in the time we are questioning, interpreted the Gospel story and action in response to what was then a new time. In other words we need to ask: how was the action of Mary MacKillop missionary in her time? How did she challenge the people and the institutional Church to see the action of God with new eyes, the eyes of their place and their time? This questioning needs to enable us to see how she challenged the people of her time to ground Jesus' message about the mission of God in the circumstances of her own place and time.

CHARISM IN THE PRESENT CONTEXT

It then follows that we are called to name what it is about the Gospel message that Mary MacKillop revealed in her historical circumstances that we are now called to reveal in ours. The heart of the message will remain the same, but its circumstances and expressions must be ones that can speak to the context of our young people today as we strive, as they do, to translate the core message of Jesus into a practical action and symbolic expression that speaks to and gives meaning to faith and mission.

Hence having named the spirit of Mary MacKillop as she lived it in her time, we need then to examine how we are called today:
- to reveal the God of compassion so that people can experience the love of God through our human action;
- to understand that God is present whenever we meet one another and wherever we are;

- to recognise that we are called to have a response to all within our community as Jesus did, and to make sure that our outreach gives preference to those who are poor, marginalised or isolated: our response is not to be conditional on the cause but to address the experience in order to bring dignity and care to those in need;
- to live simplicity of life in a manner that challenges the consumerist society in which we live, and to create a climate where we 'live simply in order that others may simply live.' It calls us to see that this embodies a lifestyle that leads us to respect our world and to be involved in a response to the environmental challenges of today that will impact on all our tomorrows;
- to see humility as an expression of truth: that the word humility is understood, not as a 'doormat' mentality but as a deep understanding of the truth of who we are. Humility is the capacity to be able to acknowledge both our strengths and our weaknesses, as individuals and as a society, so that we may use our strengths to benefit the people and the surroundings where we are and to seek help when we and others are in need;
- to spend our time responding practically to the needs of our time rather than merely naming the needs and expecting others to make the response;
- to act always with a respect for the human dignity of the other, no matter what the context of the interchange with the other;
- to engage in action which seeks to empower others to 'have life and have it to the full' so that they in their turn may express that life in the service of God and others.

In following this call we take what was at the heart of what Mary MacKillop said and did in the past, and carry it into our human experiences and cultural contexts, and we articulate their expression in word and action. We are re-establishing and maintaining a spiritual tradition as a living, evolving concept that carries what was at the heart a people's meaning and actions at one period, into the current lived situation. This is likely to require that it be re-expressed.

In the process of exploring the Josephite tradition we are involved in a deeper reflection on Scripture, our faith and our Church. This leads us to an exploration of what it means to be a Catholic, and in this case what we are called to be as a Catholic school, in the context of today's culture and human experience.

TRANSLATING THE CHARISM INTO A LIVED SPIRITUALITY OF A PARTICULAR MINISTRY

When it comes to the question of translating this expression of charism into today's lived experience, we are dealing with the question of spirituality. I have come to the following as a helpful definition of spirituality:

> *Spirituality is what we say and do as a consequence of what we believe about God, others, self and our world.*

This is true of each person's spirituality. If charism is what we believe about God, others, ourselves and our world, then the spirituality of our ministry (the school), is revealed by what we say and do as a consequence of that belief in God, others, self and our world. What we say and do in a ministry is articulated in our *policies and practices* – what we say we will do and what we actually do. Hence it is important that there be a constant testing of our policies and practices – what we say and what we do – against what we hold to be the spirit of our endeavour – the Josephite charism.

Situating the charism and its expression in the context of today's human experience and cultural setting is an exercise of articulating our current *vision* which expresses the future we seek to bring into being. The importance of a congruence between what we believe to be the special gift of the Holy Spirit entrusted to us (charism), what we say and do (spirituality), and the current experiential and cultural contexts in which we operate, is essential if our ministry is to be the place in which we participate in the mission of God today.

We examine the spirituality of Mary MacKillop (what she said and did) to get an insight into the action of the Holy Spirit (charism) in her life. At this point we can easily make the mistake of remaining with the historical story and spiritual expression of that time rather than engage with what was at the heart of that spirituality (the charism) and find an expression of that in a new time and a new cultural context, and hence create a spirituality for our time. If a spiritual heritage is to continue to be an expression of God's mission in and through our spirituality today, it must be renewed and re-imagined in the light of today's world and in the context of our current cultural reality. If we acknowledge the Church and Catholic education to be in a liminal time, a time of immense change, then we need to be returning to the question of purpose – the mission of God in our lives today. The mission of God is what charism expresses. Hence, we need to renew and re-imagine, in today's times, our spiritual heritage.

The continuing Josephite spiritual heritage, which was developed by those who gathered around that expression of God's action in the world of Mary MacKillop's time, needs to be re-imagined in today's world. In the Catholic story, mission was once thought of as the prerogative of the hierarchical Church directing missionary groups (usually religious congregations) to carry out missionary activity. With a development of the view that mission is God's action through a community (Church) and that 'Church' is defined since the Second Vatican Council as the People of God, then the 'spiritual heritage' (in this case the Josephite spiritual heritage) needs to be re-imagined in new ways. It is a question of how that spiritual tradition is adjusted to today's understanding of mission (God's work in our world) and today's understanding of Church as People of God.

When mission is understood as the call of the People of God, the charism gifted through the person and action of Mary MacKillop and carried on through mission as it was understood in the past, needs now to be enshrined in new ways. It is a question of a refounding of how people are called to gather around a particular expression of God's mission, and of what structures best define and determine that spiritual tradition in today's world. We are not here talking about managing an organisation or a work. We are focusing on how the mission of God is continued in a new understanding, and on who is called and how they are called to give expression to the missionary action of God in our world today.

Such efforts to reframe the expression of the mission of God were called for in the Second Vatican Council when it reframed the concept of the Church from a canonical concept of institutional groups (clergy, religious and laity) to the concept of the Church as People of God. The impact of this insight gifted to the Church leaders at this great Council of the Church is yet to be fully understood and fully realised. I see one aspect of it as a call to express the spiritual traditions in new ways. Gerald Arbuckle illustrates the movement of communities from a liminal situation to a new integration. He clearly states that the first response to liminality, when uncertainty about identity emerges, is to move to structural change. However, structural change will not lead us to a new place. What is required is a refounding phase rather than a restructuring phase. Restructuring deals only with 'what is'. Refounding calls us to a time

- where we recognise that interior attitudinal change is required;
- where we take time to rediscover our roots, not to resort to nostalgic movements but to discover again what it is that we are readjusting to a new time and a new cultural reality;
- where we listen to each other and engage with each other in a way that enables the prophetic voice to be recognised.[8]

---

8   Gerald Arbuckle, *Out of Chaos*, (Marwah: Paulist Press, 1988), 16.

While structures are necessary for the charism to operate, the charismatic voice must not be bridled by the emergence of new structures before the community to whom it has been entrusted has had time to consider how all the followers of Jesus are called to respond to the issues of today's world and to today's new cultural identities. An emphasis on *refounding* will lead to a deeper exploration of what it means for all members of the Church to respond as disciples of God's mission in today's world. Structures need to be the servant of God's mission in our midst, and structures which enabled the expression of God's mission through particular spiritual traditions need to be reviewed in the light of today's circumstances.

REFLECTION ON EXPERIENCE

A group of leaders in those South Australian schools which carry the Josephite spiritual tradition are currently seeking to explore together how the values expressed in this particular tradition can enable God's mission to flourish in the contemporary context. They are giving witness to the fact that the Holy Spirit is now gifting movements of people, and that in our time, charism is of necessity carried in a *wider movement than solely through the agency of the religious congregation to whom it was first entrusted.* If the movement of South Australian leaders is to successfully embed the Josephite spiritual tradition in the daily life of schools, it will be essential that these leaders ensure that the structural changes necessary to take Catholic education into the future are such as to enable this movement, and other similar movements, to continue faithfully their vital work in our time and place. In working with leaders I have come to realise that we are in the midst of a major new time of the Holy Spirit. I have also come to the realisation that in our time, as in other times of great change in human history, the Holy Spirit plays a very long game. It is a time for trust, discernment, and brave initiatives.

Bernie Graham sdb

Bernie Graham is a Salesian priest, ordained in 1989. He is an experienced educational and school leader having been principal in three Salesian schools, one in each of Tasmania, Victoria and New South Wales. He holds qualifications in education, theology and leadership. Bernie is currently the Vice-Provincial of the Australia-Pacific Province of the Salesians of Don Bosco with the particular responsibility for all Youth Ministry undertaken in the Province. This responsibility includes assisting principals, teachers, youth leaders and young people to understand and appreciate the Salesian charism and its educational pedagogy.

7

THE HISTORY, PEDAGOGY AND SPIRITUALITY OF ST DON BOSCO: RE-IMAGINING AND RESPONDING IN A NEW ERA

Bernie Graham sdb

CHARISMATIC FOUNDER

16 August 2015 marks a significant milestone in the Salesian story as we celebrate the two hundredth anniversary of the birth of St John Bosco affectionately known to us as Don Bosco – 'Don' being the Italian title to refer to a priest. Don Bosco is the founder of the Religious Congregation of the Salesians of Don Bosco and also the wider Salesian Family or Salesian Movement which includes other Religious Congregations and many groups of lay collaborators. Salesian spirituality and the particular Salesian charism which guides and underpins the Salesian work and mission have developed as a result of Don Bosco's work, his mission, his insights, his teachings and his guidance.

An authentic spirituality and religious charism which has a focus on an apostolic ministry, and particularly a ministry to and for the education and evangelisation of the young, must, of its nature, be dynamic, one which speaks to new generations of educators and of young people, one which makes meaning and inspires the young and their teachers in our ever changing world.

The Rector Major (Congregational Leader) of the Salesians of Don Bosco, Fr Pascual Chavez[1], has taken advantage of this particular bi-centenary commemoration as an opportunity to call for a renewed reflection on Don Bosco and his legacy to the Church, and also a renewal in the way we respond to and live out the 'Salesian Spirit' that Don Bosco has bequeathed to us. In a three-year program of preparation for the bicentenary, Don

---

1 Rector Major at the time of writing.

Chavez has guided the Salesian family, religious and lay, young and old, in a reflection on the three key elements which he identifies as integral to the Salesian charism (Don Bosco's History, his Pedagogy and his Spirituality) with a view to a renewed commitment to living the charism in the new era and new places that the Salesian Movement now finds itself.

Don Bosco began his priestly ministry among the young (boys) on the streets of Turin in 1841. Many young men had come flocking to this rapidly developing and expanding industrial city, the capital of the Kingdom of Savoy, from the valleys and farmlands of Piedmont in search of work and a livelihood. It was in a period of great social and political upheaval in that part of the world. On Sundays and on other public holidays when these youngsters had nothing to do, nowhere to go, and with few family or other social structures to guide and support them, Don Bosco would gather them together. He likened them to 'sheep without a shepherd' – falling into petty crime, victims of unscrupulous employers, lacking in education, and certainly with little formal religious, spiritual or moral education or guidance. Don Bosco's ministry began as a 'roving oratory' gathering the boys for games, fun, instruction and liturgical celebrations wherever he could find space – in squares, in courtyards, in churches, in vacant fields, even for a time in a cemetery! The 'oratory' has become the archetype for Salesian youth gatherings – a place of welcome, education, evangelisation and play. Eventually Don Bosco was able to establish a permanent 'home' for his boys in the rough suburb of Valdocco on the outskirts of the city. It was here in the 'Pinardi Shed' in Valdocco that the Salesian ministry of the 'education of the young' grew and developed, both as an educational enterprise, but more significantly, as a spirituality, as a 'way of life', as a means of bringing into being Don Bosco's great dream – that all his students could learn to be 'Upright Citizens and Honest Christians' [Don Bosco 1854]. For Don Bosco, education and evangelisation were two sides of the same coin. Here we 'educate by evangelising and we evangelise by educating'; meeting the human needs of the young and also their spiritual needs so that they truly could become upright citizens and honest Christians, and make a valuable contribution to their community and country and to the Kingdom of God.

From these simple beginnings, the Salesian Family, the Salesian Movement, has grown to become one of the largest groups of educators of the young in the Church, spread through every continent and to the majority of nations. Whilst this 'vast movement of peoples' has many benefits and advantages, it also poses many issues for us as we work at remaining faithful to Don Bosco's intent and dream, particularly translating his spirit into the many different cultures and settings throughout the world, and meeting the educational and spiritual needs of the young in the 21st century.

RE-IMAGING THE SALESIAN CHARISM

It is with these challenges in mind, that the Rector Major invited all those involved in the Salesian mission of the education and evangelisation of the young – Salesian priests and brothers, Salesian sisters, lay collaborators, teachers, and also (and especially) the young themselves – to prepare for this bicentenary in a particular way:

> It [the Bicentenary of Don Bosco's Birth] is a very special event for us, for all the Salesian Family, and for the whole Salesian Movement, which requires an intense and profound process of preparation, so that it may prove fruitful for all of us, for the Church, for the young and for society' (Letter of the Rector Major 31/01/2001).

2015 is not to be just another significant anniversary marked by events, celebrations, gatherings, memorabilia and nostalgia. The Rector Major is insisting that this be a time of great renewal and recommitment to the charism and spirituality we have received from Don Bosco, and of discovering anew its beauty and richness, so that it can prove fruitful, and thus inspire and bring life to the members of the Salesian Movement, the Church, the young and society in general.

Pascual Chavez identified three key aspects of the Salesian charism which he believes need to be reflected upon if we are to understand and live the charism in its fullness – Don Bosco's history, Pedagogy and Spirituality. Each of these three key aspects is integral to living the charism today. Firstly, it is important to study the history of Don Bosco, to know his story, the origins and location, the formation and situation which gave birth to the charism. Secondly, as an educator, Don Bosco's pedagogy, his style of educating, his way of ministering is a fundamental element of the Salesian charism. And thirdly, his spirituality and theology which give the truly Christian and Gospel-based inspiration to the charism.

And so for each of the three years leading up to 2015, the Rector Major asked all members of the Salesian Movement to study and reflect on one of these key aspects:

- In 2012 the focus was on 'Don Bosco and his History'
- In 2013 the focus was on 'Don Bosco and his Pedagogy'
- In 2014 the focus was on 'Don Bosco and his Spirituality'

Various resources, materials and reflections, both formal and informal, have been prepared or recommended to guide the study and reflection in each of these three key aspects.

One of the resources Pascual Chavez specifically used was the annual 'Strenna' (a traditional 'new year's message' or annual motto provided to the Salesian Family by the Rector Major each year) and its accompanying letter of introduction in each of these three years to highlight the theme to be studied and reflected upon. I will use these three Strennas here as an illustration of the importance of the three key aspects to the Salesian charism and as an example of how the members of the Salesian Family and Movement were asked to reflect upon them in the current time and context in order to make them relevant, alive and pertinent for today.

DON BOSCO AND HIS HISTORY

The Strenna for 2012 was:

> **Let us make the young our life's mission by coming to know and imitate Don Bosco.**
> 'I am the Good Shepherd. The good shepherd lays down his life for his sheep' (John 10:11).

The 'history' of Don Bosco – his story, his actions, his context, his life – was to be studied, not with the purpose of just knowing what he did, or where he worked, or how he educated and ministered, or for whom he undertook his ministry. The invitation was to imitate him. For the charism to be both true to the founder's intentions and also respond to the needs of the young of today, the study of Don Bosco's history should lead us to imitate him with minds and hearts clearly focused on the young, who are the subjects of the mission of the Salesian Movement.

The scriptural quotation which underpins the Strenna provides us with the image of the Good Shepherd. Don Bosco, as any saint or founding figure of a religious charism, was not just an educator, not just a social worker, not just a builder of community, but was first and foremost an evangeliser, and an evangeliser whose fundamental motivation was to imitate the Good Shepherd: laying down his life for his boys, leading them to fresh waters and green pastures, protecting and nurturing them, calling each by name.

> The study of Don Bosco is an essential condition in order to be able to communicate his charism and propose his current relevance. … If we do not know Don Bosco and we do not study him, we cannot understand his spiritual journey and his pastoral decisions; we cannot love him, imitate him, and invoke him; in particular, it will be difficult for us to inculturate his charism these days in the various contexts and in the different situations in which we find ourselves.
>
> (Letter of the Rector Major 2001).

DON BOSCO AND HIS PEDAGOGY

For 2013 the focus was on 'Don Bosco and his Pedagogy' and again the Strenna brought to our attention the key elements.

> **Like Don Bosco the educator, we offer young people the Gospel of Joy through a pedagogy of Kindness.**
> 'Rejoice in the Lord always; again, I say rejoice' (Philippians 4:4).

Don Bosco brought to the educational world of his day new pedagogical insights which were not based so much in theory but in practice, insights which he developed over a lifetime as an educator. In fact his educational method only found its way into written form towards the very end of his life, in the 1880s, but it had been practised for decades by Don Bosco and his followers in the many and varied educational enterprises he established. Known as the *Preventive System,* Don Bosco's pedagogy was often more 'caught' than 'taught'.

This pedagogy, the *Preventive System*, is both an 'educational method' *and* a 'way of life' – a spirituality; it is both a way of educating the young in spiritual and temporal matters as well as a way of living out our relationships with God and with others. With its three key components – 'Reason, Religion and Loving Kindness' – the fundamental premises of the Preventive System are:

- love of the young person: 'that you are young is enough for me to love you very much' (Don Bosco 1847);
- respect for the young and their particular culture: 'love what the young love and they in turn will come to love what you love';
- an environment of joy and kindness: 'here holiness consists of happiness';
- a family atmosphere: 'the youngsters should not only be loved, but they should know that they are loved' (Don Bosco 1884).

The Rector Major challenged us:

> *A deeper study of Salesian pedagogy is certainly necessary, on the one hand so it can be updated according to the sensitivity and demands of our time. Today in fact the social, economic, cultural, political and religious contexts in which we find ourselves living out our vocation and carrying out the Salesian mission have altered profoundly. On the other hand, to be faithful to our Father's charism, it is necessary to make the content and approach of what he offered in educative and pastoral terms our own. In the context of today's society we are called to be holy educators like he was, giving our lives as he did, working with and for the young.*
>
> (Letter of the Rector Major 2012).

DON BOSCO AND HIS SPIRITUALITY

The third and final aspect for consideration during 2014 was 'Don Bosco and his Spirituality' and again the Strenna draws our attention to the significant elements of it.

> 'Da mihi animas, cetera tolle'
> **Let us draw upon Don Bosco's experience so we can walk in holiness according to our specific vocation.**
> 'The glory of God and the salvation of souls'

The Latin motto that begins the 2014 Strenna is the motto of the Salesian Congregation, which translates as *'Give me souls, take away the rest'*. Don Bosco's total focus was to ensure that the souls and lives of the young were to be totally connected with and committed to God, both in this world and for all eternity. And so, whatever he did – whatever tasks he undertook, whatever projects he initiated, whatever programs he conducted, whatever decisions he made – was all done to ensure that the young developed their knowledge of, relationship with, and love of God. Don Bosco developed his spiritual understanding gradually, bit by bit, throughout his life (as he did with his pedagogy) – formed by his experiences, shaped by his encounters with others, deepened through his study and reflections, honed through his prayer and devotions.

Don Bosco's spirituality draws heavily on that of St Francis de Sales, his patron, and from whom comes the term 'Salesian'. St Francis' spirituality can be characterised as apostolic, pastoral, optimistic, charitable – the foundation of Christian humanism. Don Bosco's 'Salesian' spirituality comes out of a pastoral and an educative charity – pastoral charity because it seeks the salvation of souls, and educative charity because it finds a resource in education that allows it to help young people to develop all their energies for good. The motivations underpinning Don Bosco's spirituality are his passion for God and his passion for the young.

One of St Francis de Sales' great legacies to spirituality in general (and there were many others besides), a legacy with which Don Bosco fully concurred, was his belief that each and every person could find God and develop a deep relationship with God within the normal course of life and the particular vocation to which that person is called, *whether one is a gentleman, workman, servant, prince, widow, maid or married woman* (cf. St Francis de Sales *Introduction to the Devout Life*). God is to be found in the everyday events and activities of life. Don Bosco fully believed this was the case also for the young and so tailored his spirituality toward a youth spirituality.

Again the Rector Major challenged us to consider Don Bosco's spirituality from a very wide perspective:

> *Salesian spirituality is made up of various elements: it is a lifestyle, prayer, work, relationships with other people, a community way of life, an educative and pastoral mission based on a pedagogical legacy, an approach to formation, a characteristic set of values and attitudes, a particular focus on the Church and society through specific areas of involvement, an historic inheritance of documents and writings, a characteristic language, a typical series of structures and works, a calendar of festivities and celebrations that are proper to this spirituality...*
>
> (Letter of the Rector Major 2013)

Salesian spirituality has many facets, and they all need careful consideration when pondering the spiritual legacy of Don Bosco and bringing it to the lives and faith of the young today.

VIBRANT LIVING OF THE CHARISM

The invitation by the Rector Major to all members of the Salesian Movement to participate, over three years, in a deep period of reflection, consideration, renewal, study and prayer on the fundamental and foundational aspects of our Salesian charism is most timely and significant. It is an undertaking across the whole congregation, the whole Salesian Movement, educators and young people, in and for a whole range of contexts, cultures and settings. The program also assumes that the Salesian charism is by nature dynamic, vibrant, evolving and adaptive. The world of Don Bosco and the young to whom he ministered is very different to the worlds of the young spread across our globe in 2015. However, his charism, his pedagogy and his spirituality need to speak as loudly today as then, and to be vehicles for the young of today so that they might also become 'upright citizens and honest Christians'.

SALESIAN CHARISM: AN AUSTRALIAN EDUCATIONAL REFLECTION

As we approach 2015, the great challenge for those involved in the Salesian educational mission in Australia[2] is how to take the beauty, insights, foundations and spirit of the Salesian charism inherited from Don Bosco and present it and live it in a way that is both relevant to and challenging of the young and their educators in settings in Australia.

---

[2] There are eight schools and one specialist educational facility which formally belong to the 'Schools in the Salesian Tradition', and there are also primary schools that were formerly under the care of the Salesian Sisters, and primary schools in parishes administered by the Salesians.

Every two years a Salesian Educational Leaders' Conference is held for the Leadership Teams of the Salesian schools. The theme for each conference explores some element of the Salesian charism with a focus on how to interpret and inculcate that aspect into the current situation and time.

CHARTER FOR SALESIAN SCHOOLS IN AUSTRALIA

For the 2003 Conference a very practical outcome was planned – to write a Charter for Salesian Schools in Australia. Up until a couple of years before this, all of the schools still had principals who were members of the Salesian congregation, and there was a community of Salesians working in each school. However, as times evolved, the principalship of all schools has been transferred to lay leaders, and not all schools still have a Salesian on staff. Therefore the bond holding all the schools together as a charismatic group was no longer the physical presence of Salesians in each setting. The idea of establishing a Charter which would be adopted by all the schools as a commitment to the continuing development of and involvement in the Salesian charism was one practical element (among others) for ensuring the continuation of the Salesian charism in a new era.

Constitution 40 of the Salesian Constitutions, to be found in the Section entitled 'Criteria for Salesian Activity', uses four wonderful metaphors to describe the characteristics of a Salesian ministry or activity if it is to truly reflect the charism of Don Bosco.

> Don Bosco lived a pastoral experience in his first Oratory which serves as a model; it was for the youngsters a home that welcomed, a parish that evangelized, a school that prepared them for life, and a playground where friends could meet and enjoy themselves.
>
> As we carry out our mission today, the Valdocco experience is still the lasting criterion for discernment and renewal in all our activities and works.
>
> (Constitution 40)

The four metaphors which give expression to the characteristics were adopted as the framework upon which the Charter would hang:

A Home that welcomes
A Parish that evangelises
A School that prepares for life
A Playground where friends meet and enjoy themselves

The welcoming 'home' represents family, nurture, safety, community and belonging. The evangelising 'parish' represents prayer, liturgy, catechesis, sacraments and church. The life-engendering 'school' represents learning, development, skills, commitment and endeavor, the vibrant playground (the genius insight of Don Bosco) represents friendship, fun, activity, acceptance and mutuality.

These metaphors are already a synthesis and recasting of the Salesian charism, and for the Charter they would be given even newer, fresher and more specific focus.

The three days of the conference involved presentations, discussions, workshops and reflection on these metaphors and how they conveyed the key elements of the Salesian charism. The Charter that emerged was the result of the input of many people, Salesian and lay collaborators, coming from all the different school settings in Australia. With the specific setting of a 21st century Australian school as its focus, the Charter gave expression to the Salesian charism in our unique time and place. By its adoption each individual school community has committed to its implementation.

The shared reflections and wisdom of the group brought to life a new and distinct expression of the Salesian charism.

CHARTER FOR SALESIAN SCHOOLS IN AUSTRALIA

Preamble:

In keeping with the spirit of Saint John Bosco, whereby 'education is largely a matter of the heart' that leads young people to 'know that they are loved', the Salesian school community of today is challenged to be:

- A home that welcomes
- A parish that evangelises
- A school that prepares for life
- A playground where friends meet and enjoy themselves

A home that welcomes by:

- Being committed to the care and support of all young people, especially the poor and marginalised
- Cultivating relationships based on genuine affection, openness and acceptance of others
- Fostering a spirit of joy and hope, based on the 'Good News' of Jesus Christ

- Encouraging an attitude of optimism and a conviction that life is fundamentally worthwhile

A parish that evangelises by:

- Having a strong and vibrant program of religious education, liturgical celebration and sacramental encounter
- Addressing the spiritual yearnings of young people and adults
- Giving priority to the faith development and formation of staff
- Providing students with significant experiences of faith in action and apostolic involvement

A school that prepares for life by:

- Encouraging a passion for life-long learning and a quest for excellence
- Developing a sense of meaning and purpose, which expresses itself in a spirit of service and self-giving
- Proclaiming the challenge of community building, commitment to others and responsible decision-making
- Cultivating resilience, resourcefulness and adaptability as important skills for life

A playground where friends meet and enjoy themselves by:

- Being present to each other in an active, engaging and constructive manner, in fidelity to the Salesian Preventive System
- Building positive and inclusive relationships between each other
- Having a rich experience of interaction and sharing, especially between students and staff
- Creating occasions for celebration and festivity

Faithful to the tradition of Saint John Bosco, the Salesian school community is constantly challenged to re-interpret and re-enliven his educational vision in every generation and circumstance, according to the requirements of the contemporary situation and the needs of young people, to whom he once said: *'I have only one wish: that you be happy in this world and the next'*.

CONCLUSION

The Salesian Mission entrusted to the Salesian Family by Don Bosco is the education and evangelisation of the young. The young live in a world that is constantly changing. As they grow they need to learn and adapt; their circumstances and experiences place before them challenges and opportunities. The Salesian charism flowing from Don Bosco's History, Pedagogy and Spirituality must continually be renewed, revitalized and reimagined as each generation of young people and their educators encounter it.

The program of preparation for the bicentenary of Don Bosco's birth outlined by Pascual Chavez is an attempt by the Salesian Movement at the worldwide level to undertake this renewal across all cultures and settings. The preparation of the Charter for Salesian Schools in Australia is an example of an attempt within a particular culture and time to localise and personalise the charism.

Peta Goldburg rsm

Peta Goldburg, a Brisbane Sister of Mercy, is Professor and foundation chair of Religious Education at Australian Catholic University. Peta is an experienced educator, having taught in primary, secondary and tertiary settings. Recipient of a Carrick Citation for Excellence in Teaching and ACU's Excellence in Teaching Award, Peta is known nationally and internationally in her field. Widely published, she is the national president of the Australian Association for Religious Education and has twice chaired the writing of the Study of Religion syllabus for senior secondary students in Queensland. Her current research is focused on Catholic schools and identity and curriculum in Catholic Education.

8

SPIRITUAL TRADITIONING: THE MERCY OF GOD THROUGH THE ACTIONS OF CATHERINE MCAULEY

Peta Goldburg rsm

INTRODUCTION

Throughout the nineteenth century, many apostolic religious orders were founded to meet the specific needs of the Church and society. The Sisters of Mercy was one such religious order. For close to one hundred and seventy-five years the mission and vision of Catherine McAuley has spread throughout the world. Today, although direct involvement of the Sisters of Mercy in ministries is limited, Mercy education continues to flourish under committed lay leadership. Schools educating in the Mercy tradition incorporate the charism of the dedicated women who began their schools. This chapter will briefly explore the story of the founder Catherine McAuley to identify what inspired her and will then examine how the founding charism is continued in schools today.

THE FOUNDER: CATHERINE MCAULEY

When Catherine McAuley founded the Sisters of Mercy in Ireland in 1831 she did so to continue the work she had begun as a lay woman eight years earlier, which was working with the poor and destitute women and children of Dublin. Catherine operated in a particular context: she responded to the needs of her time in the light of the Gospels as she understood them. She was convinced that through the provision of education, life could be improved for Dublin's poor and destitute. Her emphasis on the education of women happened when education institutions for girls and young women were few. Her vision did not stop with education but expanded to include establishing welfare services and improving hospitals and the offering of means of gainful employment. Her motivations and actions were a clear example of the 'preferential option for the poor' long before Catholic Social Teaching named it as such.

When Catherine McAuley opened the *House of Mercy* in 1824 she intended it as a refuge for women in distress and a space where destitute women and girls could improve their situation. It contained school rooms and an oratory and its doors were open to the city's poor and needy. The location of the house, Baggot Street, Dublin, ensured that the poor were visible to the rich and that the young women would have employment opportunities in the local area. When other women joined her, they taught the poor children, nursed the sick and cared for people during terrible times such as a cholera epidemic.

Catherine exhibited many admirable qualities. Her willingness to take risks, especially for the sake of the poor and vulnerable, was criticised by some as 'lacking prudence'.[1] Her advocacy of the powerless is what led her to establish the House of Mercy and to give practical expressions of charity and solidarity with the poor and suffering. She trusted in the providence of God but did not expect God to intervene with situation-altering miracles, but rather depended on God for guidance through prayer. While she and those with her worked extremely hard, many have described her work as charity. In fact, what she did more appropriately fits under 'justice' because rather than open a soup kitchen, although the Sisters did this at times, she taught skills to enable people to earn their own living, and in her own way she gradually changed some of the structures which had kept some people in oppressed situations.

It was not long before Catherine received invitations to establish communities across Ireland and even in England. Each time she created a new foundation she made it independent because she wanted each new convent to respond to local needs and believed that the best place for decisions to be made was at the local level. The organisation she chose to implement was specifically designed for mission and ministry. When the Sisters of Mercy arrived in Australia, they replicated the pattern of leadership and autonomy begun in Ireland and continued to respond to the needs of local communities through the provision of education and health care. Within a relatively short period of time there was a proliferation of primary and secondary schools run and staffed by Sisters of Mercy. With the development of diocesan Catholic Education offices in the late 1960s and 1970s, many local Mercy primary and secondary schools became part of the growing diocesan education system. Today, a small number of schools (predominantly secondary) remain under the

---

[1] Mary Sullivan, *Practical Sayings of Catherine McAuley* (Dublin: Mercy International, 2010), 2.

sponsorship of the Sisters of Mercy. These schools are staffed by lay people who work to extend the mission of the founding Sisters.

Catherine McAuley offers one example of a person's whole-hearted response to the Gospel call of mercy and justice. Today, while the context has changed, the call is not so terribly different. There is still an urgent need to respond to the needs of the poor and homeless, the sick and the dying, and the most vulnerable in our society. Mercy requires justice and makes justice possible. The requirement of true mercy is the wisdom to understand concrete realities, contexts, relationships and the claims they make on us in justice. But mercy also makes justice possible. Mercy enhances the knowledge that is needed for justice and motivates actions that respond to the claims of justice. Because mercy involves beholding the value of others and suffering with them in their need, it opens reality to the beholder and offers a way of seeing that evokes a moral response. Mercy, therefore, illuminates justice and propels it to action. The mercy of God is intended to flow through individuals to others. In the words of Thomas Aquinas, 'mercy is the fulfilment of justice'. Merciful people seek to do as much as possible for the person in need – this means that mercy institutions should not be guided by the minimum requirements of law but by the generosity of God.

CHARISM

Charism, from the Greek word *charisma* meaning 'gift', is the grace of God given to all believers, by virtue of their baptism, which is to be shared with others. Paul, in 1 Corinthians, highlights the particular connection between charism and the role of the Holy Spirit as well as the inter-relationship between charism, ministry and work.

> Now there are varieties of gifts, but the same Spirit; and there are varieties of services, but the same Lord; and there are varieties of activities, but it is the same God who activates all of them in everyone (1 Cor 12:4–6).

A charism has to live rather than be a pious ideal or a myth. Understanding a founder's charism is key if ministries inspired by the founder are to be genuine. A specific charism is given to a founder at a certain time in history and is shaped by the founder's historical and cultural condition, their temperament and limitations. The charism is the founder's way of reading the Gospel at that particular time. So in that sense a charism is always time bound.

Today, no one can know the exact way the founder thought and felt but it is important to approach the intention of the founder through historical documents so that the vision which the founder initiates can be investigated.

Having clarified the intention underlying the historical expression of the charism, the congregation and its ministries need to discern the radically different ways the charism is to be lived out to realise its potential in today's world. The charism of a religious community determines its identity, way of life, spirit, spirituality, structure and mission.

Susan Sanders identifies seven characteristics of charism. In general, she describes them as:
- special gifts that equip the faithful for a way of life or a specific ministry in the church;
- originating with the Holy Spirit;
- given to founders of religious congregations;
- transmitted from founders to followers;
- authenticated by the Church's pastors, who share responsibility with religious congregations for preserving them;
- distinctive;
- used for the ongoing renewal of the Church.[2]

While some charisms are more intellectually and spiritually rich than others, no individual charism has the depth and variety of intellectual and spiritual traditions of the Church as a whole and therefore we need to emphasise Gospel values and then how these are lived out through a particular charism.

For women and men in religious orders, charisms function multi-dimensionally by grounding and focusing their sponsored ministries and by shaping the culture, style, and ethos of both their communal and ministerial lives thereby distinguishing the work and character of their religious communities. The charism of the Sisters of Mercy impels its members toward the compassionate service of the poor, sick and uneducated. When institutionalised, the Mercy charism is expressed in ministries such as health care, education and welfare. Since the Second Vatican Council, religious orders have paid particular attention to the charism of their founders in the hope of the preservation and transmission of that charism within their institutions.

Both Grace[3] and Lydon[4] highlight the important role charism played in the development of the Catholic education system in England during the years after the Counter-Reformation. Today, however, they are also acutely

---

2 Susan Sanders, 'Charisms, congregational sponsors and higher education', *Journal of Catholic Higher Education*, 29(1), 3–18.
3 Gerald Grace, *Catholic schools: Mission, markets and morality* (London: RoutledgeFalmer, 2002).
4 John Lydon, 'Transmission of the charism: A major challenge for Catholic education', *International Studies in Catholic Education*, 1(1), 42–58.

aware that as the numbers of religious in schools decline, the challenge of prophetic witness through the lens of charism proves increasingly difficult. Lydon states that [because] 'modelling or emulation constitutes the most effective means of maintaining a distinctive charism, transmission of the charism to lay people takes on a greater urgency'.[5]

Other researchers have suggested that many Catholic institutions may have lost sight of the Catholic dimension of their identity and allowed charism to supersede all else. Morey and Piderit observed that many staff in church-based institutions are more likely to talk about and even express affection for the charism of the congregation that founded the institution than they are to talk positively, knowledgably, or even at all, about the Catholic identity of their ministry.[6] There may be several reasons for this. Some staff may have antipathy for aspects of Catholicism, others may not have sufficient theological knowledge to understand Catholic theology or Catholic Social Teaching. Charisms are sometimes misconstrued as being 'different' or apart from Catholicism. But in reality, charisms could be the entry point for discussions that lead people into conversations about Catholic theology, Catholic social teaching, and sacramental and moral life. Perhaps by encountering the charism of Catherine McAuley some people may be better able to access the Church's teachings of simplicity, stewardship, compassion and service. In this way, a charism may serve as an introduction to Catholic teachings, but charisms should never be a substitute for Gospel teaching and Catholic tradition. Neither should the founder replace the person of Jesus as the centre piece of a new spirituality. If people focus too much on Catherine McAuley and the Mercy charism, then a false dichotomy is created between this dynamic woman and the gospel that motivated her. Jesus must remain the focus while we draw strength and direction from examining carefully the way Catherine McAuley lived out the corporal and spiritual works of mercy.

EDUCATION AND THE MERCY TRADITION

The founding mission of Mercy schools was education of the poor and marginalised for their social advancement alongside education of the 'non-poor' and privileged so that they would be informed, and through their work for the poor and marginalised work on behalf of justice. Like many teaching religious orders, the Sisters of Mercy were founded for specific needs of the nineteenth century, and the congregation spread rapidly throughout the western world to America, Australia, Newfoundland, New Zealand, and

---
5   Ibid, 53
6   Melanie M. Morey and John J. Piderit, *Catholic higher education: A culture in crisis* (Oxford: Oxford University Press, 2006).

South America. The sisters responded to the need to educate and provide healthcare assistance to socially marginalised Catholics. Education in many ways is liberation, and the benefits of the education provided can and often do extend beyond the student. Catholic education in a Mercy tradition should perform a similar function to what Cardinal Newman believed was the purpose of universities – to liberate the oppressed and to act as a leavening influence in the world.

Initially, Mercy ministries were almost completely staffed by members of the religious congregation, and then later if they were not completely staffed by religious, the employees were normally of the Catholic faith and had been formed in the tradition of the order. Catholic identity was strong and explicit. However, over the last fifty years there has been a steady decline in the number of women and men joining religious orders, and the ability of religious orders to continue to staff their ministries with religious is at an all-time low. Many Mercy schools no longer have sisters as members of the staff and if there are sisters at the school they are more likely to be there on a part-time basis and in pastoral roles rather than teaching or leadership roles. The staff at these schools, while agreeing to support the mission of the school, may be of many faiths or no faith, and even those who belong to a religious tradition may be detraditionalised. Boeve describes someone as detraditionalised when s/he identifies as being Catholic on the census form, for example, but in reality they know little of the tradition and participate infrequently in its rituals and the sacramental life of the Church.[7] It is within this cultural context that I distributed a survey to Mercy secondary schools in Australia in 2014.

SURVEY RESPONSES

The survey invited the principal or their nominee to respond to the following questions.
- *How does your school articulate the charism of the Sisters of Mercy?*
- *How has this articulation changed over time?*
- *What forms of witness has the charism given rise to, and how have these evolved over time?*
- *Have there been discernible stages in this evolution?*

The response rate was not overwhelming, but nevertheless the responses provide some insight into how leaders within the institution engage with the founding charism and promote it within their schools. The responses can be

---
7 Lieven Boeve, *God interrupts history: Theology in a time of upheaval* (New York: Continuum, 2007), 21–23 et al.

categorised into three main areas: staff formation into the charism; student initiation into the charism; and mission engagement related to charism.

Staff Formation

It is only in more recent years that staff formation specifically related to charism has occurred in many Religious Institute schools. Within the last ten to fifteen years, presentations on Mercy charism have become an intentional part of the formal, comprehensive and systematic process of staff induction and development. While programs vary from school to school, they range from a one-off introduction to the founding story of Catherine McAuley, to more in-depth series of sessions which introduce teachers to a Mercy way of being in the world. In some instances, Sisters of Mercy are invited to present at these formation sessions. Most schools also set aside one day per year for continuing formation of staff within the Mercy tradition: these sessions vary from reflection days, to ministry visits, to guest speakers from Mercy mission projects in other parts of the world. In some schools, staff participate in a pilgrimage formation experience to Ireland with the hope that through the experience they will gain a better understanding of the motivation and mission of the institution.

For staff, professional development opportunities provide some insight into the charism, but charism is bereft without a sound grounding in theology. One of the challenges facing school communities now and into the future is how to present Mercy charism in a meaningful way to a detraditionalised generation which is rapidly becoming religiously illiterate.

Student Formation

In the survey responses, all of the schools were able to articulate clearly what programs were offered to students. Particular effort was devoted to new cohorts of students at the beginning of the year. Within the first few months at the school, students are introduced to the founding stories of the school and the wider Mercy story, frequently this unit was part of the Religious Education program. In many instances, the life of Catherine McAuley and the founding sister/s of the local community were the focus of attention, and in some cases Mercy presence across the world was highlighted. It is interesting to note that as fewer Sisters of Mercy are visible within the school environment, there are more visible symbols related to the founding story appearing in schools: these symbols include images, statues and heritage displays related to the founding of the tradition in that location. A careful audit of these types of programs and iconography needs to take place to ensure that there is a balanced relationship between Mercy characters and stories and their place and function within the overall Catholic Christian tradition.

Another feature of student formation was special prayer assemblies and whole school Masses for days of significance to the Sisters of Mercy. These commemoration days included the Feast of Our Lady of Mercy (September 24) and Foundation days as well as other days of remembrance which in earlier generations may have been celebrated only by the Sisters.

More so than in the past, some reference to the Mercy charism has been used as a feature of advertising materials for the school and other official documents and publications. Most school documents from prospectus to yearbooks contain explicit references to the founding tradition and charism. In some school diaries, the Suscipe of Catherine McAuley was included in the section of commonly used prayers.

Mission Engagement

In many ways, the responses related to mission engagement were more expansive than information provided for the previous two areas. School responses included a multitude of justice-based activities which were directly related to Mercy initiatives and ministries as well as other programs which appeared to be more general. Some schools limit their engagement for the particular purpose of focusing on one or two projects per year which are directly related to ministries sponsored by the Sisters. Throughout the year, a Sister involved in the ministry may be invited to address students and staff.

It would appear that at least on the surface, the charism is more easily expressed through practical social justice projects, Mercy Action Programs and service learning programs than in other forms. If Mercy charism is to be exemplified, then careful attention to the difference between charity and justice should be applied so that systematic analysis and social change are considered alongside the immediate response to need. Catherine's spirituality was centred on Jesus, which motivated her compassionate service, and she reminded the people working with her that 'it is for God we serve the poor not for thanks'; therefore, it would be important that the schools ground their justice-based programs first in the Scriptures and Catholic Social Thought and not make them appear as a unique expression of Catherine McAuley alone.

SPIRITUAL CAPITAL

Members of religious orders speak about charism and focus some of their energy on the passing on of that charism to others. The charism is not fixed in an abstract definition but is the animating force for the actualisation of mission in the lives of people. Grace uses the term 'spiritual capital' to describe this animating force and motivating power for mission and ministry within Catholic institutions.[8] The idea of spiritual capital emerges from the work of Bourdieu, who identified three forms of cultural capital: the embodied state, the objectified state, and the institutionalised state.[9] As a form of cultural capital, spiritual capital also exists in these three forms.

In the *embodied state*, spiritual capital is the knowledge, abilities and credentials an individual has amassed in religion through explicit education and unconsciously through socialisation. Spiritual capital is exemplified in the way people act in the world and therefore is a measure of position as well as disposition.

In the *objectified state*, spiritual capital takes on material and symbolic modes such as ritual objects and exegetical texts as well as theologies and ideologies. Objectified capital is measured by the 'goods consumed' and in a religious mode this implies knowing the way in which sacred objects relate to the tradition.

Spiritual capital also exists in an *institutionalised state* through the power that churches and other religious organisations exercise within society. In the context of a school, the embodied state is evidenced by the knowledge people have about the charism and in the ways the charism infuses daily interactions. The objectified state is evidenced through the iconography related not only to the charism but also to the tradition, and the institutionalised state is visible in the way the school exercises the ideas of justice and mercy and its effort to impress this on the wider society.

Grace makes the point that 'spiritual capital' is different from 'religious capital', stating:

> *Spiritual capital can be a source of empowerment because it provides a transcendent impulse which can guide judgement and action in the mundane world. Those within education whose own formation has involved the acquisition of spiritual capital do not act simply as professionals but as professionals and witnesses.*[10]

Spiritual capital, however, is not developed in a vacuum: it requires high levels of theological literacy which are demonstrated by a well-developed understanding of theological knowledge and the ability to communicate it effectively to others. Spiritual capital, according to Grace, while drawing on theological literacy, also includes the dimension of personal witness to faith. When spiritual capital is compared with charism it is more like a sustaining reservoir for every day Christian life and work rather than a lens through which to focus mission.

---

8   Gerald Grace, *Catholic Schools: Mission, Markets and Morality*, 236.
9   Pierre Bourdieu, 'The Forms of Capital' in John Richardson (ed), *Handbook of Theory and Research for the Sociology of Education* (New York: Greenwood Press, 1986).
10 Gerald Grace, *Catholic Schools: Mission, Markets and Morality*, 65.

Mercy schools possess an enormous wealth of spiritual capital but as Verter (2003) reminds us, spiritual capital can be amassed and exchanged but it can also be squandered. Mercy spirituality is about encountering the love of God – a love that makes possible the love of self and love of neighbour. Mercy charism consists of three practical components: it focuses on the poor in order to find ways to liberate them; it reflects God's loving kindness; and it combines contemplation with action to create a strong base from which to restore others to wholeness. Catherine McAuley did not have at her disposal the body of Catholic Social Thought (CST) developed over the past one hundred years and its terminology of the common good, human dignity, and option for the poor, but her actions and initiatives in ministry are a clear demonstration of Catholic social thought, albeit long before it was recognised as a formal body of teaching within the Church.

CHALLENGES FOR THE FUTURE

A contemporary education within a Mercy tradition should deepen and expand students' aspirations beyond professional advancement and therefore must include an explicit integration of commitment to justice into the educative process. Ideally, students should leave Mercy schools religiously literate with a well-developed understanding of justice and Catholic social thought and a willingness to advocate for the marginalised in society.

Arbuckle speaks of the need to 'refound' Catholic institutions. Refounding, he says, is the 'process of story-telling whereby imaginative leaders are able to inspire people to rearticulate the founding myth and apply it to contemporary needs'.[11] Leaders of Mercy schools, and indeed all involved in Mercy education including system schools which retain something of their Mercy heritage, need to be people who are able to articulate the founding myth of Catherine McAuley and bridge the gap between a nineteenth century explanation of the charism and that required in the contemporary context, in order to bring to life Catherine McAuley's legacy and spiritualty reflected in the works of mercy.

---

11 Gerald Arbuckle, *Catholic Identity or Identities?: Refounding Ministries in Chaotic Times* (Collegeville: Liturgical Press, 2013), 93.

Chris Smith

Chris Smith is the National Director of Identity and Liberating Education for Edmund Rice Education Australia (EREA), where he supports schools in nurturing the Catholic ethos and Edmund Rice charism. EREA has the governance and management responsibility for nearly 50 schools enrolling over 35000 students nationally and is a canonical entity within the Church. Prior to 2010, Chris held a number of school-based appointments in Anglican and Catholic schools including two principalships. He has been a member of a number of Catholic education and Archdiocesan committees in Tasmania and was founding Chair of the John Wallis Foundation, established to continue the mission of the Missionary Sisters of Service.

9

EDUCATING FOR LIBERATION AND POSSIBILITY – THE EDMUND RICE VISION FOR EDUCATION ALIVE TODAY

Chris Smith

Recently, I was driving away from the second of two meetings I had held that day with leadership teams of Edmund Rice Education Australia (EREA) schools. In both cases, I had been introducing a process used to invite schools into a reflective time, considering the ways in which their schools were being authentic to the expressed mission of EREA schools, one based on the story of Jesus and guided by the charism of Blessed Edmund Rice.

Even without going through the full process with them, I know that these schools are good schools, well grounded in the Catholic tradition and imbued with the Edmund Rice charism. Both have strong demand for places at the school, both have dedicated staff and both will be integral to the shaping of the futures of the young people in their care.

ABf they are dramatically different places.

One is a large, relatively high-fee school that offers a well-structured and rich academic and co-curricular program. Liturgical celebrations are powerful; social justice programs of all kinds are well supported; the story of Edmund Rice is taught and well known. Its year begins with certainty about enrolments, resources and programs. Its long history brings a confidence and prominent position in the educational setting of the city.

The second is actually a network of small schools. There are no fees charged here. Religious education is not overtly taught; liturgy may comprise reflection and sharing. There are no uniforms or other high profile signs of community membership. In these schools, there can be uncertainty about the year ahead, such as who and how many will attend on the first day, and the programs that will be necessary to meet their needs. These are some of the Flexible Learning Centres, part of EREA Youth+, the arm of EREA providing education to disenfranchised young people outside mainstream education.

What is it about a spirituality that fosters two such diverse communities and so many in between? How can those responsible for guiding the ongoing evolution of charism-inspired schools promote a sense of shared mission and identity? How are the foundational stories kept alive?

EDMUND RICE – CALLED TO LIBERATE

There are a number of informative histories of the life of Blessed Edmund Rice, and whilst some of the factual details and interpretations may vary, what emerges is a clear picture of a man with a deep faith and spirituality who combined a life of prayer and reflection with one of action in meeting the needs of the poor.

In many ways, Edmund's life was a gifted one. He was born into a loving and moderately well-off family; he enjoyed the benefits of a good education complemented by a vocational training in commercial studies, his area of interest. He lived at a time when the penal laws were being relaxed, particularly in the area where he lived, so he was able to practise his faith, something he did through regular Mass attendance, meditation, prayer and reading. He was apprenticed to his uncle who ran a highly successful providing business in Waterford, and after a time took over this business, enabling him to become a man of significant financial means. He courted and married a young wife whom he adored, and the couple were soon expecting their first child.

Yet, from his young days, Edmund was someone who looked beyond his own privileged circumstances:

> *Deeply aware of the Father's providential presence in his life, Edmund Rice was moved by the Holy Spirit to open his whole heart to Christ present and appealing to him in the poor.*[1]

Tragedy struck in the early years of Edmund's marriage when his wife died, leaving him with a newly-born daughter. Whilst the tragedy seems not to have caused him to question his faith, it did bring an uncertainty about his future directions and a time of prayerful discernment as he considered whether a contemplative life or one of action was the best way for him to nurture and express his deep faith. His chosen path combined both.

Edmund's decision was to confront the stark reality of poverty such as that evident in the boys outside his window on the docks of Waterford.

---

1   Christian Brothers Charism Statement 1982.

His approach was guided by his life experience – being loved by his family, enjoying opportunities to pray and to express his faith, having access to education, his business acumen, his position in society, his work with the poor and his joy at being a husband and a father, even though these brought an experience of personal tragedy. Inspired by the message of Jesus, his path was to seek liberation for young boys by offering an education that was not only unique in its availability but also in its style:

> What Edmund Rice was setting his mind to was a mission that was radical indeed – it wasn't just handouts of food and clothes, or special kindnesses to exceptional needy families; it was equipping young people mentally, morally and religiously, to stand on their own feet, and change their lives for themselves and in time, to struggle for change in the society that caused and allowed them to be poor.[2]

A few young men joined with Edmund in the early days when his school was based in the rudimentary surroundings of a stable. Conditions were not easy and the behaviour of the boys challenging. Helpers came and went, but Edmund's approach, no doubt influenced by his own fatherhood, saw the boys begin to see that he valued and respected them as special in the eyes of God. A community formed, which later became a religious community, and Edmund expanded his educational initiative in the establishment of Mt Sion, an imposing school building on a prominent site – surely another message to the poor boys about their importance in his eyes.

Edmund's work soon grew into further schools, and his faith in God's providence encouraged him to send his brothers to other parts of Ireland and, eventually, to other countries. His influence is seen by many as having brought about long-term change in the culture and society of Ireland:

> …the Brothers effected a transformation of Catholicism and the modernisation of Irish society, by providing their pupils not merely with a useful education, but with a moral vision which supported the creation of a new Ireland.[3]

Many would argue that the influence in other countries has been similar and is particularly evident in Australia, where the Brothers have been involved in nearly 120 educational establishments since the dynamic and inspiring Br Ambrose Treacy led the building of the first Australian school on Victoria Parade in Melbourne in 1871. Christian Brothers' schools

---

2 Anthony J. Shanahan cfc, *A Quiet Revolution* (Perth: Christian Brothers, 2005), 16.
3 Daire Keogh, *Edmund Rice and the First Christian Brothers* (Dublin: Four Courts Press), 2008, 110.

have been central to the increased social mobility of Catholics and in the promotion of Catholic faith.

The spiritual foundations of an Edmund Rice education, also expressed by the Christian Brothers in articulating their ministry, are identified as: *Presence*, leading to a respectful sense of the sacred and a belief in the divine equality of all; *Compassion*, nurturing authentic community, solidarity with the poor and a responsibility to serve; *Liberation*, underpinning the provision of an education which is relevant and which encourages critical reflection on society.[4]

These spiritual foundations and the stories of Edmund Rice and the Christian Brothers continue to inspire and guide the journey today. The leaders of the Christian Brothers challenge schools to be authentic to the very soul of an Edmund Rice inspired education:

> *I see no value in a centre of learning which churns out numberless school leavers each year and is passively part of a society torn apart by division of race and partisan politics ... Our schools exist to challenge popular beliefs and dominant cultural values, to ask the difficult questions, to look at life from the standpoint of the minority, the victim, the outcast and the stranger.*[5]

CONTINUING THE STORY – EDMUND RICE EDUCATION AUSTRALIA

Edmund Rice Education Australia (EREA) was established by the Christian Brothers in 2007 to govern and manage the schools owned by them at that time. Whilst EREA was given the operational management of schools in October 2007, it was at the start of 2013 that it became a civil and canonical entity in its own right. As well as outlining these responsibilities, the purpose of EREA was expressed in foundational documents in part as:

> *Edmund Rice Education Australia's work of evangelisation shall build on the sound traditions of the Christian Brothers and ensure the continuation of the charism of Edmund Rice in school ministry as Church Mission.*[6]

At the end of 2013, EREA comprised 47 registered schools in all states and territories, with a total enrolment of over 35,000 students. There are capital city schools, some with nearly 2000 students, boarding schools, an agricultural college, regional colleges, schools for students with special needs,

---

4   Denis McLaughlin, *The Price of Freedom* (Melbourne: David Lovell Publishing, 2006), 388.
5   Philip Pinto cfc, Congregation Leader, address to teachers, New York, 2002.
6   *Canonical Statutes of Edmund Rice Education Australia, 2011.*

primary schools and campuses, single sex and co-educational schools, and one stand-alone child care centre. Also included in the 47 are 14 Flexible Learning Centres, each a registered school offering a flexible education for between 50 and 150 young people disenfranchised from the education system and from many aspects of society.

EREA is governed by a Council which holds the canonical authority of EREA as canonical stewards and the civil authority as Trustees of Edmund Rice Education Australia. The Council is appointed by the Congregational Leader of the Christian Brothers. The EREA Board has responsibility to the Council for the strategic direction and management oversight of EREA. An Executive structure, led by an Executive Director, is based around three mission areas: Identity and Liberating Education; Community Engagement and Support; Stewardship and Resourcing.

In addition to the schools governed by EREA, the Member schools, there are Associates of EREA. These are schools which also have a history of connection with the Christian Brothers and which desire to keep that story and the charism of Edmund Rice guiding the education they offer through relationship with EREA.

JOURNEY OF POSSIBILITY

In November 2000, the Inter-Province Leadership Committee (ILC) of the Christian Brothers established the National Planning Committee for Schools' Governance (NPCSG). This committee began to plan for the implementation of a direction informed by a number of themes, central to which was a desire by the Congregation to set new directions towards serving those at the margins of society. There was a recognition that the school systems under the governance of the provinces of the Christian Brothers had matured to a level at which different governance arrangements could be contemplated. The vision for the role of laity driven by Vatican II was complemented by an acknowledgement on the part of the Christian Brothers of the many committed, faith-filled and competent lay people within their schools. There was also the practical reality for the Brothers that numbers were declining and ages increasing, meaning that fewer Brothers were able or motivated to be involved in the ongoing high-level governance demands of schools.

In the period leading up to 2007, the National Planning Committee engaged in comprehensive dialogue with school and congregational communities to shape the new governance structure, which became EREA. From the beginning, the motivating force was mission, leading to the emphasis taken in developing policies, strategies and structures to support mission, including in the area of identity and formation. A significant step was the proclamation of the *Charter for Catholic Schools in the Edmund Rice Tradition* in 2004. This followed a period of broad consultation with the school and congregation communities to try to articulate the particular cultural characteristics of schools which were then known as Christian Brothers' schools. Eleven such characteristics were identified: Holistic Education, Spirituality, Faith in Action, Community, Pastoral Care, Service of Others, Being Just, At the Margins, Compassion, Stewardship and Reflective Practice. The Charter, launched at national, regional and school gatherings, was well received and owned by schools as an articulation of the unifying bonds within a group of distinctly different schools across the country.

The National Planning Committee took a number of initiatives to support the Charter. These included the development of *Foundations for School Ministry as Church Mission*, a theological reflection on the core beliefs underpinning the charism of Blessed Edmund Rice, the life and ministry of the Christian Brothers and the subsequent tradition of service to the Church and wider community over the centuries. *School Renewal*, a process to authenticate schools as Catholic schools in the Edmund Rice tradition by inviting reflection and review of school culture using the lens of the *Charter for Catholic Schools in the Edmund Rice Tradition,* was trialled and implemented. The development of a Policy statement and theological underpinning for Formation, *Opening our Hearts to the Reality of the Sacred,* and a *Formation Framework* guided the establishment of an initial suite of core formation programs to induct staff into a Catholic school in the Edmund Rice tradition and to form leaders at all levels.

TOUCHSTONES IN SCHOOL PRACTICE

The understanding of the foundations of an Edmund Rice education provides an exciting challenge to EREA as it seeks to remain true to, as well as to grow, the charism in a contemporary setting. There are a number of ways in which schools are supported in addressing this challenge.

The Charter for Catholic Schools in the Edmund Rice Tradition is seen as the central document which guides everything at the individual school level as well as for EREA as a whole. The 2004 Charter was reviewed, and a revised Charter launched in 2011. This Charter identifies four *Touchstones* of a Catholic education in the Edmund Rice tradition:

Liberating Education – *an education that liberates the heart and mind;*

Gospel Spirituality – *an education firmly based on Gospel values and inspired by Jesus;*

Inclusive Community – *an education within a welcoming community which celebrates difference;*

Justice and Solidarity – *an education which encourages questioning, solidarity and action.*

The Charter articulates a culture based on this set of *Touchstones* which, while being embraced across all schools, will be evident in different expressions across the diversity of schools forming EREA. A common language and symbolism reinforces the sense of shared mission for leaders, staff, students and families while not taking away from the individuality of each community.

There is strong ownership of the *Touchstones,* and schools have them exhibited in different ways, including in some very creative and inspiring sculpture and garden interpretations. Principals frequently use them as a focus for newsletter or assembly messages, and a high level of Charter and Touchstone literacy within school communities is evident. By its aspirational nature, the Charter calls every community to ongoing improvement; by its universal acceptance, it gives a common language linking schools of widely varying geographical and social profiles. The ongoing preparation of resources to support the Charter is aimed at ensuring a freshness of engagement and interpretation.

As each *Touchstone* can also be seen as being aspirational, schools are encouraged to reflect upon their position along a continuum. For example, the question a school might ask of itself regarding inclusivity will not be, 'Are we an inclusive community?' but, 'Where do we think we are on a spectrum of inclusivity, and wherever we are, what is holding us there, and what can we do to become more inclusive?'

The *Touchstones* are easily linked to the charism and story of Edmund Rice and the way in which he ran those very early schools in Ireland, setting a tone that went beyond the simplicity of the practice. As an example, one of Edmund's counter-cultural practices was to shake the hands of the boys in the morning and afternoon. It was a simple act, but in the society at the time, it was a powerful statement of his belief in the divine equality of all and in the dignity of all human beings. How the boys must have felt lifted in spirit and esteem!

There are many similar stories of Edmund's respect and determination to help boys look beyond their circumstances as he led them to become aware of their being very special in the heart of a loving God. There is a richness that comes from hearing the stories that began our history:

> *It seems the case that many Catholic schools have lost contact with their cultural narrative. When this happens it becomes difficult to anchor values in a meaningful way within the community .... Leaders have a very real obligation to ensure that the story is kept alive, celebrated, and has a trajectory which leads to hope.*[7]

---

[7] Jim and Therese D'Orsa, *Leading for Mission: Integrating Life, Culture and Faith in Catholic Education* (Mulgrave: Vaughan Publishing, 2013), 125.

EMBEDDING THE *TOUCHSTONES*

The genesis for the Charter was the perceived need for a document to guide schools in their ongoing movement towards full authenticity as Catholic schools in the Edmund Rice tradition. For many, it articulated what was felt in their minds and hearts. It set a path, but a number of structures and processes help the Charter to be a lived reality within the life of the school.

Formation

The National Planning Committee developed a Formation Framework to guide the planning and delivery of formation. The Oceania Province of the Christian Brothers had a similar framework. In 2013 the decision was made to produce a common framework for the Oceania Province and EREA to recognise the shared understandings of charism and mission, as well as to affirm the ongoing close relationship between the two entities.

There are four core formation programs for EREA, each spanning two to three days and offered regionally in partnership with Formation staff from the Oceania Province:

- **Galilee** for those new to Edmund Rice ministries, inducting them into Catholic education and the Edmund Rice, Christian Brother and EREA stories;
- **Into The Deep** for those in middle leadership, or who aspire to leadership, helping them to understand the ministry of leadership within a Catholic education in the Edmund Rice tradition;
- **Break Every Yoke** for senior leaders;
- **Mt Sinai** for long-serving staff to allow them to reflect on their gifts and on the value of their contribution to the school, whatever their role.

Schools are expected to have a formation plan in place for staff. EREA office staff along with Oceania staff can work with schools in developing and implementing this plan. School boards also engage in regional or school-based induction and formation programs as well as their regular meetings. A Board Formation manual provides resources for use at their meetings.

Identity Leadership

The principal is the acknowledged leader in the identity of schools as Catholic schools in the Edmund Rice tradition, but for mission and identity to flourish, it is hoped that all members of the school community take an active role in nurturing its development. Complementing this is the appointment and focused support of Identity Leaders in each school.

The concept of Identity Leadership has been developed to encourage the appointment of a staff member who will support the principal in this key role. Ideally, the appointee to the Identity Leader role (howsoever named in different schools) will be a member of the school Leadership Team. The concept of an identity team covering all areas of Catholicity, spirituality, charism, Religious Education curriculum, liturgy and social justice activities has been embraced by a number of schools. Identity Leaders are supported in their roles by two regional gatherings and a national gathering each year.

An online interactive Identity Matrix allows schools to look at how each of the Touchstones of the Charter might be expressed in various areas of the school: curriculum, pastoral care, leadership, administration, extra-curricular and others.

School Renewal

School Renewal offers the school community a structured time to focus on the way in which the Charter is a lived reality in the school: in its structures, policies, practices and culture.

Whilst the outcome of School Renewal is accreditation as a Catholic school in the Edmund Rice tradition, the process is one of mentoring rather than inspection. Schools engage in a consultative process within their communities, reflectively considering the synergy between the culture of the school and the *Touchstones* of the Charter. A team then visits the school over a three-day period to validate the reflections, conclusions and suggested directions by interviewing a broad cross-section of the community. A written report contains commendations and recommendations relating to each of the *Touchstones*.

Participation in School Renewal each five years is a valuable formative experience for the school community. It brings the community to a place in which the Charter becomes the lens for viewing all aspects of the school. Whilst there is a focus on affirmation, schools are also challenged to look for continuous improvement related to each of the *Touchstones*: How can we be more inclusive? In what ways can Gospel spirituality be more central to all that we do? School boards are involved in the consultation stage and also receive a briefing on the final report.

Immersion Programs

Compassion for the poor drove Edmund's response, and a preferential option for the poor is central to the philosophy of EREA. All senior leaders in EREA are encouraged to participate in an immersion during their first contract period, and opportunities offered include immersions in India, South Africa and East Africa. An indigenous immersion opportunity is also offered. These immersion opportunities complement the many student immersion opportunities offered by schools.

Framework for Justice and Peace

The *EREA Framework for Education in Justice and Peace* (2010) provides a structure for schools to incorporate social justice issues into their curriculum and other endeavours. Whilst there is a strong history of support through fundraising in all schools, this is complemented by service learning programs and immersions so that students have an opportunity to be in solidarity with the marginalised. EREA office staff members provide resources and planning support to schools so that Justice and Peace initiatives can be central rather than peripheral to the experience of students. There are regular symposiums in justice and peace: recent ones have developed understanding and underpinnings of immersions, service learning and advocacy.

National Networking

As EREA is a national network of schools formed from schools governed by four different Christian Brother provinces, a strong emphasis in the early years has been to reinforce a national identity as a way of growing in shared understanding of the charism and the mission as Catholic schools in the Edmund Rice tradition. National gatherings of principals, deputy principals, business managers, identity leaders, junior school leaders and boarding school leaders provide rich opportunities for shared formation, networking, collegial solidarity and sharing of best practice. National gatherings are frequently based in or near schools, allowing participants to experience the environment of another Edmund Rice school.

The fifth year of EREA, 2012, saw the inaugural EREA Congress being held. Having aims akin to those of a congregational Chapter – a time for reflection, celebration of the past and discernment of new directions – the Congress engaged delegates from all EREA schools along with representatives from the Christian Brothers, international Christian Brother educational offices, Catholic Education Offices and other religious orders. Delegates were reminded by the Congregation Leader of the Christian Brothers and the Executive Director of EREA, in particular, about faithfulness to mission, inclusivity and a preferential option for the poor.

Advocacy

Integral to the liberating education offered by Edmund Rice was leading students to question the status quo of poverty and division in the hope that they would feel motivated to bring about change in the world.

The Christian Brothers have positioned themselves to advocate on a local and international stage, the latter through Edmund Rice International in Geneva. Parallel to this, recent years have seen an increased focus on advocacy in schools. Schools encourage students to question and look for steps which can bring about change. Edmund Rice International provides formation opportunities in advocacy to EREA and hosts a group in Geneva each year as part of an Ireland and Geneva Edmund Rice experience. At the local level, a school network, Edmund Rice Advocacy (ERA) for Change, an initiative of one Queensland school, is now incorporated into the programs of a number of others. ERA helps students see how they can meaningfully advocate while at school and as individuals after school.

CHALLENGES TO MISSION AUTHENTICITY

Religious congregations and their lay partners must be alert to the challenges to the authenticity of their missions. Structures and processes are established to highlight aspects of mission risk and the possibility of mission drift. Drift that is slow and gentle may be harder to identify and counteract, particularly if new directions have become institutionalised and form the reality for those engaged in the work. The drift may be evident at different levels of an organisation: individual institutions (schools in the case of EREA), senior leadership level or in governance.

For EREA, a key question must be: What will help us stay true to our direction? How can our vision of being a mission-driven, Gospel-focused and charism-charged organisation become a reality? Is the spirituality of Edmund Rice, inspired by Jesus, challenging us to liberate? And with a deep faith in divine providence is it guiding us where we are heading?

EREA has identified a number of potential areas of mission drift at the school and organisational levels. Significant ones include a movement towards a corporate rather than a mission focus with an associated emphasis on compliance and risk management to the detriment of trust in providence. There can be a loss of connection with Church, an overemphasis on the charism of the founder above the story of Jesus, or a narrow focus on educational outcomes to the detriment of providing a liberating education in line with the aspirations of Edmund and the message of the Gospel. Enhancing mission creates a challenge for leadership succession, with an increasing number of leadership aspirants who may not have strong personal connections with the Congregation or an affiliation with institutional church.

Many of the programs and structures in the sections outlined earlier in this chapter, such as formation, School Renewal, Identity Leadership and the emphasis on a national network, are influential in counteracting these tensions which potentially impact upon the nature and direction of EREA.

The governance structure of EREA, comprising a Council with specific responsibility for faithfulness to mission, provides mission-focused scrutiny, reinforced at the executive level in recent times by the evolution of all directorates to more mission-focused roles, titles and language. In addition, relationship with church is a strategic focus for EREA.

Along its journey, EREA has been influenced by the directions of the Christian Brothers as reflected in their international (Munnar, India 2008) and Oceania (Brisbane, 2008) Chapters. Both have provided inspiration, and EREA looks forward with great interest and a spirit of shared vision to the outcomes of succeeding Chapters at both levels.

CONCLUSION

If charism is seen as a gift to be shared; if it is to respond to the needs of a particular time; if it is to be lived and explained by ongoing generations of leaders and community members in ways that inspire, excite and confront, then we cannot rely upon a process of osmotic transfer. Story can lose its power. It can lose its link to the reality of today if it is not revisited and consciously connected to today's society, in which the needs may differ in detail, but not in essence. There must be constant self-questioning and challenge:

> We must not let fear, attachment to the past or seduction by other agendas deter us from being single minded in our commitment to a vision for Edmund Rice education in which we proclaim education as liberation, as a means of experiencing full humanity and the vehicle of 'good news' to those who are at the margins of our society. Let us continue to challenge one another and have those difficult conversations as we journey into deeper authenticity. To do anything less is to betray the mission we have been given and the foundations upon which we stand.[8]

It is hoped that the stories of Edmund Rice and the Christian Brothers, and of those who, over time, are imbued in the charism, will continue to guide EREA in living out its role to nurture the fullness of life which Jesus promised.

---

8 Wayne Tinsey, Executive Director, EREA, Concluding Address 2012 EREA Congress.

Michael Green fms

Brother Michael Green is currently the National Director of Marist Schools Australia and Executive Director of Marist Ministries for the Province of Australia, and is based in Melbourne. He has been involved in Marist education for forty years as a teacher, school principal, administrator, author, and course presenter. Michael's studies have been in the disciplines of history, theology, scripture, and education. His doctorate, which explored the charismic culture of Australian Marist schools, brought together the sociological concept of culture and the theological dynamic of charism. As well as his scholarship in Marist history and spirituality, he has a particular interest in the ways in which the spiritual families of the Church can contribute to its vitality and renewal.

Darren McGregor

Darren McGregor is currently the Foundation principal of Marist College Bendigo. Prior to this he was principal at Catholic College Bendigo for ten years. After being educated in Sale by the Marist Brothers, Darren has been involved in a range of Marist activities ranging from Youth Ministry in the 1980s through to membership of the National Ministry Council during the formation of the Australian Province. He has been heavily involved in the ongoing exploration and discernment around the role of all Marists in the living out of the Marist charism in Australia. Darren and Jane McGregor live in Bendigo and have four children and one grandchild.

10

LOOKING FOR NEW WINESKINS: THE MARIST EXPERIENCE

Michael Green fms and Darren McGregor

SETTING A CONTEXT

It is almost a quarter of a century since the then Superior General of the Marist Brothers, in a landmark Circular that discussed the growing role of lay people in Marist life and mission[1], posed the question: If the Institute were not experiencing such a downturn in the number of Brothers in some parts of the world, would it be so concerned with fostering the vocation and involvement of lay people? As someone enthused by the Second Vatican Council, he answered his own question with a decisive YES! The Council's defining teachings on the *universal call to holiness* and the *essentially missionary nature of the Church* meant that no one in the Church could tolerate an arrangement that allowed lay people to sit off to the side in any kind of auxiliary, second-rung, or passive role. Indeed, there was really no such thing as a 'lay Christian' or a 'lay disciple' at all.[2] The Church's renewed appreciation of itself as *communio* and its rejection of an implied hierarchy of holiness among its members were recasting the place of consecrated life in the broader life of the Church.[3] Over the last two decades, the Marists have been among those spiritual families of the Church[4] which have

---

1 Brother Charles Howard, *The Champagnat Movement of the Marist Family, a grace for us all*. Circulars of the Superiors General. (Rome: Marist Brothers, 1991).
2 For a more extensive consideration of this, see: Michael Green, *'Lay Spirituality' – Would Jesus have understood the concept?* Paper given at the 'On Sacred Ground' Conference: Lay Leadership in Catholic Human Service and Diocesan Organisations. Novotel Hotel, Brighton Beach, Sydney. 23rd September, 2011.
3 Pope John Paul II's encyclicals *Christifideles laici* (1987) and *Vita consecrata* (1996) along with *Educating Together in Catholic Schools: A Shared Mission between Consecrated Persons and the Lay Faithful* (Congregation for Catholic Education, 2007) provide some sharp discussion on the complementary roles of consecrated and lay life in the spiritual, communitarian and missionary life of the Church.
4 The term is the one favoured by the Congregation for Catholic Education. See *Educating Together in Catholic Schools: A Shared Mission between Consecrated Persons and the Lay Faithful*, 28–30.

been deliberate and strategic in reimagining how their particular spiritual heritage might be appropriated more broadly within the post-Conciliar Church as it strives to share in God's mission in the world. They are now on the threshold of a significant step in defining who they are as an ecclesial movement and how they sit within the broader Church.

The most fundamental challenge for any spiritual family, and arguably the most telling litmus test of its integrity, will be its alignment with mission, God's mission. In the sense that Bevans and others propose God *as* mission[5], this means essentially alignment with God. To share in the life of God – God who is love – is to encounter Christ who reveals this love.[6] This is the heart of mission because this is where the Reign of God is rooted. Before all else, therefore, spiritual families should be *schools of spirituality*. They will be also schools of community and schools of mission, but first of all they need to be graced spaces in which people can learn Christian discipleship. People encounter Christ there, personally and profoundly. They experience conversion of heart. They learn to pray. In such spiritual families, people can become prophets and mystics; indeed prophets and mystics hold wisdom and authority in these groups. It is a misunderstanding of the Church's spiritual families – including those associated with the so-called 'apostolic' religious institutes – to begin with what they do, or to focus on their works as their *raison d'être*. That is not the essence of the mission they undertake. While the personal charisms of founders have been invariably associated with addressing a pressing human need, there is a deeper way of understanding what they were about. All founders of the great spiritual traditions of the Church acted out of a prior and intense God-encounter in Christ.

In the *Constitutions of the Marist Brothers*, the charism of their founder, Saint Marcellin, is defined simply in terms of his being called by the Spirit, from his deep personal experience of being loved by God, to bring Christian education to young people, especially the most needy, in order that he could help 'to make Jesus Christ known and loved'.[7] It is the last clause that Marists claim as their bedrock. A reference text on their Marist spirituality puts it this way:

---

5 See, for example, Stephen Bevans, 'The Mission has a Church', *Compass*, 43, 3, 2004, 314; S. B. Bevans and R. P. Schroeder *Constants in Context: A Theology of Mission for Today* (Maryknoll NY: Orbis, 2004), Stephen Bevans, 'A Theology of Mission for the Church of the Twenty-first Century: Mission as Prophetic Dialogue' in Stephen Bevans and Katalina Tahaafe-Williams (eds), *Contextual Theology for the Twenty-first Century* (Eugene OR: Pickwick Publications, 2011).
6 See the opening three paragraphs of Benedict XVI's Encyclical *Deus Caritas Est* (2005) for a sense of this Christ-encounter.
7 *Constitutions of the Marist Brothers* #2. (Marist Brothers, Rome 1986; 2010).

> *The founding Marists understood their mission as a sharing in Mary's work of bringing Christ-life to birth in the lives of young, and being with the Church as it came to be born.*[8]

The heart of Marist self-identity is not to be found in networks of schools or in excellence of education or in wonderful care of young people. At its heart is Christ or, more pointedly, a community of educators whose lives have been transformed by Christ and who, with Mary, see themselves helping to bring about God's reign in themselves and in their world. At least that is the rhetoric. The challenge for the Marists – as for all spiritual families – is that those who describe themselves as *Marist* have this congruence with the life of God. The consequent challenge is for them to be mystics and prophets – people of both prayer and action – and to be a community that inspires, forms, and sustains them as such.

Today's Marists, with all Catholic educators, are charged with 'integrating faith, life and culture' in the teaching and learning experiences and other programs they share with students.[9] It is what *Evangelii Nuntiandi* understood as incarnating God's reign within a cultural and real-life context, a theme that is commonly enough taken up by contemporary mission theologians.[10] The actual culture in which they go about this is of course a post-modern one which often attracts descriptors such as pluralist, relativist, fractured and secularist. Some in the Church despair of this post-modern world and retreat from it in what Sivalon calls a 'romantic conservatism'. While anecdotal evidence suggests that contemporary Marists are not typically to be found among that group, the challenge remains as to how the Marist movement can be assured that its members are going to be, in the spirit of *Gaudium et Spes*, a respectful but redemptive presence *within* post-modernity: how they are going to evangelise their culture and evangelise the culture of their schools, and how they are going to bring the heart of God to their ministry.

---

8 *Water from the Rock: Marist Spirituality flowing in the tradition of Marcellin Champagnat*, #11 (Institute of the Marist Brothers, 2007). See also #26.
9 The term was introduced by the Sacred Congregation for Catholic Education in its signature document *The Catholic School* (1977) #41, and was subsequently picked up by the *Marist Brothers' Constitutions* (1986) #87.
10 See, for example, the treatment of 'inculturation' by Bevans in 'What Has Contextual Theology to Offer the Church of the Twenty-first Century?' in Bevans and Tahaafe-Williams, op.cit., and John C. Sivalon, *God's Mission and Post-Modern Culture: The Gift of Uncertainty* (Maryknoll N.Y: Orbis, 2012), 13ff.

THE FOUNDATIONS OF MARIST SPIRITUALITY

In addressing this challenge during the last two decades, Marists have returned to their founding intuitions for inspiration. The Marists began, like so many of the Church's spiritual families, as a renewal movement. The founding intuitions were to share in the eternal 'work of Mary' as they called it, indeed to be *as Mary*. Their conviction was that the ecclesial tepidity, ignorance, scandal, regression, fractures, and secularism of post-Revolutionary France would be most compellingly addressed by an essentially Marian approach. Modern Marist theologians describe this in terms of the 'Marian principle' of the Church, something very much in sympathy with the theology of von Balthazar.[11] The Marian way is to nurture, to unify, to reconcile, to heal, to believe, and to embrace the lives of those whose sense of a loving God has been most damaged or never really born. Within this broader movement, one branch – that led by Marcellin Champagnat – became specifically concerned with realising the Marist dream through the Christian education and care of young people. The particular strand of Marist spirituality that evolved from the personal charism of Marcellin was one marked by a profound experience of God's abiding presence and love, by trust in God, by a deep personal love of Jesus and his Gospel, by community living in a family spirit, and by a humility expressed through simplicity.[12] Marists take Mary's *Magnificat* as their manifesto, setting out into the 'hill country' of young people's lives, filled with hope and joy, bringing them news of the justice and mercy and faithfulness of God.[13] Like Mary, first disciple, their lives are centred on Christ, and their hearts are moved by the young.[14]

Marist education was a by-product rather than the starting point of the Marist movement. There was no move to create a new philosophy or mode of education. This is important because it points to a fundamental principle for how the formation and association of today's Marist educators should be undertaken. 'Marist education' is simply how and why Marists do education. While Marist education has developed its distinctive features and characteristic emphases, and while not for a moment undervaluing the evangelising and educative effectiveness of these, it would be a mistake to see them as the essence of Marist education. Its essence is to be found, rather, where all charisms born of the Spirit have their source: in *Missio Dei*. For

---

11 A Circular of the present Marist Superior General, Brother Emili Turú (2011) explores this theme: *He Gave Us The Name of Mary*. (Rome: Marist Brothers, 2011).
12 *Water from the Rock*, Chapter 1, summarises these six features of Marist spirituality.
13 Cf. Luke 1:39–56
14 From the description of Marist spirituality in *Marist Schools Australia: An Introduction* (Marist Brothers' Province of Australia).

someone to be a genuine Marist educator, that person needs to be Marist. And to be Marist, is to be caught up in God's mission in the world, living this out through the graced way of Christian discipleship which was introduced by Saint Marcellin and which has been enriched by successive generations of Marists as they have contributed to its accumulating wisdom, its body of literature, its inspirational stories and sacred places, its heart-lifting art and music, its way of prayer, its family sense of Christian community. That is, as Marcellin's charism grew into a spirituality which could be articulated and appropriated, it provided ever-broadening ways for Christ-life to be incarnated in time, in place, in culture. But its basis is the Christ-encounter, lived out in a community of people similarly inspired. If the movement were to lose touch with this centre, or if the glue that held the Marist family together became something other than their shared sense of a praying Christian community, then they would no longer be genuinely Marist in the sense that the founding generation understood it. They would no longer be bringing the mind and heart of God to the culture of their schools and the young people in them. They would be diminished in their capacity to be the prophets and mystics whom Marcellin would have wanted.[15]

CURRENT DIRECTIONS

A key priority for Marist leadership in Australia and in other parts of the world is the imperative for Marists to be formed, sustained, and associated in ways that have both integrity and effect. Strategies for formation (both early and ongoing) and structures of association have emerged as the two most critical strategic emphases. This priority is premised at least on these convictions:

i   that Marist spirituality is a graced and accessible path of Christian discipleship, and its expression through a distinctive approach to the education and care of young people remains a very effective means of evangelisation at the service of the Church;

---

15   There has been a renewed appreciation of the primary prophetic-mystical foundations of the ministry of St Marcellin Champagnat, replacing an earlier focus on his indefatigable and rigorous apostolic zeal. This is a particular emphasis of the present Superior General, Brother Emili Turú, (E. Turú, *op.cit.*) and has been well explored in the doctoral dissertation of Brother David Hall, (2010) *Friends of a Compelling God: Forming Australian Marist School Leaders in Uncertain Times*, unpublished D.Min dissertation submitted in the CTU, Chicago. The concept of capacity to be prophets and mystics may be considered as a distinctive perspective on Gerald Grace's concept of 'spiritual capital'. See Gerald Grace, 'Renewing spiritual capital: an urgent priority for the future of Catholic education internationally' *International Studies in Catholic Education*, 2, 2, 2010, 117–128.

ii that the Marist spiritual family, if it is to be effective in mission, must first be a school of spirituality for its members, inspiring in them an encounter with the living Christ and a response lived out in a Eucharistic Christian community;

iii that the broader embrace of people now attracted to the Marist way, in the spirit of Vatican II, needs to have a validated space in the Church, with structures and formation strategies that assure its future integrity, and its ongoing ecclesial accountabilities.

If Marist education is how and why Marists do education, then the self-evident need is to have Marists. Since the early 1990s, there has been in the Australian Province an extensive and ever-growing suite of formation opportunities, academic courses, pilgrimages, immersion experiences, retreats, seminars, conferences, assemblies, and other provision of resources, all with the strategic aim of pursuing this purpose. These have been complemented by youth ministry programs and solidarity initiatives. They have continued to expand and are always being evaluated and improved. Thousands of people have participated in them. These formation and gathering experiences have given Marists a language to describe, and to appreciate more deeply, both the spiritual path and the style of Christian education to which they have been intuitively attracted. It has validated and enhanced their self-identity as Marists, an identity that in earlier generations was restricted only to Marist Brothers. The buzz-words for the wider group, which certainly includes the Brothers in a special place but is much broader than them alone, have been 'communion' and 'co-responsibility'.

While there is always more to do in formation, the critical next step is the determination of the most appropriate means for giving structure, definition, and canonical legitimacy to this sometimes amorphous group of people who see themselves as the Marists. Their defined and assured place in the Church is important for two reasons:

i They need to understand themselves as an expression of the one universal Church and not devolve into some kind of sect or club. Pope Francis has warned strongly against any 'privatisation' of the Church by particular groups.[16] While Marist formation programs have been increasingly alert to the need for a Christocentric approach in all that they offer, and to avoid the 'cult-of-the-founder trap' that is always lurking for charismic traditions, it is equally important for any spiritual family to ensure its ecclesial communion.

---

16 See his General Audience, 25 September 2013. The Pope points out that a mark of any genuine Christian community is its inclusivity rather than exclusivity – that any Christian may feel 'at home' within it.

ii The Church quite reasonably also needs to be assured that these 'Marists' are trustworthy and reliable partners in mission – that they have, *inter alia*, clear purposes that are congruent with the Gospel of Jesus, that they have solid formation strategies, that they have appropriate means for choosing and renewing leadership, and that they are sustainable and viable as a group. While the Holy See and local bishops have a responsibility to welcome, to nurture, and to support both old and new charismic groups[17], they have a concomitant responsibility to exercise a pastoral vigilance over them as part of the Church.

The way chosen for this to occur is to form a public association of Christ's faithful, the membership of which will be inclusive of Marists broadly, with the Brothers inevitably forming a smaller fraction of the whole. In deciding to go down this canonical path, the Marists have opted for a concept of juridical personality that is different from that being favoured by many other apostolic groups: this new association will be, in the terms of Canon Law, an 'aggregation of people' rather than an 'aggregation of things'. The reason for this should be evident from all that has been written above: the Marists are convinced that it will be as a recognised ecclesial movement that their particular spiritual tradition will have most salience in the service of the Church. This move represents an invitation for all people who feel called to share in God's mission in a distinctively Marist way to live that call, collectively and individually, in a more self-conscious and intense way than perhaps ever has been the case before now.

A CASE-STUDY

The potential contribution of a charismic tradition to the evangelising effectiveness of a Catholic school is immense.[18] What might all of this look like in practice? One way of approaching that question is to take the case study of a new school, one which is shaping its identity and taking

---

17 *Lumen Gentium* #12 challenges the Church to accept this multifaceted giftedness of the Spirit 'with gratitude' because it is God's way of building up the Church.
18 For elaboration of this, see some other writings of the author, e.g. M. Green, 'Charismic Contribution in Liminal Times' in the preceding book in BBI's Mission and Education series *Leading for Mission: Integrating Life, Culture and Mission* (Mulgrave: Garratt Publishing, 2013); Michael Green, *Charisms: What possibilities and challenges do they offer principals for developing culture and spirituality in Catholic schools?* Monograph published by Marist Schools Australia (2008); M. Green, (2009) *Lay Spirituality and Charism*. Keynote address at Catholic Education Conference, Townsville; Michael Green, (2008) Charisms: What possibilities and challenges do they offer principals for developing culture and spirituality in Catholic schools? For a recent study, see Jennifer M. Elvery, *Understanding and Implementing the Marist Charism from the Middle: The Experience of Middle Leaders in a Marist School*. Unpublished Ph.D. thesis submitted in Australian Catholic University, Brisbane, 2013.

its place in the Church in the emerging context that has been described. Let us consider Marist College Bendigo, a mainstream P–12 school in a developing area, which has enrolled its first students in 2014. In establishing a new Marist school, two principles are being given strategic priority: (a) the gathering and formation of a community of educators who are intuitively attracted to Marist spirituality and pedagogical practice as their preferred way of sharing in God's mission; and (b) the building and assuring of a complementary and integrated relationship with the local Church in ways that are mutually valued and ongoing. These principles, of course, are being pursued hand-in-glove with other educational priorities that should shape the formation of any good twenty-first century school. But let us focus on how the seeds for evangelising mission of the College are being sown.

Building a Marist-inspired Community of Mission

The choice of the foundation staff has been a carefully undertaken process. First, in the appointment of a principal, priority was given to identifying someone whose personal faith has been strongly influenced by the Marist way of Christian discipleship, for whom this was consciously important, and who felt confident in leading an educating community to be a Marist community of mission. The successful applicant wrote this as part of his application:

> *The Marist way is where my heart lies. I have come [while principal in a school of another tradition] to a deeper appreciation of how integral Marist spirituality is to my core self. I deeply yearn to have the opportunity to build a community based on this spirituality. I wish to devote my personal and professional life to doing all possible to make Jesus known and loved.*

He saw his role as foundation principal in terms of drawing a group of educators around the story of Marcellin and forming them in Marcellin's Marian intuitions, in order that they would be captured by the same love of Jesus that Marcellin had and be drawn to make Jesus known and loved with the same passion and approach of Marcellin:

> *I see that one of my key responsibilities is to be a Marist leading others to become Marist. My heart is at home within the Marist family. I feel drawn to a relationship with a Christ seen through this lens on the Gospel and I have a strong desire to understand the deep discipleship of Mary. For me to lead a school, therefore, seems only possible out of this charism. Leading from the heart can only be done authentically for me in a Marist school. Staff members can then gain from my leadership a Marist style. This is first seen and felt through prayer, language, and relationships.*

In inviting applications for the first teaching staff, the newly-appointed principal drew on the motif of the most recent General Chapter of the Marist Brothers, which called Marists to go 'in haste with Mary' to 'new lands', a challenge to align with Mary of the *Magnificat*. Applicants were asked to comment on what this meant for them in the context of the new school. All had had some experience of Marist education and Marist staff spiritual formation; all would have already seen themselves as part of the Australian Marist family. The principal was looking for people who had a sense of what it meant to have the Gospel in their hearts, and would want to draw on a Marist spirituality to give it expression in their teaching, their relationships, and their personal lives, including their faith life. Let us consider some extracts from their applications:

Applicant 1

'Remember that the young people you teach are your brothers and sisters, your own likeness, bone of your bone, another you. These young people have the same heavenly Father, the same destiny, the same end, the same hope. They are called to the same happiness. They are your travelling companions in time. They will be heirs with you, sharing the joys of the homeland of heaven with you.' St Marcellin.

So reads my crumpled piece of paper, weathered with pin holes and blu-tack smudges from a life following me from office to office. I first came across this piece of paper at a staff gathering early in my teaching career I couldn't believe we were being given this... 'brothers and sisters'... 'travelling companions'... it sounded like what I had dreamt teaching could be but would not have said aloud. This piece of paper sparked a desire to find out more about the Marist tradition and to be part of what they do. And so began my journey of discovery of the Marist charism which has led me to write this reflection ... how I wish to be involved in the move to a 'new land' at Marist College Bendigo.

Applicant 2

Marcellin Champagnat's educational approach was a simple one: to teach children one must love them and love them equally Marcellin also worked hard to ensure each school became a happy place where everyone was welcome – 'the family spirit'. Given the small beginning of this college in terms of size, we are presented with a wonderful opportunity to ensure that this Marist charism is evident in all that is put in place from the very start. This ethos strongly corresponds to the values which underpin my own life as a teacher, my commitment to my work, my relationships with staff, students, parents and the community, and my determination to model these values in all of my daily roles and personal life – particularly in terms of service to others.

Applicant 3
I have had the absolute privilege of joining a Marist pilgrimage where we journeyed to the hills of Lavalla, where on the ground floor of a house we sat around a table carved by the hands of Marcellin Champagnat and prayed, it was a powerful experience that still remains an experience best felt by the heart.

My passion for this application comes not simply from my pedagogical connection to the learning and pastoral requirements as stated in the position description, but from my excitement at joining the Marist community in its work with the young people and the new staff in this charism that is dynamic, relational and comes to life as we share it.

The principal clearly had a very solid core from which to build an educating and evangelising community – one which was intuitively attracted to Marist spiritualty and pedagogical principles, of people with strong self-identity as Marists, not in any overly sentimental or emotive way, but in one that was considered, informed, and centred in Christian faith. Staff faith formation began from the start – in conjunction with other educational planning – with regular prayer, readings, a residential retreat, a spiritual journal, and associated initiatives. It would be surprising if all of this group would not become active members of the new canonical Marist association. Over time, as the College grows, the staff will become inevitably more diverse, but it is envisaged to have always at its heart a community of people who are authentically and deeply Marist in their spirituality, their association with one another, and in their distinctive way of educating and evangelising.

Ensuring Ecclesial Integrity

As a lay-led and lay-staffed Marist school from its foundation, it has been important to set in place *modi operandi* that ensure, first, that the College will remain closely integrated into the life, mission and structure of the local Church and, second, that the local Church will value, support and nurture the Marist spiritualty and educational traditions at the heart of its service. This is being done in two ways: by fostering strong, collaborative and honest relationships with local Church leaders and agencies, and with these being supported by robust written agreements.

The relationship between the Marists and the diocese is framed as one where respective responsibilities are undertaken in a complementary and cooperative way. This begins and is sustained at the level of personal relationships which are founded on good will. It is then expressed through a mutual recognition of what each brings to the partnership. For example, the Marists do not seek to replicate the services and expertise offered by the diocese's Catholic Education Office, or to develop different general policy frameworks or industrial agreements from those of other Catholic schools in the diocese. At the same time, by way of further example, the Marists have seen that it is important that canonical and civil authority for the College, including employing authority, is vested in them, so that they can recruit, form, and be responsible for the development of staff in their distinctive spiritual and educational tradition. A range of respective responsibilities, accountabilities and understandings are included in the main agreement between the Marists and the local bishop. They are premised on the proposition that there is a contemporary way for a diocese and a canonical entity of pontifical right (a religious institute or another kind of public juridical person) to form a partnership to establish and conduct a Catholic school. Such an arrangement provides a way for local churches to continue to be enhanced by the spiritual traditions of the Church.

CONCLUSION

Like so many of the spiritual traditions of the Church and the ecclesial families that continue to live out a creative fidelity to them, the Marists were founded in a time and place when the Church was in considerable trouble, rather than when it was enjoying stability and apparent prosperity. Members of such movements tend to be energised by need rather than be dispirited by it. Such hard-wiring for mission offers the Church much in this period of post-modernity and apparent Church diminishment. At their best, these movements can contribute a great deal to bringing the mind and heart of God to the actuality of human experience; their members sit easily and intuitively with what might be seen as the first *evangelion*: 'Fear not. The Kingdom of God is very near to you.' These words of Jesus reveal a profound truth about God, and about God as mission. They are followed, of course, by the imperative to 'repent and believe this Good News.' It is an invitation to recognise the God of love already at the core of human life and of all creation, and to be different as a consequence.

The apostolic commission which emanates from this is something that the Church has sought to embrace in the two millennia since the Jesus event, not least through the founders of apostolic movements, such as Marcellin Champagnat, who have read the signs of their times and responded in ways that spoke compellingly to the people of those times. But for someone to be an apostle, there needs to be a prior and an ongoing means of Christ-centred discipleship and community. The rich spiritual traditions of the Church do all three in accessible and effective ways; that is why they have grown from being personal charisms into ongoing spiritualities. The ones that will continue to offer salience to God's mission in the Church, including in Catholic education, will be those that continue to be accessible and effective for people who are seeking ways to live out their Baptismal call, that continue to read the signs of the times, and that foster the sense of *communio* as Vatican II imagined it.

The strategic priorities for the Marists, in their focus on Catholic education, are being shaped by this thinking. They have, therefore, a major focus on faith formation and theological education, on building their community as Marists, and on professional learning in Catholic, and more specifically, Marist education. They seek to foster and to sustain an ecclesial movement of Christ's disciples, whose enthusiasm and capacity as both evangelisers and educators are enhanced by their drawing deeply on Marist spirituality and Marist pedagogical principles.

Gerard Rummery fsc

Gerard Rummery is a De La Salle brother who taught in secondary education in Australia before continuing postgraduate studies in Moral and Religious Education in Europe (1969–1972). His doctoral thesis – *Catechesis and Religious Education in a Pluralist Society* – was the basis for a book of the same name, published E.J. Dwyer (Sydney) 1975 and by *My Family Visitor* (US), where it won the prize for Religious Book of the Year. Gerard provided significant leadership in catechetics in the post-Vatican II period. He was editor of the Australian catechetical journal *Our Apostolate*, subsequently *Word in Life* and now the *Religious Education Journal* of the Australian Catholic University of which he was an Adjunct Professor. He has conducted national catechetical workshops in England, Ireland, Philippines, US and Australia.

11

THE COMING OF THE TEACHING BROTHERS[1]

Gerard Rummery fsc

SHARING THE STORY

On 6 June 1694, the young French priest, Jean-Baptiste de La Salle, recognising that 'God, who guides all things with wisdom and serenity, whose way it is not to force the inclinations of persons, willed to commit me entirely to the development of the schools as one commitment led me to another which I had not foreseen at the beginning'[2], took twelve of his followers and vowed with them to associate themselves for the rest of their lives in providing a completely gratuitous education for the 'children of the artisans and the poor'. In this society at this time, the word 'children' usually referred to boys.

Some eight or nine years previously, de La Salle had asked members of his growing community of teachers what name they wished to be called. De La Salle's early biographers record that the community – not de La Salle – renounced the title of 'teachers' [maîtres = masters] and chose to call themselves 'Brothers'. They understood 'brotherhood' as being '*brothers* to one another and *older brothers* to their pupils'. In making this choice, they gave themselves both an *identity and a mission*.

In communities of men established by the Desert Fathers (3rd century AD) and the first communities of the Benedictines (6th century), there had always been this concept of brotherhood expressed progressively in terms such as the Latin word *frater* and subsequently by equivalent terms in modern languages. In these instances, the word signified the fundamental

---

1 The first teaching Brothers emerged at a particular moment in the 17th century in France, the predominantly Catholic country in Europe, when there were already important teaching congregations of women. This article shows the origin and development of a particular congregation of teaching Brothers, the De La Salle Brothers.
2 John Baptist de La Salle (presented by various editors), *The Spirituality of Christian Education* (Mahwah: Paulist Press, 2004), 109–120.

status of the person in the community, irrespective of whether some members received ordination. Within monastic communities, each 'frater' was assigned to general duties of prayer and work, and to particular assignments according to his education and talent.

Brotherhood for de La Salle's Brothers was *much more specific*. In establishing their rule, the new congregation made a clear choice that they *would not be priests* but would live their brotherhood through the mutual support of one another in the community, while at the same time spending their lives in the Christian and gratuitous education of the poor.[3] Both their identity as 'brothers to one another' and their mission as 'older brothers to their pupils' were *complementary and inseparable*.

IMPLICATIONS OF BEING 'OLDER' BROTHERS

Innovative practices flowed from the idea of being 'older brothers'. At a time when corporal punishment was practically synonymous with schooling, the Brothers determined that the basis of their teaching flowed from building a relationship which was consistent with being the 'older brother' to each of their pupils, and caused them to determine 'that corporal punishment is absolutely forbidden'. Pupils were addressed by their baptismal names, and the singular person was used, as in the family. While the singular forms ('thou' and 'thee') have become archaic in English usage, the Brothers' use of the first name instead of the family surname was in itself an assumption of the family relationship already present through the meaning given to the word 'Brother'.[4]

Historians recognise that de La Salle's major contribution to education was his insistence on the training of teachers, both for members of his own brotherhood, and for teachers working but also for training teachers who taught in country schools. De La Salle's practical experience of twenty-five years teaching in Catholic schools was set out in the text provisionally known as *The Conduct of the Christian Schools*[5], which was first circulated as a manuscript between 1706 and 1717 and later given definitive form by de La Salle himself before his death in 1719. For two successive summers (1705 and 1706), a group of experienced Brothers was asked to reflect on the first twenty-five years of the Brothers' experience, and to formulate their most successful teaching methods and practices. Over the next ten

---

3 Rule #1705. *Rule and Foundational Documents* (Landover Maryland : Lasallian Publications, 2002), 14.
4 For example, in French: 'Qu'est-ce que tu penses, Jean-Louis?' But if Jean-Louis was not paying attention he would be addressed more formally, 'Qu'est-ce que vous pensez, Jean-Louis?'
5 John Baptise de La Salle, *The Conduct of the Christian Schools* (English translation) (Landover Maryland: Lasallian Publications, 1996).

years, De La Salle Brothers (as they were popularly known) were asked to suggest improvements before the text was re-printed.[6] The process of critical reflection used to develop this seminal work in Catholic education proved influential in shaping both thinking and practice in male and female teaching congregations in France (and in many other countries) as the new teaching congregations developed and spread during the 19th century.[7]

There are many significant changes between the first manuscript of 1706 and the printed version of the *Conduct* in 1720. Most astonishing is the development of the 6th chapter with the title, *Correction – not Punishment*, which begins by pointing out six ways 'in which the behavior of a teacher becomes *unbearable* to his pupils'. Not only is the 'unbearable' aspect clearly depicted, but each of the six examples is followed by a statement as to why it is unbearable. Probably the most striking statement deploring the first unbearable behavior ['the teacher's penances are too rigorous and the yoke imposed by the teacher too heavy']ced[8] simply states, 'Often children do not have enough strength of body or of mind to bear the many difficulties with which life presents them'. It would be difficult to find in any historical period a more compassionate observation about the lives led by the children of the poor. The observation derives not from any theory but from close contact with the daily life of the poor in 17th century France.

The statement is more striking in that it is *all-encompassing*, noting not just the weakness of the body, but also that of the mind. It was to such children that the De La Salle Brother was called to be the 'older brother'.

TEACHING IN FRENCH AND THROUGH FRENCH

De La Salle's schools taught in French rather than Latin, which was then the custom. When the bishop of Chartres, a personal friend of de La Salle from seminary days, remonstrated with him over this innovation, he responded by acknowledging to his friend the importance of Latin, but also stating quite firmly that, in the two years at most that poor boys could attend school, it was important to give them some mastery of their native tongue. For de La Salle, prayers were in Latin, the Mass was in Latin, but French was the language of instruction.

---

6   Apart from Jacob Comenius's guide for his Moravian Brethren, *The Conduct of the Christian Schools* is the first manual of teacher-training in western Europe.
7   Thus the first Sisters of Charity who came to Australia brought with them a handwritten translation of the original *The Conduct of the Christian Schools* in English, with the addition of chapters on Music and Needlework for teaching girls, prepared by Sister Mary Hennessy.
8   *The Conduct of the Christian Schools*, 136.

Following the publication in 1691 of the first Academy French dictionary, a notable attempt to standardise the spelling and pronunciation of the French language, the De La Salle Brothers' schools developed a small 30-page document called a *syllabary*. From this, pupils learned the correct pronunciation of their language and were also trained to write and spell it correctly. Acquiring skills in pronunciation and in spelling widened the possibility of their being employed.

TEACHING WRITING

Unlike other fee-paying Catholic parish schools of the time, which concentrated on teaching reading to the children of the growing middle class, de La Salle's schools were gratuitous, free, open to all who wished to come, and from the very beginning insisted on teaching not only reading but also writing.[9] This immediately put de La Salle into conflict with the guilds of the 'Writing Masters' who insisted that they alone were authorised by the Church to teach writing. In their view, De La Salle Brothers' schools threatened their livelihood.

As the 'older brother', the Brothers sought to ensure that their pupils attained a standard of reading and writing that made them employable in a historical period in France that coincided with the growth of large towns and cities. Again and again, especially in Paris, the schools of the Brothers were attacked, sacked and closed by court orders supporting the Writing Masters. But de La Salle was stubborn about the importance of writing, and showed himself willing to accept various compromises, so long as the schools could continue to function as he desired.

The emphasis which de La Salle gave to preparing the poor boys for employment can be seen in the structure of the school day. There were prayers at the beginning and end of the day, frequent attention to recalling the 'presence of God', and the catechism lesson which was conducted during thirty minutes. But the greater part of each day (six hours) was devoted to the teaching of reading, writing, elementary arithmetic, politeness, and good manners. In his many writings, de La Salle frequently reminds his Brothers of their duty to teach all these subjects *with the same care that they instruct their pupils in their religious duties*.

Jean-Baptiste de La Salle's Brothers in France were often mistakenly

---

9. De La Salle's congregation was also unique in accepting that unless the *petites* écoles offered something more than religious education, parents would not send their children to school – hence their strongly vocational focus. In the great majority of schools, 'reading' literacy rather than 'writing' literacy was the priority. 'Petites ecoles' was the name given to parish schools for the poor. Joseph Bergin, *Church, Society and Religious Change in France 1580–1730* (New Haven and London: Yale University Press, 2009), 308.

referred to as 'the Brothers of Christian Doctrine'. While the Brothers certainly gave a high priority to teaching their students about the Catholic religion and its practices (doubling the time given in other schools of the time), the teaching of religion always went hand in hand with all the other subjects and activities of a school that aimed to prepare boys to be employable in the society in which they lived.

ANSWERING NEEDS

This attention to preparing their pupils to be able to earn their livelihoods because of the education they received is probably best expressed through noting how schools devised their programs according to the obvious needs of their pupils in a particular place. It is significant that the sons of merchants in the boarding school in Rouen were taught what we would call 'elementary book-keeping'. When schools were opened in the sea ports of Calais and Boulogne for the children of fishermen, elementary navigation was added. Prior to the French revolution, the schools in Marseille taught both Italian and Spanish, needed for persons engaged in commerce, while the school at Metz taught German and the school in Rouen, English.

TOUCHING HEARTS

In a society in which there was much violence, e.g., thieves having the word *voleur* (thief) burned on their forearms, the Brother's duty, as de La Salle insisted, was 'to pray for the gift of being able to touch hearts'.[10] His writings also challenged his Brothers to 'win hearts' and even 'to conquer the hearts' of their young charges. In his view, relationships were the key to ensuring that this kind of education could be successful.

A particularly important practice designed to 'touch hearts' was what became known as the 'Reflection'. At the end of the morning class, before the pupils went home for a midday meal, the desks were cleared of all books, and for a period not exceeding three minutes, the Brother was to speak from what was important in his heart to the hearts of his pupils – he spoke as the 'older brother', and he put his trust in his listeners and spoke of something that was important *for himself and for them*. The Brother left the objectivity and security of the teaching subject to reveal his vulnerability in personal matters and beliefs, which he was willing to share with his pupils. He revealed himself in this way as the 'older brother', advising, guiding and encouraging each one of his pupils to live as a child of God.

---

10   Cf. Meditations 42 & 43 for Pentecost Sunday and Monday.

THE ATTACKS OF THE 'PHILOSOPHES'

The schools of the De La Salle Brothers came under sustained attack from certain French philosophers of the 18th century. While history rightly acknowledges the importance of the 'philosophes'[11] in attacking privilege and a society ruled by an 'absolute monarch', it has usually overlooked the limited nature of their vision, especially with regard to the education of the poor. As Jesuit schools gradually diminished in France because of political difficulties leading to the suppression of the order in 1773, the De La Salle Brothers' gratuitous schools were seen by many people as 'the successors of the Jesuits'. Thus, the Breton educator, de La Chalotais, writing to Voltaire in 1762, says of the spread of the schools:

> *The Brothers ... have come along to destroy everything. They teach reading and writing to people who need nothing more than to draw and use the plane and the file, but who do not want to do this any more. They [i.e. the Brothers] are the successors of the Jesuits. The good of society requires people to go no further than their occupations. Every man who looks beyond his own little trade will never carry out his duty with courage and patience. Among ordinary people there is no need to know how to read and write except for those who live by these means or who these means help them to live.*[12]

Voltaire replies:

> *I thank you for forbidding the education of labourers. As I cultivate the land myself, I need workmen and not tonsured clerics. Send me above all some of these ignorant Brothers to hitch up to my ploughs and guide them.*[13]

This reference to the 'ignorant' Brothers was typical of the insults of the time because the Brothers, who neither learned nor taught Latin and Greek in their schools for the poor, were looked down upon by those who had done such studies. Thus we find another of the 'philosophes', M. de Langouria, a minor philosophe[14], claiming that it was necessary 'to chase out these 'ignorantins' (ignoramuses), these Brothers with flowing sleeves, because these bizarre fellows teach the people to hold the pen which is such a dangerous tool in certain hands'.

---

11 The 'philosophe' was the name loosely given to those who were against the prevailing order of a society where an absolute monarchy and the Church had such power. Some of the best-known philosophes were Voltaire, Rousseau, D'Alembert, Diderot and the Encyclopedists.
12 *Essay on National Education*, 1762, 419. Translated from Rigault Georges *Histoire Generales des Freres des Ecoles Chretiennes* Tome II, 417–421.
13 Letter of 28 February, 1763 in ibid.
14 Cited by Lucard in *Annales, II*, 274.

The sociological term 'upward mobility' had not been coined in de La Salle's time, but by educating poor boys in skills that their parents often lacked, his schools enlarged the employment possibilities open to their pupils. In *The Conduct of the Christian Schools*, there is a chapter on *Absences*. In it, de La Salle asks his Brothers to convince parents to keep their child at school because 'a child who has learned to read and write, however limited the child's intelligence… is capable of doing anything'.[15] The confidence underlying such a statement can astonish us even today.

GROWTH AND EXPANSION OF THE ORIGINAL SCHOOLS

The original De La Salle schools were concerned with what could be called 'basic literacy' and teaching the children their religion. Their success gradually led to the years of schooling being extended, especially through the foundation and growth of boarding schools, throughout the 18th century.[16] As pupils now attended school for some six or seven years, it became necessary for the Brothers to be more thoroughly trained in the subjects to be taught. The fifth successor to Jean-Baptiste de La Salle, a Brother Agathon (congregational leader from 1777 to 1798), opened *scholasticates*, what today we would call training colleges, in which Brothers studied in programs in the natural sciences, mathematics, writing and languages for two or three years. It was the same Brother Agathon who wrote the treatise called *The Twelve Virtues of a Good Master*, which took on a life of its own and became the standard text in teacher-training institutions in many European countries until the eve of the Second World War.[17]

In the 19th century, in the aftermath of the French Revolution, there begins a rapid flowering of congregations of teaching Brothers.[18] Very quickly, many of these congregations of Brothers were called on to open schools in the colonies of the countries in which they originated, often following in the wake of poor immigrant families. In this way they developed a 'missionary outreach' that remains integral to their mission

---

15 *The Conduct of the Christian Schools*, 161.
16 When the Brothers were temporarily suppressed in 1792 during the French Revolution (along with all other religious congregations, convents and monasteries), they were running eight such establishments.
17 Saint Don Bosco, as a young chaplain to the Brothers' school of Santa Barbara in Torino, came to know this text and kept a copy on his desk. The translation into English done by the Irish Christian Brothers in the 1840s is referred to in a text written about the Victorian goldfields in 1855.
18 E.g., the Christian Brothers of Ireland founded by Edmund Rice (1803); the Patrician Brothers founded by Bishop Delaney (1808); the Marist, or Little Brothers of Mary founded by Marcellin Champagnat (1817); the Brothers of Christian Instruction, founded by Jean-Marie de la Mennais and Gabriel Deshayes (1817), and some 13 other congregations in Europe.

to the present day. However, the form of this outreach has changed in response to new needs and circumstances.

CHARISM, HERITAGE AND THE CULTURAL TRADITIONS OF TEACHING BROTHERHOODS

Charism is a gift or personal quality often associated with the person of the founder of a religious congregation. Well-known founders of religious congregations of men include Saints Jean-Baptiste de La Salle, Marcellin Champagnat and Blessed Edmund Ignatius Rice. This personal charism usually developed and manifested itself in the framework of a community initiated by the founder, but the congregation then developed its own charism as it survived the death of the founder and stabilised itself through a Rule approved by the Church. The mission of the congregation was often spelt out implicitly rather than explicitly in this rule.

As more and more religious congregations became international, they developed within their overall heritage particular practices and traditions as they established themselves in different societies. Periodically, through international meetings such as General Chapters, this 'heritage' has been examined and revised, most notably in the overall appraisal called for by the document, *Perfectae Caritatis* (Decree on the Adaptation and Renewal of Religious Life) from the Second Vatican Council (1962–5), which asked all congregations to look back to their origins to see how faithful they had been to the founding vision.

THE ANTHROPOLOGICAL CORNERSTONE OF 'BROTHERHOOD'

De La Salle's first group of teachers gave the group a sense of identity which is still the cornerstone of a teaching brotherhood. In the historical circumstances of 17th century France, it was only through a *community* supported by a basic standard of living that a completely gratuitous education could be offered to the sons of the poor. The insistence on gratuity and on the school being open to all who wished to come was fundamental. It is worth reflecting that such openness to all made it possible for the very poor and the better-off to be seated next to one another on the same benches, when other schools of the time had the 'poor' and the 'better-off' carefully separated. De La Salle's writings frequently reminded his Brothers that both groups were in their classes and, if any distinction needed to be made, they should favour the poor over the better-off. In various writings and in different expressions, de La Salle reminds the Brothers that all these 'pupils… young people' are 'entrusted to your care', that 'ignorance of the truths of religion... would be criminal for you since it would cause ignorance in those who are entrusted to you', and that 'your work does not consist in making your disciples to be Christian but in helping them be true Christians'.[19]

HOW IS DE LA SALLE'S CHARISM OF 'BROTHERHOOD' HELPFUL FOR CATHOLIC SCHOOLS IN AUSTRALIA TODAY?

As the membership of religious teaching brotherhoods has declined, there has been a great deal of attention given to sharing the historical mission of the congregation with lay people, usually under the title of 'shared mission'. Thus, for example, in 1967, in an important restatement of their identity following the teaching of the Second Vatican Council and their own General Chapter, the De La Salle Brothers acknowledged:

> *The school will be moulded into community only through a staff rich in diversity and the unity of its members. For this reason the Brothers work closely with lay teachers... Lay teachers should be completely involved with the whole life of the school, with catechesis, apostolic organisations, extra-curricular activities, and administrative positions.*[20]

Reading this confident statement almost fifty years later reminds us that today the majority of people working in what was once known as 'the Brothers' school' are not members of the brotherhood, and that the leadership of the school may well be entrusted to a lay person. Is it possible to extrapolate from this anthropological cornerstone of 'brothers to one another' and 'older brothers to the young' and apply the principles in a new way?

As has already been stated, these two foundation aspects of 'brotherhood' are complementary. It has not been difficult to enlarge the original self-definition to 'brothers *and sisters* to one another' and 'older brothers *and sisters* to the young', as more and more women have taken an important place in the staffs of schools founded by brotherhoods.[21] Many schools that were once only for boys are now co-educational. There is no difficulty in recognising the general appreciation of the important contribution made by women to the education of boys in schools of the brotherhoods.

But the first part of the definition is just as important: how can the schools of the brotherhoods develop school 'communities' in which all

---

19   *Meditations* 37.2 and 173.2.
20   *The Declaration of the Brother of the Christian Schools in the World of Today*, D 46.3
21   The 2012 international statistics for De La Salle institutions in some 80 different countries show that there are 89,000 lay teachers, some 45,000 of whom are women.

members are prepared to commit themselves to that aspect of the school's mission that calls on them to be 'brothers and sisters to one another'?

TOWARDS A DIFFERENT FUTURE

Many religious teaching congregations continue to develop new ways of 'sharing' their charism with lay colleagues. This sharing is noted and commended in the document (Vita Consecrata) which was issued following the 1994 Vatican synod[22] on consecrated life:

> Today, often as a result of new situations, many Institutes have come to the conclusion that their charism can be shared with the laity. The laity are therefore invited to share more intensely in the spirituality and mission of these Institutes. We may say that, in the light of certain historical experiences such as those of the Secular or Third Orders, a new chapter, rich in hope, has begun in the history of relations between consecrated persons and the laity.[23]

For example, some international programs of the De La Salle Brothers, formerly intended only for the Brothers, have now, for over twenty years, been opened for complete or partial participation by lay men and women. In the past fourteen years, there have been two International Assemblies of three weeks at which two-thirds of the delegates were lay women and lay men from some eighty countries around the world. The assemblies were prepared by lay people and presided over by lay people, and the resolutions regarding Lasallian education were passed on to the Brothers' General Council for implementation. It is not surprising that the overall direction of these resolutions was for better formation programs for lay people in the history and charism of the Institute, programs increasingly recognised by academic institutions at graduate and postgraduate level.

In Australia from 1990 to 2012, residential programs were run from Sunday evening to Friday lunchtime at the Lasallian Centre in Narooma, NSW. A total of over 3,000 teachers, front office staff and youth leaders have taken part in these programs. Individuals who were particularly interested have been given the opportunity to attend programs at a higher level. An online course as part of a Master's degree in pastoral studies or religious education was validated by the Australian Catholic University or Notre Dame University, and has been successfully followed by over fifty participants, most

---

22 The Catholic Church's synod or international meeting in Rome of bishops from around the world in October 1994 was based on a working paper written after a worldwide consultation of religious congregations.
23 *Vita Consecrata* #54e.

of whom are now in leadership positions. To ensure the government and administration of many works formerly entrusted to the Brothers (and to Sisters), boards have been created that guarantee the autonomy of the work and its continuation in the spirit of the original foundation.

SHARING THE CHARISM

The history of the individual brotherhoods and sisterhoods in Australia shows that there have been similar stages in their attempts to share their charism with lay people.[24] The first, and the most important, is the sharing of the story of the founder in the historical circumstances which led to the foundation, growth and spread of the congregation. It is a 'human' story of exceptional women and men whose lives were lived in obedience to their understanding of where God's Spirit was leading them in their desire to share the Gospel with young people. Modern biographies, retreats, staff formation activities, international study sessions, pilgrimages 'in the steps of the founder' have all contributed to a better understanding and appreciation of the values enshrined in the charism.

These first steps are all offered by way of *invitation*. The invitation is to come to know the common story and to share the values which the congregation has incorporated in its organisation and the direction of its works. Each individual is then challenged to adopt these values personally and to be willing to share them and maintain them in 'partnership' with others in the 'community' of the staff. All can thus contribute to the overall mission of the school in spite of their particular beliefs and practices.

Experience teaches that it is important to recognise that, just as the personal charism of the founder passed through a kind of 'mutation' to become the charism of the congregation, and that this charism manifests itself in similar but distinct forms in different societies, so too the charism shared with women and men who will never be vowed members of the original foundation also tends to 'mutate' into *recognisable but distinct forms* according to different circumstances. This is most obvious where international sisterhoods and brotherhoods maintain works in countries where the majority of teachers are not Christian, but who find unity and direction from the story of the founder and the growth of the congregation. It is a timely reminder of the discussion by Ormerod[25] that both mission

---

24 For example, Boystown Beaudesert, originally founded by the De La Salle Brothers for court-committed boys had a staff of some 12 Brothers, and is now refounded to serve many and diverse social needs with the services of some 500 lay persons. The Brothers are represented on the board, but the CEO is a lay person.
25 Neil Ormerod, 'Identity and Mission in Catholic Organisations', *The Australasian Catholic Record*, 2010, No 87, 430–439.

and ministry may be required in a traditional Catholic school, whereas the mission of a Catholic school in societies in which Catholics are a small minority, according to the late Cardinal Cordero of Karachi, is primarily one of presence and example.[26]

If attention to founding charisms in Catholic schools is regarded as a distraction from direct teaching about Jesus Christ in schools today, an opinion which is sometimes heard, something important may be lost. Each brotherhood and sisterhood exemplifies a particular way of living the spirituality of a Christian educator. The human story of a wealthy man like Jean-Baptiste de La Salle devoting his life to teaching the neglected poor boys of his society has been inspirational since it was first shared with Muslim, Hindu, Buddhist, Confucianist and Shintoist teachers in Asia in the 19th century. As his followers continue to share this story today, the very 'incarnational' aspect of this story needs no further gloss. The Brothers are known and respected as dedicated Christians. In a broader sense, the continuing existence of the educational works founded by different brotherhoods and sisterhoods continues to offer the 'human' gift of education based on Christian principles and values that originally inspired founders and foundresses.

STRAITJACKET OR RESOURCE FOUNT?

Exploring the diversity of charisms exemplified in the history of the many teaching congregations in Australia is a constant reminder that God's gifts are shared against a historical background. In Australia, for instance, this historical background includes the independent stance taken by Church leaders following the exclusion of any government support by the 19th century Education Acts; the pioneer courage of women who brought education to so many outback towns; the full primary and secondary education offered in inner-city schools on minimal or no fees through the Great Depression; the thousands of Sisters and Brothers who, after a full teaching day, struggled to obtain their university qualifications through evening lectures and residential schools so that the education they offered would be better for all their pupils. This collective effort shaped the lives of individual women and men who, in their own lives, tried to live the Gospel journey exemplified in the lives of their founders and contribute to the mission of their community.

While at one level this history is inspirational, at another level it points to particular emphases and collective experiences that embody the enduring

---

26 Opinion conveyed to me in a personal meeting with Cardinal Cordero in Karachi in March 1984.

principles of good Catholic education based on relationships, respect for differences, and an agreed set of practices, all of which challenge teachers to unite in upholding the 'heritage' embodied in the De La Salle ideal to be 'older brothers and sisters' to new generations. In a time of rapid social and cultural change, 'tradition' can easily become a straitjacket. However, viewed as a valued heritage, it also reminds us that we are heirs to a gift, a charism, that offers us the 'freedom of the children of God'.

It is this heritage of rich and diverse charisms that offers all who work in Catholic education the distilled wisdom of human experience and practical holiness in fulfilling the mission to educate the next generation. Charism seen as God's gift to a community, and as a special call to witness to the Gospel, gives us confidence that, while we may not know quite yet where the path we tread leads as we track over new territory, or what difficulties may lie ahead, we have a valuable and most important mission to pursue, and that God will continue to accompany us on this journey in new and surprising ways.

Chris Gleeson sj

Christopher Gleeson is a Jesuit priest and member of the Australian province. He has spent most of his working life as a teacher and administrator in Jesuit schools. Over the years Chris has written four books for parents and teachers. He is currently Director of Jesuit Publications (now Jesuit Communications) in Melbourne. He is also inaugural Director of both the *Faber Centre* of Ignatian Spirituality and the Archdiocesan *Santa Teresa* Spirituality Centre in Brisbane. In January 2011, Chris took up his current role as the Provincial's Delegate for Education and Mission Formation, and in October 2012 was asked to be the Jesuit Conference Asia Pacific (JCAP) Secretary for Primary and Secondary Education.

12

CHARISM AND MISSION IN THE IGNATIAN SPIRITUAL TRADITION

Ministry without passion is mission diminished

Chris Gleeson sj

As one who often speaks to groups of educators about the Ignatian charism, I like to begin by showing a brief clip from the film *Billy Elliot*. Those who have seen the film would remember that it is set in the north of England in County Durham, during the seemingly endless, violent 1984–85 strike against the Thatcher Government's closure of British coal mines. Widower Jackie Elliot and his eldest son and fellow miner, Tony, take a very dim view of eleven-year-old second son Billy's poor record in boxing class, which worsens when they discover he has secretly transferred to the neighbouring, otherwise girls-only-attended ballet class.

Despite the encouraging view of his dancing teacher that Billy has the talent to audition for the Royal Ballet School, his father, Jackie, disapproves vehemently – until he catches sight of Billy dancing in the gymnasium and realises his son is truly gifted; he will do whatever it takes to help Billy realise his dream. Jackie even attempts to cross the picket line to pay for the trip to London, but older son, Tony, blocks him. Instead, his fellow miners and the neighbourhood raise some money and Jackie sells his wife's jewelry to cover the cost of taking Billy to London to audition for the Royal Ballet School.

The brief film clip captures the moment at the end of the Review Board interrogation at the Royal Ballet School when, faced with the frustration of Billy's nervous, monosyllabic answers to their questions, one board member asks him finally: 'What does it feel like when you're dancing?'

Billy sparks up as he tries to put words around his passion: 'It's like fire in my body....it's flying like a bird....it's like electricity.' It is a magical, very moving, and ultimately successful response. Indeed, it reminded me of what the philosopher, Martin Buber once said famously: 'When two people relate to each other authentically and humanly, God is the electricity that surges between them.'

Charism is more than a lens into the story of the Gospel. Like Billy Elliot, when we speak about a charism, we seek to try and put some words around the passion, the fire and electricity it provides. This, it seems to me, is the purpose of this piece – to reach a better understanding of what fuels the Ignatian mission. After all, passion is God's fire in us, as Father Ron Rolheiser OMI has written so eloquently.[1]

CHARISM, PASSION AND MISSION

At the 56th Conference of the Union of Superiors General in 2002, the President, Fr Claude Maréchal AA, set out a fascinating template to describe the charism of a religious congregation. He suggested that the genius of the founders of religious congregations was to reinterpret the Gospel in a way that was attractive to a new generation. He proposed that the characteristic features of such charisms are:

- a story to enter;
- a language to speak;
- a group to which to belong;
- a way to pray;
- a work to undertake;
- a face of God to see.

This is an excellent template or framework that all schools could use to examine their fidelity to their spiritual tradition.

From the perspective of the Ignatian tradition, we can ask ourselves:
- do we tell the story of Ignatius and the Jesuit tradition?
- do we use in an intelligible way, the characteristically Ignatian language which captures so many of our core ideas and values?
- do we provide a strong group identity to which students and staff wish to belong?
- do we have prayer and a way of learning prayer at the heart of all we do?
- what are the particular works we undertake – teaching and learning, certainly, but also service of the poor?
- does the school reveal a face of God for people to see?

---

1 Ronald Rolhheiser, *Forgotten Among the Lilies – Learning to Love Beyond Our Fears* (New York: Doubleday, 2005), 63.

In terms of mission, our current Father General of the Jesuits, Adolfo Nicolás, spoke to a group of Jesuit and Ignatian school educators in Manila in 2009 as follows:

> In Jesuit education we do not have small goals, but an enormous dream: to assist our students to achieve what (my predecessor) Fr Kolvenbach described as 'the full growth of the person that leads to action—action, suffused by the spirit and the presence of Jesus Christ, the Man-for-Others.[2]

He outlined the scope of this dream in 2012:

> The mission of God has no limits. It's God's mission, so the whole world is a beneficiary of that mission. We (Jesuits) try to go beyond Australia, beyond Asia and the Pacific, beyond whatever limitations we might see in our concerns or in our possibilities.[3]

St Ignatius saw his schools as *platforms for mission*. In the *Constitutions*, he frequently expressed the hope that, through the Society's educational work, capable zealous leaders would be poured into the social order in numbers large enough to leaven it effectively for good.

IGNATIAN SPIRITUAL TRADITION

Let me retrace my steps at this point and, especially for the uninitiated, endeavour to give a little background to what we might call education in the 'Ignatian spiritual tradition'.

The great Jewish author, Elie Wiesel, wrote once that 'God made man because he loves stories'. Ignatian education has a rich story. It derives its name and spirit from St Ignatius Loyola, the founder of the Society of Jesus, the Jesuits. After his early and very worldly years as a career soldier, a life-changing injury in a battle against the French in 1521 opened the way for Ignatius to hear God calling him to follow a radically different path in life. He was transformed by the experience, placing his whole life in God's hands, and so came to find God at the centre of everything he pursued and achieved. The centrality of God is therefore at the core of the Ignatian story of which Ignatian education is a vital part.

Ignatian education can be seen as an offshoot of Jesuit schooling, which began in 1548. At the behest of the local community, the Society opened its first secondary school in Messina, Sicily, in 1548 – just eight years after

---

[2] Father General, Alfonso Nicolás SJ. July 2009, on the occasion of the 150th anniversary of Jesuit education in the Philippines.
[3] Fr Alfonso Nicolás SJ, at St Ignatius' College, Riverview, Sydney, Jan 25th 2012.

its foundation by Pope Paul III in 1540. When St Ignatius died in 1556, the number of schools entrusted to the Jesuits' care had grown to 33, expanding to 372 schools in 1615. This spread of influence and their attempt to systematise education in the 1599 *Ratio Studiorum* (Plan of Studies) earned the Jesuits the somewhat pretentious title of 'The Schoolmasters of Europe'. Indeed, early Jesuits viewed their ministry, described in the words of Spanish Jesuit educator Juan de Bonifacio, as: 'Institutio Puerilis Renovatio Mundi' – 'the education of youth is the renewal of the world'.

While the first Jesuits got into education 'through the back door', as historian John O'Malley SJ has described it[4], they then gave themselves wholeheartedly to creating an educational system that would respond to their apostolic goal enunciated in the *Constitutions*: 'The end of the Society and of its studies is to aid our fellowmen to the knowledge and love of God and to the salvation of their souls'.[5]

In 1599, after fifty years of educational experience in schools, the Society published a document that would set down norms for the educational apostolate: the *Ratio Studiorum* mentioned above became the *Magna Carta* of Jesuit education. In the Middle Ages, the Augustinians also had a document known as *Ratio Studiorum*, and other orders had similar documents which were intended for the training of members of the orders.

The *Ratio* of the Jesuits was different, however, in that it was meant as much for the education *of lay students* as for Jesuits, but it was different also because the 'plan of studies' now included the humanities – literature, history, drama, and so forth – as well as philosophy and theology, the traditionally clerical subjects. The Jesuit *Ratio* assumed that literary or humanistic subjects could be integrated into the study of professional or scientific subjects; that is, it assumed that the humanistic program of the Renaissance was compatible with the Scholastic program of the Middle Ages.[6]

As John O'Malley points out, the *Ratio* had benefits and defects. While it set standards, for instance, it discouraged innovation.[7] Despite this, it had an impact far beyond Jesuit institutions because it was seen as a coherent and lucid statement of ideals, methods, and objectives shared broadly by educators in early modern Europe. For the Society of Jesus, the *Ratio*

---

[4] John O'Malley SJ, 'How the First Jesuits Became Involved in Education', in Vincent J. Duminuco SJ (ed.), *The Jesuit Ratio Studiorum – 400th Anniversary Perspectives*, (Fordham University Press, 2000), 64.
[5] George E. Ganss (ed.), *The Constitutions of the Society of Jesus* (St Louis: The Institute of Jesuit Sources, 1970), Part IV, #446.
[6] The development of the Jesuit philosophy of education is charted by Jose Mesa SJ, 'The International Apostolate of Jesuit Education: Recent Developments and Contemporary Challenges,' in *International Studies in Catholic education* (Vol.5, no.2, 2013), 176–189.
[7] John O'Malley, 'From the 1599 Ratio Studiorum to the Present: A Humanistic Tradition?', in Vincent J. Duminuco (ed.), *The Jesuit Ratio Studiorum*, 136–138.

Studiorum symbolised a certain maturing in its commitment to education, which had great repercussions for the future of Catholicism. The schools were often at the centre of the culture of the towns and cities where they were located: typically they would produce several plays and even ballets per year. Some maintained important astronomical observatories.

With the *Ratio*, the Jesuits distilled the best educational practice of their time, while at the same time incorporating the apostolic criteria they had learnt in experiencing the *Spiritual Exercises* of St Ignatius. The curriculum of the early Jesuit schools included important elements of the Italian humanism of the day, including the formation of character through study of the classics. The *Ratio* leaves no doubt about the apostolic character of education as proposed by Ignatius in the *Constitutions*: 'One of the primary ministries of our Society is to teach all subjects that are in keeping with our Institute for the purpose of moving people to knowledge and love of our Creator and Redeemer'.[8]

Stepping ahead to our own time, Pope Francis, in mid–2013, told Ignatian educators: 'Educating is not a job but an attitude. It is a way of being'.[9] While Ignatian education has its roots in Jesuit schooling and educational tradition, its hallmark is the *Ignatian spirituality* that drives it.

Over the years, many religious congregations have adopted the Ignatian spirit for themselves and infused their schools with its inspiration. In more recent times, numerous Catholic diocesan schools, understanding the need to have a rich story with which they can identify, have committed to following the Ignatian way. Because Ignatius wrote the *Spiritual Exercises*, the core of Ignatian spirituality, *as a layman* rather than as a cleric, Ignatian spirituality is very appealing and accessible to lay people. Its practical value for decision-making in everyday life is now well documented.[10]

IGNATIAN EDUCATION AND IGNATIAN SPIRITUALITY GO TOGETHER

Clearly, Ignatian education and Ignatian spirituality are of a piece. While there have been many attempts over time to develop this tapestry, perhaps the most helpful has been a new charter produced by the Jesuits for their own and associated Ignatian schools in 1986 – *The Characteristics of Jesuit Education*. The *Characteristics*, composed by an international commission that met over four years and consulted worldwide, drew on a number of sources: the life and writings of St Ignatius Loyola (1491–1556), the narrative of

---

8 *Ratio Studiorum*, Rules of the Provincial, no. 1
9 Pope Francis, *Address to Italian and Albanian teachers and students in Jesuit Schools 6/6/2013*.
10 For instance, see Chris Lowney, *Pope Francis: Why he leads the way he leads – Lessons from the first Jesuit Pope* (Chicago: Loyola Press 2013).

Jesuit education, and on what was seen as best in contemporary practice. What follows here is an attempt to summarise the *nine defining characteristics of Jesuit education* that educators who identify with the Ignatian tradition worldwide have found very valuable.[11]

The World is God's Creation

'The world is charged with the grandeur of God' (G.M. Hopkins SJ). God is at the heart of his creation, which shares in his mystery, and God is at work in human culture and human history. Ignatian education is therefore conducted in a spirit of reverence and from a radically religious perspective: facilitating the discovery of, and encounter with, God is its core-value. We seek to transcend false dichotomies between religious and secular, sacred and profane, and the religious dimension permeates all aspects of life in the school.

Cura Personalis

Ignatian education, driven and guided by Ignatian spirituality, has always seen the human person in the context of their eternal destiny – as the central focus of the enterprise – and insists on individual care and concern for each one (*cura personalis*). Relationships and pastoral structures reflect this focus. Through the curriculum, co-curricular activities and the environment of the school, our mission is to help students to grow holistically and lay the foundations for life-long growth – liberated from ignorance and the other forces which inhibit growth, learning to think for themselves, finding their own distinctive 'voice' and becoming ever more fully their unique self.

Moral Values

We are defined as persons above all by our values, by the habitual moral choices we make. Ignatian education is essentially value-oriented. Ignatian pupils are to be people of conscience, able and willing to stand up and be counted in the name of the truth, prepared to use their skills of self-expression and advocacy for those who may have no voice, and committed to choosing the path that is right, not the one that is merely popular or fashionable.

---

[11] I draw heavily here on work done by an Irish Jesuit colleague and dear friend, Father Bruce Bradley, who described his in-house February 2004 summary in these words: 'What follows, including the headings, is an attempt to express the essence of the 'characteristics' in summary form.'

Jesus Christ as Model

For Ignatian education, Jesus Christ is at once the human face of God and the model of all human life, responding totally to the Father's love. He is our conscience incarnate, the pattern of authentic humanity, the centre of history. His way of compassionate love is not *a* way but *the* way. This conviction is reflected in the provision of pastoral care for all involved, aimed at encouraging spiritual growth and the development of a personal relationship with Jesus Christ. It is also reflected in the practice of communal prayer and worship and the celebration of the sacraments as constitutive parts of the school's rhythm of life. Service programs are consciously promoted as a way of imitating Jesus Christ, the Man-for-Others, in his complete self-dedication to building the Kingdom of God.

Faith That Does Justice

Ignatian education is intended as a preparation for a life of active social commitment. Ignatian students are encouraged to understand their own 'place' in the world in terms of educational and socio-economic opportunities, and to use these opportunities in compassionate service of others, especially those whose opportunities have been less than theirs or who are the victims of poverty and injustice. In the *Spiritual Exercises*, the map of his own conversion which Ignatius composed for the guidance of others in their journey to God, he taught that 'love is shown in deeds'. Religion is deeply personal but not private: faith which does not express itself in love for others and the passionate quest for justice lacks authenticity. We aim to facilitate the emergence of young women and men who will exercise leadership in terms of these values and seek to be agents of change, not more or less passive upholders of the *status quo*.

Part of the Church's Mission

Ignatian education has its roots in the Jesuit education tradition which Ignatius established to advance the Church's mission to which he was intensely loyal. This mission is to spread the Gospel of Jesus Christ and, in this way, to build the Kingdom by serving and humanising the world and giving glory to God. Living by the Gospel is not a merely individual pursuit. Jesus founded a community, called his followers into community, and committed himself to the imperfect structures and institutions of communal human living.

Striving for Excellence

Ignatius discovered his own need for education when he was already an adult. He eventually found the best education available in the world of his time in the Sorbonne in Paris. The first Jesuits were all fellow-students there. Ignatius insisted on the highest standards for the formation of young Jesuits and applied the methods of the Sorbonne (the *modus Parisiensis*) to achieve this. The commitment to excellence – in terms of intellectual rigour and all aspects of the enterprise – is at the heart of Ignatian educational philosophy.

Working as a Community

As Ignatius came to grasp God's love revealed through Jesus Christ and began to respond by giving himself to the service of the Kingdom, he shared his experience and attracted companions who became 'friends in the Lord'. Ignatian schools are intended to be communities of life, work and worship. Staff, religious and lay, collaborate in service of shared values, a common task and an overarching vision, as reflected in the *Characteristics*. Pupils are encouraged to respect and care for one another as friends and companions, in the spirit of the Gospel. The school community embraces not only all those within it – pupils, teachers and members of the wider staff – but also, very particularly, parents, along with board members, past pupils, and others associated in any way with its operation.

Adaptable and Open to Growth

In the course of his conversion, Ignatius learned discernment, the capacity to reflect prayerfully on his experience at the most profound level and learn from it. The habit of reflection is part of the Ignatian approach to education, as to everything else. Hence, the *Characteristics* document itself and the process which produced it: reflection on experience worldwide, extensive consultation to share best practice wherever it was to be found, and dissemination of the fruits of this deliberation to all Jesuit and Ignatian schools. In the same spirit of constant self-improvement, each school is called to adapt and develop in the light of our shared wisdom and the local circumstances in which each one operates, and members of staff are encouraged to avail themselves of opportunities for their own continuing formation.

In 1993, the *Characteristics* document was augmented by the publication of *Ignatian Pedagogy* which set out to demonstrate the practical efficacy of the *Characteristics* in the everyday classroom. When the authors of *Ignatian Pedagogy* were searching for the best practical methods to promote the Ignatian mission, they found something very helpful in the proceedings of the General Congregation (their international policy-making body). The 33rd General Congregation called for a review of all the society's ministries and asked Jesuits to review their endeavours 'through a constant interplay of experience, reflection and action'. These three words: *experience, reflection and action*, lie at the centre of both the *Spiritual Exercises* and the teaching model articulated in *Ignatian Pedagogy*.

CHALLENGE OF RENEWAL

Twenty years on, the Society of Jesus has called for a new document on reading 'the signs of the times' to ensure that our schools are keeping pace with contemporary religious, cultural and social developments. Reading the signs of the times is seen as a prelude to renewal and transformation.

While the purpose of Jesuit schools has not changed over time, the context in which these schools operate and the challenges they face today require a fresh look at the distinctive characteristics of Jesuit education as part of our on-going conversation in our living tradition. The Jesuit school leaders are challenged to imagine and propose elements that could now be used to reinterpret and perhaps re-express our distinctive characteristics. As the Father General notes '…for this we need tremendous imagination and creativity – an openness to other ways of being, feeling, relating'.[12] He sees that an important element in this renewal process will be formulating an answer to the question: 'How can we present Ignatian spirituality, a spirituality of reflection, to a generation that is used to instant information and instant response?'

The Australian Province's response to this call has been to establish what we have termed *The Ignatian Ethos and Identity Review*. The Review Handbook asks the school to look at itself through five interrelated lenses:
- *Mission* – How is the school Catholic and Jesuit?
- *Formation* – How does the school form the various members of its community in the Ignatian tradition?
- *Programs in Practice* – How do the school's curricular and co-curricular programs reflect the emphases of our guiding documents such as *The*

---

12 Fr Adolfo Nicolás SJ, *Challenges to Jesuit Higher Education Today* (Mexico City: April 23, 2010), 5.

Characteristics of Jesuit Education (1986) and *Ignatian Pedagogy: A Practical Approach* (1993)?
- *Global Networking* – How does the school address the challenges of becoming a more effective global apostolic network? In the words of the 2012 Jesuit Schools International Colloquium in Boston, 'national boundaries must no longer define our ways of working together'.
- *Adherence to Current Province Goals* – How does the school support current Province Goals as enunciated in the Province's Mission Statement and by the Provincial in letters to the Province, his addresses to school conferences and Province Gatherings?

These five lenses focus on the characteristics that should be clearly present in every Jesuit and partner school. They can be used in different forms of evaluation:
- A *comprehensive review* of mission by a visiting Review team leading to a comprehensive Report;
- An annual *'dashboard' Review* of the Report's 'Recommendations' conducted by the School Council – ensuring that the Review Report remains a 'work in progress' each year.

While the *Ethos and Identity Review* has been a very useful instrument for embedding the Ignatian charism more deeply in our schools, there have been other successful methods of achieving this goal. Some examples are:
- all schools have an Ignatian Coordinator, sometimes with the authority of a deputy principal. These coordinators come together as a group twice a year under the direction of a facilitator to share their resources and deepen their understanding and knowledge of the charism;
- since 2010, every new employee in the Province – for both educational and non-educational ministries – has been required to complete a four-day induction experience over two years into the main tenets of Ignatian spirituality. Further formation experiences like silent retreats are also offered to deepen their understanding and commitment to the charism;
- additional mentoring and more focused Ignatian formation experiences are also provided for leaders in the educational ministry, like School Council and School Executive Team members;
- priority is given to ensuring that Ignatian spirituality themes find their way into the ritual of school meetings.

CHARISM COUNTS AND MAKES A DIFFERENCE

In the Australian Province of the Society of Jesus, there are five Jesuit-owned schools and five *Jesuit Partner Schools* – schools which are not owned or controlled by the Society, but which are committed to embedding the Ignatian charism in everything pertaining to their school culture. Perhaps the most successful example of this Jesuit Partner School alignment is St Ignatius College, Geelong, in regional Victoria, just an hour's drive from Melbourne. Previously known as Catholic Regional College, Geelong, the school originally comprised three campuses, two in central Geelong and a third newer campus at Drysdale, a beautiful rural village some twenty minutes from Geelong. For various reasons, the school began to lose significant numbers and, faced with the prospect of closure, the authorities made the difficult decision to terminate the city campuses and consolidate on one site at Drysdale at the end of 2005. In addition to undertaking significant planning to support the consolidation exercise, school authorities believed that they needed to reimagine themselves if they were to survive as a Catholic school and, with approval from the Catholic Education Office, approached the school leaders at the Jesuits' Xavier College in Melbourne for assistance. The school leaders of the consolidated school at Drysdale saw themselves in need of a story, a new identity, a group to which they might belong – some of the qualities of charism to which we have already alluded in the first part of this chapter.

The school was rebadged as St Ignatius Geelong, and its leaders committed, in a *Memorandum of Agreement* in late 2006, to following the Ignatian spiritual tradition. The college's story in the past eight years has been quite remarkable. With excellent leadership and with ongoing support from Xavier College, they have transformed a school teetering on the edge of collapse into a robust school community with waiting lists of students at most levels. Their academic results in the Victorian Certificate of Education in 2013 were excellent, and the school has become something of a 'buzz word' around the City of Geelong.

In concluding, I would need to add that while the Ignatian Charism should be the passion that fuels our education ministry, not everyone will necessarily be fired by it. As British Jesuit Adrian Porter insightfully observes:

> *Different people will engage at different levels with the enterprise of Jesuit education. While one will attend discussions and prayer groups and be a leading carrier of the torch of Jesuit ethos, another will teach his subject well and in so doing contribute to a fundamental of Jesuit education namely that God is to be found in all things, even mathematics and rugby.*

> However, the fact that people place themselves at different 'distances' from the heart of what is happening does not mean they do not need to be formed. Many of our teachers have themselves come through an education system without the overarching structure and underlying values which can give meaning and sense to their lives and their work as teachers of the young.
>
> We need to invite people to participate in conversations and events which will allow them to be formed – as human beings, as teachers, as role models for the young, as Christians and as Ignatian educators.
>
> That invitation, however, must be to a variety of pathways so each can find his (or her) own mix of comfort and challenge. There should never be one exclusive way for teachers in Jesuit schools to contribute to the Jesuit character of their school.[13]

That said, it is important to remind ourselves finally that our charism is only an effective pathway to the degree that it helps us to focus more on Jesus and to see the world through His eyes.

MINISTRY WITH PASSION

To return to where we began, Jesus is the Man of great passion: 'I have come to bring fire to the earth, and how I wish it were blazing already!' (Luke 12:49). In Mark 6:34, we hear it said that 'Jesus saw a large crowd and he took pity on them because they were like sheep without a shepherd.' There is the passion of Jesus throwing the merchants out of the temple, of course, but there are countless episodes of Jesus meeting people with great love in the Gospel stories. There is the Widow of Naim, who had lost her only son – Luke tells us: 'When the Lord saw her he felt sorry for her' (Luke 7:13). With the Rich Young Man, Mark tells us that Jesus 'looked steadily at him and loved him' (Mark 10:21). And finally, what about that wonderfully passionate scene by the lakeside after Jesus' Resurrection when Jesus asks Peter three times: 'Do you love me?' (John 21:15–17).

> *Ministry without passion, without the fuel and pathway of charism, is mission diminished.*

---

13 Adrian Porter SJ, 'The Identity of Ignatian Leadership and Ignatian Formation', paper delivered at the Congress of Directors of Jesuit Schools in Europe (Loyola), October 2005.

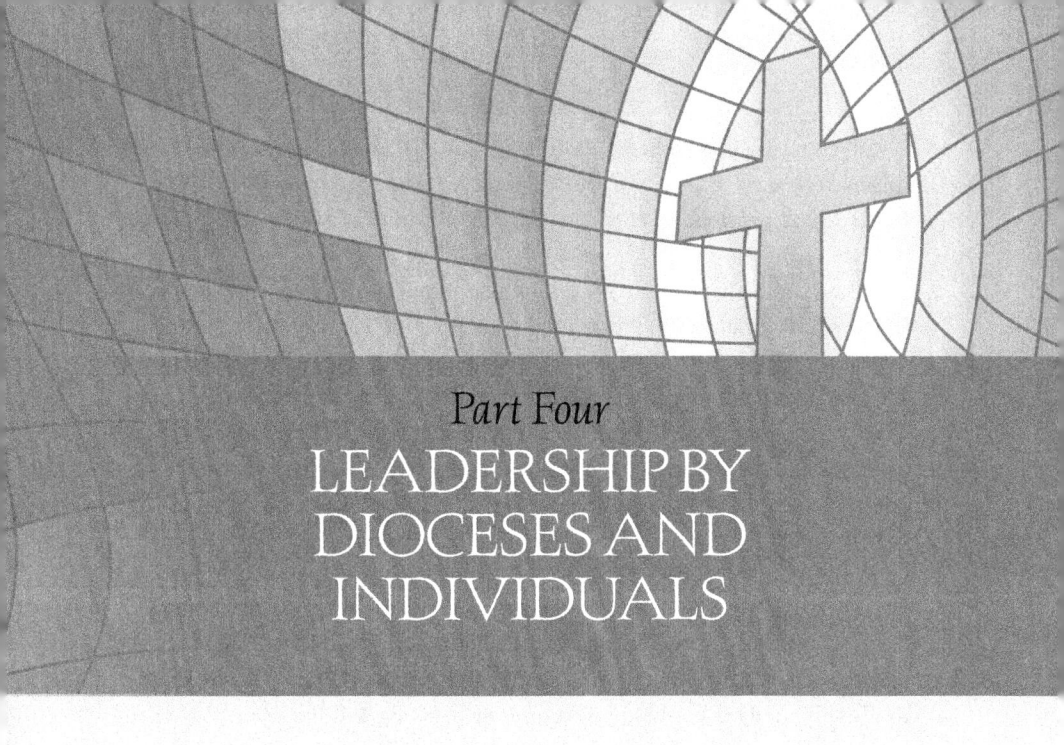

Part Four
LEADERSHIP BY DIOCESES AND INDIVIDUALS

This section details four case studies in which there have been significant efforts made by systems, or individual leaders working within systems, to create the 'critical mass' of 'mature Christians' needed to sustain the religious identity and mission of Catholic schools. The chapters indicate the variety of possible approaches with their accompanying rationales and strategies.

Efforts to situate Catholic schools within the contemporary Catholic spiritual journey in Australia seem to lie between two extremes. At one end of the scale are school systems that do very little at system level, delegating the task to principals on the justification that the system lacks the funds to do anything worthwhile. At the other extreme are systems that offer so many options that the whole project of teacher formation lacks direction and loses focus. Doing everything seems to return a similar result to doing nothing, although it is harder to criticise leaders for not trying!

As the chapters in this section illustrate, helping people develop an inner life requires discipline, focus, collaboration, creativity and persistence by leaders. The task is not something achieved solely by academic study since spiritual growth relates to the biblical heart – that centre of ourselves that determines what we choose to know, how we feel, what we choose to value, and so how we behave – summed up by missiologists as 'our worldview', the centre from which we make sense of life and respond to its challenges.[14]

---

14 Paul Hiebert, *Transforming Worldviews: An Anthropological Understanding of How People Change* (Grand Rapids: Baker Academic, 2008).

Efforts to project teachers and students into the contemporary Australian spiritual journey have a narrative dimension, a strategic dimension and a leadership dimension. All three are important as the following case studies indicate.

In the first (Chapter 13), John Graham outlines the approach taken by the Catholic Education Office in the Diocese of Lismore. After a long period of trial and error, the schools of the diocese chose to adopt the Ignatian spiritual tradition as the vehicle for the spiritual formation of staff. The chapter charts the resilient determination of school and system leaders in using this spirituality to develop the inner life of teachers as a way of consolidating the mission and religious identity of Catholic schools across the diocese.

In Chapter 14, Cathy Day outlines a quite different approach based in a particular reading of the Catholic spiritual tradition. Here the aim has been to develop the inner life of teachers and students through the practice of a particular style of Christian meditation. The work done in the Townsville Diocese has proved ground-breaking and has been adopted by other dioceses in this country and overseas. The approach highlights the necessity of having a clear focus in encouraging people to explore the inner dimension of Christian life. Cathy's account reinforces the notion that charism – in this case understood as a particular tried and tested means of spiritual growth – is a gift to the whole Church.

The final two chapters throw light on the role of leadership in influencing the direction the spiritual journey can take for people in local contexts.

In Chapter 15, John McGrath outlines the path chosen by Bishop David Walker, very much a 'hands-on' leader in this area, in creating the conditions to develop what he has called earlier a 'critical mass of mature Christians' needed to anchor the identity of all Catholic communities in the diocese, not just the schools. The Broken Bay Diocese has become both a leader in and model of close collaboration between diocesan and school organisations, in particular the integration of thinking and planning at the mission and strategic levels. The integrating factor is a common understanding of and commitment to *Christian discipleship*. Through his example and teaching, Bishop David has attempted, with considerable success, to help Catholics hold the inner and outer dimensions of Christian life together as they wrestle with the challenges thrown up by the contemporary context of Christian mission.

In the final chapter of the section, Chapter 16, Anita Carter outlines the vision and strategy adopted by the charismatic founding principal of St Peter's College Cranbourne, Terry Feely, to develop a unique spiritual tradition in the school. His was the task of starting 'from scratch', a situation many school principals now find themselves confronting. Terry's efforts were pioneering in their time and still provide a model that others might emulate. He found himself operating outside the support systems offered by religious congregations[15] and chose to chart his own path with the blessing of the local Catholic Education Office and parish. Terry brought a strong theological background to the task as well as the resources of the Celtic spirituality which nourished him as he grew up in Scotland.

All the examples covered in this section chart *possibilities* open to Catholic schools and systems in facing the challenge of reinvigorating people to participate whole-heartedly in the Australian Catholic spiritual journey in these blessed, albeit chaotic, times.

---

[15] Terry Feely's previous leadership experience had been within the Brigidine spiritual tradition which he openly admired.

John Graham

Dr John Graham is Assistant Director – School Evangelisation and Catechetical Services at the Catholic Schools Office Lismore. Prior to this he was a Senior Lecturer at the Australian Catholic University, Sydney. John has taught in secondary schools and served two terms as a Commissioner on the New South Wales Catholic Education Commission. John has lectured and published widely both within Australia and internationally. His current research interests relate to the leadership role of the Catholic school principal in facilitating notions of 'school community'. Research interests also include student discipleship, formation, and parental partnership. He has a particular interest in the ways in which the student voice can be better utilised to inform educational policy and practice.

13

PARISH SCHOOLS EMBRACING IGNATIAN SPIRITUALITY

John Graham

THE CHALLENGE

Throughout the 1990s and until the present, Catholic education authorities in the Diocese of Lismore have been increasingly challenged as how best to provide staff with opportunities to both grow in holiness and fulfil their proper vocation in Catholic schooling.[1] Central to a response to this challenge was to offer a formation of the heart that provided opportunities for staff members to experience a spiritual encounter 'with God in Christ which awakens their love and opens their spirit to others'.[2] The response to this challenge needed to be a 'solid, organic, and comprehensive formation in the Church's faith'.[3]

A growing sense of urgency developed across Australia from the mid-1980s regarding lay educators' sense of vocation and commitment to the mission of Catholic education. Without a strong sense of vocation directed to the building of the Kingdom of God, it was agreed that it would be difficult for teachers to effectively contribute to the development of the 'culture or habitus' and 'integral formation' of students, central to the mission of Catholic schools.[4]

---

1 Sacred Congregation for Catholic Education, *Lay Catholics in Schools: Witnesses to Faith*, #65. www.vatican.va/roman_curia/congregations/ccatheduc/documents/rc_con_ccatheduc_doc_19821015_lay-catholics_en.html
2 Pope Benedict XVI cited in J. Miller, 'Challenges Facing Catholic Schools: A View from Rome', in Gerald Grace and Joe O'Keefe (eds), *International Handbook of Catholic Education* (Springer: Dordrect, 2007), 449–80.
3 Miller, 473.
4 Richard M. Jacobs, *Building Spiritual Leadership Density in Catholic Schools* (Washington: National Catholic Education Association, 2005); J. Sullivan, *Catholic Schools in Contention* (Dublin: Veritas, 2000), 98; A. Kennedy and J. Duncan, 'New Zealand Children's Spirituality in Catholic Schools: Teachers' Perspectives', *International Journal of Children's Spirituality*, Vol 11, no. 2, 288.

As the Catholic Schools Office progressively responded to the challenges of progressing the formation of lay educators, there was a clear awareness that it was doing so amidst the tensions and struggles taken up in the inherited social and cultural patterns of the current era. In particular, secular thinking has spawned its own understanding of the spiritual, in terms of finding personal meaning and affirmation of self, with disregard for religion and Church.[5] The forces of secular culture are now perceived to be so strong that unless certain actions are quickly progressed, such as the formation of lay educators, the mission of Catholic education may well 'be doomed to failure.[6] There is a danger that it may not be possible for lay Catholic educators to recognise the pervasive hold these understandings have over them.[7]

THE EVOLVING RESPONSE AND ITS ENGAGEMENT WITH IGNATIAN SPIRITUALITY

The Catholic Schools Office, Lismore, has had a long history of resourcing the religious and spiritual formation of educators employed in parish schools. The impetus behind this initiative was the mounting urgency of the situation and the clear ecclesial 'voice' promoting lay formation, combined with the growing challenges to the purposes of Catholic schools. At the same time there was a clear lack of detailed directional frameworks and maps for how to proceed with lay formation. Hence, the Catholic Schools Office committed itself to the following consultative planning process to design a solid and comprehensive approach to formation.

In the first phase of the process, from the 1980s to the mid 1990s, parish schools conducted annual Spirituality Days mainly facilitated by local clergy, Catholic Education Office staff and visiting religious. However, by the mid 1990s schools were struggling to find suitable personnel, usually Religious, to lead the mandated annual Spirituality Day. During this period, members of a Spirituality Team in a metropolitan Catholic Education Office provided three years of retreats for significant numbers of teachers. Each year there were two live-in retreat programs, *Journey* (three days) and *Wellsprings* (five days). Anecdotal evidence over ten years later from teachers who participated in these retreats has reported a life-transforming impact that

---

5 Frank Fletcher, *Falling in Love with God* (Strathfield: St Paul's Publications, 2010), 21–22.
6 Bishop Michael Putney, 'A New Ecclesial Context for Catholic Schools', in Anne Benjamin and Dan Riley (eds), *Catholic Schools: Hope in Uncertain Times* (Mulgrave: John Garratt Publishing, 2008), 17.
7 Putney, 17; James Arthur, 'Secularisation, secularism and Catholic Education: Understanding the Challenges', *International Studies in Catholic Education*, Vol 1, no. 2, 230–231.

still remains. However, this initiative could not be sustained and, despite the best of intentions and initiatives, many schools increasingly struggled with their capacity to provide quality Spirituality Days.

Consequently, action was required to support schools with more substantive religious and spiritual formation initiatives, which marked the second phase around 1997. Given that spiritual formation resource staff were not available centrally to meet the needs of the forty-five parish schools, renewal teams consisting of clergy and teachers, supported by Catholic Education Office staff, were formed for each of the four deaneries of the diocese. Their purpose was to offer a retreat day at least once a year in each deanery. Over one hundred and twenty teachers participated each year in the retreats. The evaluations for each retreat over nine years reflected significant faith enrichment for all participants. While this systemic support for schools met part of the need, significant numbers of schools still struggled to provide Spirituality Days that left teachers enriched and/or transformed spiritually.

The third phase addressed the ongoing struggle that many schools were still experiencing in providing faith-transforming Spirituality Days. A consultative process revealed that school leaders had virtually no engagement with the major spiritual traditions, which are part of the rich heritage of the Church, that they could draw upon. In order that each parish school could access sound spiritual formation on its Spirituality Day, a comprehensive four-year religious and spiritual formation program was introduced by the Catholic Schools Office called *Schools of Spirituality*.

Each year, for four years, members of the Carmelite, Franciscan, Jesuit and Benedictine religious congregations conducted parish school retreats that introduced staff to their particular spiritual tradition. This was an enormous task given the geography of the diocese, a region extending over five hundred kilometres in length. As this phase came to an end, the parish school executives were asked to identify which of the various spiritual traditions they preferred to continue with in their spiritual formation.

Parish school executives named Ignatian Spirituality as the tradition they wish to engage with and so this became the fourth phase. After the *Schools of Spirituality* phase finished, there was a period in which the Executive Director of the Loyola Centre, Sydney, conducted Ignatian retreats for various parish school staff in the diocese.

The evaluations from the Ignatian retreats confirmed the transformational impact of this spirituality upon staff. Following extensive consultation, it was decided to develop, for all parish school Spirituality Days, a six-year formation program which would be coordinated and resourced systemically. The heart of this six-year program would be the *Spiritual Exercises* of St

Ignatius Loyola, which he wrote out of his experience as a layman. It was intended that through the *Spiritual Exercises* the faith of teachers would be strengthened, Catholic identity and purpose of parish schools enhanced, religious leadership capacity matured, and richer experience gained to continue building a solid, organic and comprehensive religious and spiritual formation framework.

The *Spiritual Exercises* were chosen because they facilitate a formation of the heart whereby the movement of grace within people allows the love of God to inform all life decisions and resolutions. They create contemplatives within daily life and so address a great spiritual estrangement experienced in our times. Centred on Jesus Christ and his body the Church, they are a set of foundational exercises that enable a person to deepen the experience of God in daily life, and discern how best to serve God, others and creation. They do this through promoting conversation, by listening to oneself, others and God, discerning one's deepest desires for self, others and the workplace, and learning how to help souls more by deeds than words.[8] Aware that the *Spiritual Exercises* could prove to be quite daunting for many school executive members and staff, it was decided to provide two years of preparation prior to their introduction.

Given the varied levels of preparation among school executive members for the six-year program, four Catholic Schools Office Consultants provided accompaniment to strengthen faith leadership capacity. Through school-based meetings, executive members were supported and resourced to prayerfully reflect upon their leadership from a faith perspective. This was undertaken using *Leading Life to the Full*.[8] The accompaniment was extended to include the use of two prayer books, *Sacred Space*[9] and *Mission*[10], to strengthen personal and communal prayer. During the first term of each school year, all parish school executive members engaged in a two-day retreat, intended to deepen their sense of vocation and understanding of the content and processes for the school Spirituality Days. In doing so it was anticipated they might be better able to prepare, support and follow up all aspects of the Spirituality Days. Over the two years, each parish school executive retreat and parish school retreat day was facilitated by the Executive Director, Loyola Centre, Sydney. The topics included understanding one's baptismal gifts, seeing God in all things, St Ignatius the pilgrim, schools as places of pilgrimage, imaginative contemplation, awareness examen, discernment, images of God, and faith leadership.

---

8   David Touhy, *Leading Life to the Full* (Dublin: Veritas, 2005).
9   Irish Province of the Society of Jesus, 2009.
10 Mark Link, *Mission* (Cincinnati: RCL Benziger, 2000).

The evaluations from the 2008–2009 retreat and Spirituality Days provided a rich source of data for supporting the organic development of religious and spiritual formation. At the end of each retreat and Spirituality Day proforma evaluations were completed by participants. The evaluation sheets were framed around three open-ended statements – 'I leave here thinking/feeling/hoping…' Over the two-year period, evaluation sheets were completed by teachers (n=3200) and school executive members (n=276). Interpreting this limited data required a rigorous analysis to accurately identify the impact of the formation activities on the participants' lives. An independent consultancy group analysed the data using the QSR NVivo software to identify the major themes and code participants' responses to them. Consequently, they established the extent to which the needs, experiences and future aspirations were common to all three participant groups of principals, secondary teachers and primary teachers.

The analysis provided overwhelming evidence that each participant group experienced a deeper engagement with the purposes of Catholic Education as a result of the retreats and spirituality days. The most frequent group of positive responses related to participants' enriched interior faith lives and spiritual journeys. Within the pattern of responses, strong themes emerged. More than two thousand responses reported the experiences enhanced participants' self-knowledge, self-acceptance, commitment to reflection, a more prayerful life (particularly the Awareness Examen prayer) and deeper engagement in their faith. Affirmed in their faith and spiritually enriched, these responses indicated a pattern of strong energy to continue building the Catholic faith life and community in their parish schools, especially by providing students with access to Ignatian ways of praying. However, the data revealed a noticeable disengagement between participants and their sense of vocation. Further, connection with the Church received little prominence in the responses. This analysis contributed significantly to an understanding of the implications of an organic approach in developing a solid and comprehensive framework for religious and spiritual formation.

The organic development of the formation framework expanded during phase five when it was identified that school executive members required further support to enhance their capacity for leadership in religious and spiritual formation. Consequently, over a two-year period, thirty senior staff have participated in a thirty week Retreat in Daily Life. This retreat is an annotated version of the *Spiritual Exercises* and includes one hour of prayer daily and weekly meetings with a spiritual director. While the evaluations of this program have not yet been subjected to rigorous analysis, the anecdotally reported impact on the lives of the participants and their school communities has been very positive.

Further, the Loyola Institute took on a train-the-trainer role for the four years of the *Spiritual Exercises*. From 2010–2013, the two-day retreats for parish school executive members included an additional training component and package enabling them to facilitate their school's retreat days. Given the level of responsibility this placed on the executive members, accompaniment was provided by Catholic Education Office consultants for each school's retreat day. The consultants' accompaniment included preparatory and debriefing meetings, as well as attendance at each school's retreat day. In the four-year period from 2010–2013, over 1154 parish school executive staff engaged in this retreat program. The evaluations document a progressive integration of a strong Catholic spiritual maturation by the majority of participants, which significantly impacted on them personally, as teachers and members of the Church. As well, there was a clear voice regarding increased confidence in faith leadership of the school retreat days and in general. Finally, there was a strong hunger to keep this spiritual renewal and formation going in the Ignatian tradition.

Concurrently with phase five, phase six began. This involved the process of documenting the direction for religious and spiritual formation as just described. Taking up the directions outlined in this paper, a document was developed, entitled *Launch into the Deep – Policy Framework for Religious and Spiritual Formation in the Apostolate of Catholic Education,* to provide a common language, greater clarity and unity of purpose around formation in Catholic education. The document is located within the diocesan foundations of Catholic education and provides a conceptual base for religious and spiritual formation. Implementation of the directions in this document will guide the building up of parish schools' capacity for religious and spiritual maturity, vocational awareness, theological knowledge and missionary commitment. While the second part of the document details the six year program around the *Spiritual Exercises*, the first part provides directions regarding the rationale and meaning for religious and spiritual formation, which include the following core elements:

Christ-centred

The centre of all formation is fidelity to Jesus Christ who is the way, the truth and the life. It is about coming to know, love and imitate him and so entering into the life of the Trinity.[11]

Personal

God's self-revelation to each person is to be found in the reality of their daily lives. Formation provides ways to penetrate the veil around the events and experiences of daily life to recognise the divine presence and its invitation

---

11 Pope John Paul II, *Ecclesia in Oceania* (Strathfield: St Paul's Publications), #39.

to loving friendship. The human heart is the centre of all spiritual formation for it is from these inner recesses that a person is moved to live in God's love.

Vocational

The formative process cultivates and matures the common vocation of the baptised to love God and neighbour as oneself and to collaborate in the building of God's kingdom through active involvement in the life and mission of the Church. It is also about cultivating one's personal vocation to do God's will wherever one is placed in life.[12]

Invitational

Membership of a Catholic school community brings with it a responsibility for staff to seek understanding of its identity and mission. The school has a responsibility to invite each staff member to participate in appropriate educational and formative programs that provide this understanding. Upon engaging in these activities, the response that individuals make is a personal choice and a matter of conscience. Such was the formational approach of Jesus Christ.

Integral

Formation engages with people as total human beings. It ensures that there is no gap between the reality of daily life and a person's faith life. It is the journey to holiness, as faith penetrates and gives direction to all dimensions of life. It is also unitive as it incorporates formation in doctrine and the social teaching of the Church and cultivates the best of human and cultural values.

Communion

Christian formation is decidedly relational and significantly influenced by the community context in which people find themselves. The influence of significant people bearing witness to Christian discipleship both challenges and nurtures the faith of others. Religious and spiritual growth can be strengthened through access to the heritage of the Christian community.[13] Access to mentors, spiritual companions, animators and formators is vital for the support of teachers in their faith growth.[14] It is an experience of communion.

---

12 Richard Jacobs, *Building Leadership Density in Catholic Schools* (Washington: National Catholic Education Association, 2005), 34.
13 Maureen Dolan, *Partnership in Lay Spirituality* (Dublin: The Columba Press, 2007), 116.
14 Tilden Edwards, *Spiritual Director, Spiritual Companion: Guide to Tending the Soul* (Mahwah: Paulist Press, 2001), and L. English, 'Mentorship: Adult Formation for Educators', in *Catholic Education: A Journal of Inquiry and Practice* 2013, Vol 2, No 4, 45–64.

Life-long and Developmental

Formation is a task that a person engages in throughout the whole life journey. While primary faith socialisation is highly influential, experience shows that for many people the truly formative experiences come when they are well into adulthood and persists throughout the life cycle. Christian living is a pilgrimage which is only fulfilled through grace after death. Therefore, the life-long formation of teachers is critical for Catholic education.[15]

CONCLUSION

Catholic schooling is still at a 'crossroad' moment[16] in many ways. However, within the Diocese of Lismore it is clear that at least one of the challenges, namely staff faith formation, has clearly moved beyond the 'crossroad' and is travelling in a strong, clear and Catholic direction. Through the *Spiritual Exercises,* the faith of teachers has been strengthened, Catholic identity and purpose of parish schools enhanced, religious leadership capacity matured, and a solid, organic and comprehensive religious and spiritual formation framework has progressed significantly. A new culture of staff faith formation is coming into being.

---

15   Miller, 474.
16   Bishops of New South Wales and ACT, *Catholic Schools at a Crossroads*, 2007, http://www.cecnsw.catholic.edu.au/db_uploads/catholic-schools-at-a-crossroads.pdf

Cathy Day

Dr Catherine Day is currently the Executive Director of Catholic Education in the Diocese of Townsville. Cathy has extensive experience as a teacher and principal in Catholic schools. She holds qualifications in education and leadership, including a PhD in education. Cathy is Adjunct Professor in the School of Education at James Cook University, Townsville. Under her Directorship of Townsville Catholic education, Cathy and her colleagues have created and implemented a world-first Christian Meditation program for all Catholic schools in the diocese. Cathy has numerous educational and community involvements and is passionate about education and the arts.

14

CHRISTIAN MEDITATION – A PRAYER FOR OUR TIMES

Cathy Day

Incarnate Word, in whom all nature lives,
Cast flame upon the earth: raise up contemplatives
Among us, men who walk within the fire
Of ceaseless prayer, impetuous desire.
Set pools of silence in this thirsty land.
(James McAuley, A Letter to John Dryden).

In Catholic schools across Australia, and more recently in other countries which have learned from the Australian experience, teachers are introducing their students to the prayer practice of Christian meditation. In the Diocese of Townsville, all Catholic schools include Christian meditation in the prayer life of their students and staff. This practice was introduced in 2005, initially as a pilot program involving thirteen interested teachers. Eighteen months later, on the recommendation of these teachers, Christian meditation was introduced to all teachers in the diocese with the idea that it be taught to every student from Prep to Year 12. Through this Christian meditation initiative, teachers have been introduced to a new understanding and a re-imagining of contemplative prayer, and they continue today to provide their students with the opportunity to experience this beautiful prayer of the heart.

Such an expansive and systemic approach needed to be presented in a compelling way in order that teachers, who were already heavily burdened by constant curriculum change, would willingly commit to this new prayer practice. Prayer is and always has been a high priority for Catholic schools. What teachers seek for their students through prayer and other means is conversion not indoctrination. Whilst instruction remains an important element of teaching all children, transformation of the heart, which is the real aim of Catholic education, is made possible through the experiential approach to prayer. In particular, students must be given the opportunity through prayer to experience the intimacy of knowing God, not just knowing about God. Essentially what is compelling about Christian meditation relates to *the actual experience of meditating.*

As a prayer practice infused with the Christian tradition, the purpose of meditation is to encounter Christ in some way. Eileen O'Hea CSJ explains that prayer is the lifting up of the mind and heart to God ...

> *My turning towards the Divine Other, Christ, in some way is the interspace in our prayer where our love and desire for God and God's love and desire for us is realised.*[1]

In the stillness, simplicity and silence of meditation, children grow in self-awareness and accept the invitation from God to enter into oneness with self, with others and with God.

THE PRACTICE AND ITS ORIGIN

Teachers and students enjoy the practice of Christian meditation, but they also like to hear the story of how this prayer practice emerged and its place and importance within the contemporary Christian faith life. This knowledge is important for teachers who, like many other lay people, have limited experience of the contemplative tradition which for centuries remained within the cloistered element of the Christian story.

Christian meditation can be seen as both ancient and new. It was rediscovered as a vital contemplative prayer practice by the renowned theologian and spiritual director, John Main OSB. After a stellar career in the British Diplomatic Corps followed by a Law Professorship, his faith-filled Irish Catholic background led him to enter Ealing Abbey in London to become a Benedictine monk. His initial faithful practice of meditation began when he was a diplomat in Malaya, where he learned silent meditation with a mantra from an Indian monk, Swami Satyananda. It ceased, however, once he joined the monastery, as the method he had learned from the swami was not accepted as part of the Benedictine contemplative prayer life. Fortunately for all who have since embraced his wonderful legacy, Fr John returned to his meditation practice with the certainty of its place in Christian life through his study of the early Desert Fathers and Mothers.

Silent prayer using a sacred word or phrase was discovered in the writings of John Cassian, a Christian monk of the fourth century. Cassian, a contemporary of St Augustine, founded a house for monks in Marseilles. He spent time as a young monk in a monastery at Bethlehem near the Cave

---

1 Eileen O'Hea, *Silent Wisdom, Hidden Light* (London: Arthur James/Medio Media, 1997), 19.

of the Nativity and later listened to the Desert Fathers of Egypt for several years before returning to his monastery in Marseilles. Over the following years, Cassian meditated on the Egyptian desert spirituality which he deeply revered before writing a number of works which included the *Conferences*, a study of the Egyptian ideal of the monk. In the ninth and tenth conferences, John Main read of the practice of the Desert Fathers and Mothers of using a single short phrase (a mantra) to achieve the stillness necessary for prayer. This discovery led him to return to his previous silent meditation practice. He chose as his prayer word or mantra the Aramaic word *Maranatha*, which means 'Come Lord' and is found at the conclusion of Paul's First Letter to the Corinthians and at the end of the Book of Revelation.[2]

John Main died in 1982 but his rediscovery and development of the Christian tradition of meditation, and his insights into the simplicity and poverty of spirit associated with the silent repetition of a sacred prayer word, have continued to this day. His work has largely been continued through the efforts of Laurence Freeman OSB who lived and worked with John Main in their Benedictine community in Montreal. Fr Laurence has written extensively on the origins of Christian meditation. He acknowledges that meditation has acquired a variety of meanings in western tradition. In reference to the desert monks, however, meditation meant simply a prayer of the heart, a kind of chewing or repetition of the word. In the Eastern meditative traditions there are also many kinds of meditation but they are essentially non-discursive or imageless, silent practice. Whilst John Main certainly practised discursive meditation in pondering the scriptures (lectio divina), he brought non-discursive Christian meditation to life for all who seek this deep, imageless, interior silence using the mantra and the twice daily discipline of setting aside time for the practice. Laurence Freeman describes the teachings of John Main as slow food for the soul: he taught that meditation is a way to live the mystery of life, its grief and joy, in faith and with the power of faith that heals and raises the human being to love of God and neighbour. It is not a panacea for life's difficulties, but it is a way to liberty.[3]

In his writings, Laurence Freeman provides a compelling story of generations of contemplative men and women who through their lives and writings have left a body of work that demonstrates the trustworthiness of meditation as a form of pure prayer that helps us experience God in our lives. These contemplatives include the great mystics such as Meister Ekhart, St John of the Cross, Teresa of Avila, and the anonymous author of

---

2 John Main (edited by Laurence Freeman), *Door to Silence – An Anthology for Christian Meditation* (Norwich: Canterbury Press, 2006), xvi.
3 Laurence Freeman, *The Selfless Self – Meditation and the Opening of the Heart* (Mulgrave: John Garratt Publishing, 2009), vii.

The Cloud of Unknowing, all of whom have illuminated the power of silence and the possibility through deep silence of being drawn into the experience of divine love. *Meditation is simply the pilgrimage to the heart where we find the Spirit of Jesus worshipping the Father in love.*[4]

Christian meditation is a prayer for our time, a time increasingly defined by indifference and possibly hostility to the idea of the transcendent. Success in life is measured and defined in economic terms and is so often at odds with the Gospel worldview. John Main saw the warning signs of a complex world displaying a growing rebelliousness and resistance to the old order. He began his work of bringing Christian meditation into the wider Church community just as the Second Vatican Council began seeking *aggiornamento* or a new openness to the world and a call for 'universal holiness'. A new contemplative moment was coming to fruition and John Main was no doubt encouraged and influenced by the work of deeply spiritual people such as Thomas Merton, Thomas Keating and Bede Griffiths, amongst others.

Meditative prayer was an important aspect of each of these great teachers. Merton drew attention to the inner experience, referencing the Desert Fathers' desire to lose themselves in the inner, hidden reality of a self that was transcendent, mysterious, half-known and lost in Christ.[5] Keating devoted his time to bringing to the community the practice of what he termed 'centering prayer', with its focus on psychological patterns of wholeness. Fr Bede Griffiths was perhaps the most spiritually gifted of these great teachers. His own capacity for self-gift or agapic love, which he practised devotedly in India, was underscored by his understanding of the need for all Christians to tame their ego and move from self-centredness to God-centredness.

What these great teachers were calling for was a transformation of consciousness that required a new way of knowing. This type of knowing goes beyond the scientific, rational mind with the ego in charge to a type of knowing which comes not from outside us but interiorly through our participating in the practice of silence. A major step in spiritual development comes from being open to the process of transformation of consciousness that occurs as we practice meditation, regularly and faithfully. *Gradually the presence of love in the experience of knowing becomes the experience of love.*[6] The possibility of true faith is revealed as the leap that embraces the mystery of the divine as we experience this participatory knowing whereby our mind is stilled and we learn that our ego does not need to be so dominant.

For children and young people this experience of participatory knowing through meditation can build on their innate and not yet stifled

---
4 John Main, *Essential Writings*. Selected with an introduction by Laurence Freeman. Modern Spiritual Masters Series (Maryknoll N.Y: Orbis, 2002), 67.
5 Thomas Merton, *The Wisdom of the Desert* (New York: New Directions, 1970), 7.
6 Eileen O'Hea, *Manifesting in Form* (Singapore, Medio Media, 2011), 19.

capacity for awe and wonder. Wonder and awe form the foundation for spiritual experience. This experience is a form of pure grace – God's self-communication to the child. As a regular and disciplined prayer practice, meditation offers children an ongoing return to their original innocence. It nurtures a child's ability to retain a sense of wonder in their life, with the sensitive teacher adopting an approach of great respect for the person of each child, remembering the child's God-given aptitude for contemplation.[7]

THE WORLD COMMUNITY FOR CHRISTIAN MEDITATION

Following the example of the Townsville experience, many other schools around the world are now giving students the opportunity to participate in Christian meditation. Along with school communities, other people participate in meditation groups under the auspices of the World Community for Christian Meditation. This global community was inaugurated in 1991, inspired by the work of John Main and continued today by Laurence Freeman. The World Community emphasises the link between contemplation and action. It is an ecumenical, contemplative community with a strong commitment to inter-faith dialogue. Many members of the World Community assist teachers in schools to bring Christian meditation into the lives of children.

TEACHING CHRISTIAN MEDITATION

John Main understood that children could meditate and find joy in the practice but it has taken many years for his personal insight to become well accepted. The prayer practice has only recently come to the attention of many Catholic school leaders, and training and formation programs have now been developed and widely initiated to support teachers in bringing the practice to their students. The Townsville Catholic Education Office has developed a well-resourced and planned approach to introducing and embedding Christian meditation in its schools. This includes a Meditation website – www.cominghome.org.au. Through ongoing innovative and prayerful formation programs, teachers are given direct access to the original teaching of John Main as well as opportunities to consider contemporary understandings of how the universal practice of meditation and a contemplative stance for living are powerful and positive ways to well-being and wholeness. Teachers learn what John Main came to know

---

[7] Madeleine Simon, *Born Contemplative: Introducing Children to Christian Meditation*. (London: Darton, Longman and Todd, 1993), 14.

and understand in a profound way with respect to young people – that the contemplative dimension of prayer affirms the contemplative dimension of life at an age when children's life patterns are first established and set. For adults and children alike, the practice remains simple and accessible to all in a most inclusive way. John Main taught the practice in the following simple way:

> *Sit down. Sit still with your back straight. Close your eyes lightly. Then interiorly, silently begin to recite a single word – a prayer word or mantra. The word maranatha is recommended. Say it as four equal syllables. Breathe normally and give your full attention to the word as you say it, silently, gently, faithfully and above all – simply. The essence of meditation is simplicity. Stay with the same word during the whole meditation and from day to day. Don't visualise, but listen to the word as you say it. Let go of all thoughts (even good thoughts), images and other words. Don't fight your distractions but let them go by saying your word faithfully, gently and attentively and returning to it immediately that you realise that you have stopped saying it or when your attention has wandered. Meditate twice a day every day. For adults it is recommended that twenty to thirty minutes is set aside for each period of meditation.*

In classroom settings, the teacher makes time for meditation within the daily lesson schedule. The length of the meditation for children depends on their age. Teachers use a simple rule of thumb to time meditation – one minute per chronological year of age. Five year olds meditate for five minutes; ten years olds for ten minutes. In setting aside this time, teachers may feel anxious about taking valuable time away from an already crowded curriculum. Experienced teachers of meditation explain that in reality the benefits of having focused and attentive students actually creates time with fewer distractions impacting on students. Secondary school timetabled days can present obstacles that are more difficult to manage. Teachers, however, have come to recognise the value of meditation not only in the spiritual realm, but also in the improved attentiveness that their students display, and they find creative ways to ensure the practice occurs. As an example, a mathematics teacher will have a period of meditation between double periods of maths. The homeroom time each morning and afternoon is an ideal time for including meditation. Students themselves are also taking responsibility for setting up and conducting meditation groups in their schools.

Children learn quickly the difference between the silence of meditation and just being quiet. The emphasis is placed on stillness, silence and simplicity.

Silence means letting go of thoughts. Stillness means letting go of desire. Simplicity means letting go of self-analysis. These three concepts underpin a disciplined approach throughout the meditation. Children practice this pure prayer of the heart as a personal discipline, focusing on sitting with backs straight, eyes lightly closed, concentrating on the breath and paying attention to silently repeating their mantra. Teachers need only provide the right environment, a classroom space and time suffused with reverence and sacred beauty, and the children do the work of meditation themselves. They allow God to do the work of God within them as they experience the idea of learning *to be* through meditation. They are attentive to the wonder of themselves and of all creatures and the natural world and they revel in these moments of being, growing in awareness and friendship with God. In the holiness of each period of meditation they complete the work of Jesus in incarnating God more fully into this world.

THE CONTEMPLATIVE PRAYER AND EVANGELISATION

The Australian Catholic Bishops Conference has called for fresh approaches to stimulate a new evangelisation. Catholic schools are essential places for this evangelising freshness to be understood and fostered. The ultimate evangelising work of the Catholic school is to bring children ever more surely to get to know the person of Jesus at deeper and deeper levels. The General Directory of Catechesis states that the purpose of catechesis is 'to bring people into communion and intimacy with Jesus Christ'. An experiential approach can be the way to attune students' hearts and minds to the possibility of entering the mind of Christ. To enter the mind of Christ is to enter into the ordinary human mind that God loves into being and that is experienced through simple awareness. *This is why we meditate in order that we might settle into this ordinary mind where we become just ourselves, our true selves in which we realise our oneness with God.*[8]

Experiential catechesis is one of several pillars that are essential in supporting the total approach to Religious Education and spiritual formation. Spiritual growth in young people is made possible by experiences that are able to bring to the surface for the individual student the meaning of their own personhood and their relationship to the person of Jesus. Providing opportunities for a child to experience deep inner silence can lead them to touch the deepest mystery of faith.

---

8 James Finley, *Christian Meditation: Experiencing the Presence of God* (San Francisco: HarperOne, 2005), 192.

> It is important that even the smallest child learn to be still and silent and not just to be quiet. It is in their stillness and silence that God can speak to their hearts and they can discover the love of God for each of them personally.[9]

In reality, the teacher reveals God to the child in every aspect of classroom life, intentionally or not. Laurence Freeman reminds teachers in Catholic schools that God is and always will be a mystery and the 'question' of God will always be with us, but depending on what is in the heart of the teacher and their subsequent classroom response, *God can be the most deadening, dry and boring of questions. Or, the most quickening and illuminating of all our human questions about reality and meaning.*[10] The teacher has an abiding responsibility to bring children to an understanding that God is not distant and disinterested but so very close and so loving of each person. Many young people speak of the calm and secure feeling they experience as they pray in silent meditation. There is a feeling of being comforted and being enveloped within a completely loving embrace of a non-judgemental, understanding presence which removes all fears and anguish. Eileen O'Hea reframes this experience stating:

> The path of Christian meditation is a way into the experience of Christ's own consciousness which then allows us to be grasped by divine love and drawn into that experience of the living presence of God.[11]

Teachers who have wholeheartedly brought Christian meditation into their classrooms express delight at the response of children and great satisfaction at the inclusiveness of this prayer practice, with children of all abilities able to meditate without any sense of competitiveness, especially those who may have learning delays and difficulty controlling bodily impulses. Meditation is a way of deepening faith and love within all of their students and perhaps within teachers themselves. Daniel O'Leary states that 'to facilitate young people's growing in wisdom and age is to watch the unfolding of God in our midst'.[12] He refers to the great educationalist Jerome Bruner, who suggested that we should be celebrating a child's moments of breakthrough into fresh connecting and understanding in the same way we celebrate the child's birthday. This includes the spiritual breakthroughs. The first lesson of the teacher is to show the child that we can never know God by thought alone. In fact the teacher learns this best from participating with the children in

---

9   Bishop Michael Putney, *The Townsville Catholic Education Position Statement on Christian Meditation*
10 Laurence Freeman, *Meditation Newsletter* July 2012, 2.
11 Eileen O'Hea, *Silent Wisdom, Hidden Light*, 26.
12 Daniel O'Leary, *Begin with the Heart: Recovering a Sacramental Vision* (Blackrock: The Columba Press, 2008), 136.

meditation, where they enter the period of silence with such trust and joy in the experience itself. Children clearly demonstrate what adults know but often forget: that we can only really know God by love. In meditation, *the question that has no answer* (the mystery we call God) becomes the essence of our prayer through the heart's intelligence which is love.

The work of the teacher in what is truly a sacred contract with each child requires openness to the genuine possibility of self-transformation that can provide the teacher with the inspiration and confidence to support this evangelising process within the classroom. Ideally, teachers act in partnership with the parents in this spiritual work. Increasingly though, parents are relinquishing this responsibility to teachers, leaving the teacher to be the principal spiritual guide in the lives of children. The ultimate way they support children spiritually is through the prayer experience they provide for the children. This goes beyond the idea that prayer is something to be learned as a rote vocal prayer. *Prayer is something to be experienced*. The fruits and benefits of this prayer experience are to be deep and lasting, not fleeting, and should lead students to want to delve more deeply into the vast reservoirs of spiritual wisdom that the Christian community has accumulated.

Through Christian meditation, children can discover an inner sense of who they are as they freely enter their own inner sanctuary of silent stillness in a world that is built on incessant noise and activity. In this experience of an inner sanctuary, a young person's faith can be nurtured in the context of their developing self-awareness, increasing capacity for self-giving, perseverance in the practice and even self-transcendence. Prayer that is regular and authentic can assist children to develop an outlook which allows them to move from self to the world, from personal comfort to active compassion for a world in desperate need of peace and justice. Laurence Freeman says meditation opens the child to the spiritual vision within the matrix of love and, in quoting St Ignatius of Antioch, where we realise that the beginning is faith, the end is love, and the union of the two is God. Faith is active in love.[13] As children grow and mature, the depth of experience in silent prayer leads them to learn to be compassionate towards themselves and to see others through the eyes of Christlike compassion as well. Meditation renders the heart ever more sensitive and responsive to self and others.[14] This is surely the real heart of the new evangelisation; it is the message of Christ revealed in the way he lived his life.

CHURCH TEACHING ON

---

13 Laurence Freeman, *Jesus the Teacher Within* (London: Continuum, 2002), 98.
14 James Finley, *Christian Meditation: Experiencing the Presence of God* (Harper San Francisco, 2005), 27.

CONTEMPLATIVE PRAYER

The *Catechism of the Catholic Church* is an important source of authoritative teaching on prayer. There is great beauty in the words used to explore and explain vocal, meditative and contemplative prayer. These words can be a source of knowledge and inspiration for teachers in their living out their evangelising roles.

> *There are as many and varied methods of meditation as there are spiritual masters. Christians owe it to themselves to develop the desire to meditate regularly, lest they come to resemble the first three kinds of soil in the parable of the sower. But a method is only a guide; the important thing is to advance, with the Holy Spirit, along the one way of prayer: Christ Jesus. #2707.*[15]

THE MEANING OF SILENCE

John Main believed that one of the most important things for people living in the noise-filled and hurried world of today to remember and to recover was the meaning of silence. To do so allows a capacity to understand again what prayer really is and means. According to Laurence Freeman, liberation from desire and fear and developing inner and outer trust are the conditions of prayer as taught by the example of Jesus.[16] Without the contemplative element, any prayer may simply become merely formal, ritualistic, neurotic, compulsive and even self-indulgent. No-one should attempt to judge another's prayer, but the fruits of prayer become self-evident. If prayer does not make a difference – if it does not change the one praying first of all – something essential is missing. As we see from the experience passed on from the early desert monks, silence is the essence of prayer. Silence as the foundation of prayer brings us into relationships with others as spiritual beings. Through the silence of meditation, our prayer shifts from any tendency to self-centred request to prayer which bears the wholeness we are seeking whilst acknowledging that we do not know precisely what we are searching for.

Robert Sardello provides a clear overview of the personal benefits of silent meditation.

> *We feel a new sense of freedom and a capacity to be ourselves again. We may be shocked to notice that we had not even realised we had lost ourselves.*

---

15 *Compendium of the Catechism of the Catholic Church* (Strathfield: Australian Catholic Bishops' Conference/St Paul's Publications, 2005).
16 Laurence Freeman, 204.

> We feel a new attunement to spirit as a directly felt reality. We gain the capacity of reflection, of letting the world and things and others mirror within us, rather than ceaselessly going from one activity to the next. We realise that our activity had become an addiction. We gain a newfound creativity. Insights, new ideas, and new ways of seeing come again. But all these results are by-products of Silence and not reasons for becoming intrigued with it... We think we can find silence by being quiet for a while, going inward, getting back in touch with ourselves, disengaging for a time from all of the pressures and tensions of life. This limited view is like getting to the door of a cathedral and thinking that is the whole experience.[17]

In a world in which we are all bombarded by noise and toxically overstimulated by dazzling technology of all kinds, caring teachers must work even more deliberately to ensure that children maintain and grow in appreciation of their capacity for awe and wonder and a deeper experience of God. In his address to the 2012 Synod of Bishops in Rome, Archbishop Rowan Williams gave his unequivocal endorsement of the work of Christian meditation particularly in schools. He stated that what people recognise in such contemplative practices is the possibility, quite simply, of living more humanly – living with less frantic acquisitiveness, living with space for stillness, living in the expectation of learning and, most of all, living with an awareness that there is a solid and durable joy to be discovered in the discipline of self-forgetfulness that is quite different from the gratification of this or that impulse of the moment. Christian meditation is a prayer practice that aids in the recovery of a new humanity.[18] Such encouraging words have inspired teachers in their work of developing the inner potential of their students and thereby *setting pools of silence in this thirsty land*.

---

[17] Robert Sardello, *Silence: The Mystery of Wholeness* (Berkeley, Goldenstone Press/North Atlantic Books, 2008), 9–10.
[18] Rowan Williams, *The Archbishop of Canterbury's Address to the Thirteenth Ordinary General Assembly of the Synod of Bishops on The New Evangelisation for the Transmission of the Christian Faith* www.zenit.org/en/articles/archbishop-rowan-williams-address-to-the-synod-of-bishops

John McGrath

John McGrath is Assistant Director (Mission) in the Broken Bay Catholic school system. He has responsibility for Catholic mission and identity, Religious Education, the formation of teachers and schools, and the school system's collaboration with parishes and the diocese. He has led the Catholic Schools Office Mission Services team since 1999 and has played a leading role in the developments he describes in the chapter. John has had extensive mission and Religious Education leadership and governance experience at school and diocesan levels. He also exercises leadership at the state syllabus level and as a member of the Religious Education Committee of the National Catholic Education Commission.

15

CULTIVATING AND SUSTAINING MISSIONARY DISCIPLESHIP AS A DEFINING SPIRITUAL ELEMENT IN BROKEN BAY CATHOLIC SCHOOLS

John McGrath

Dioceses and their school systems may not have, as a particular response to the Good News of Jesus, the gift of a charism, lived and sustained over a long period by a religious community animated by its Rule. Nevertheless, the experience of the Diocese of Broken Bay shows that it is possible to develop, through contextualised mission thinking, a distinctive spiritual identity that enlivens lay leaders and teachers in their ministry as Catholic educators. The combination of the visionary leadership of a bishop and the purposeful and consistent strategies by system and school leadership over a period of more than 15 years is bearing fruit. The result is a singular expression of mission and discipleship as a renewed way of living the Gospel in a particular context.

The Diocese of Broken Bay occupies tracts of Darug and Guringai country in northern Sydney and Darkinjung country on the Central Coast of NSW. It was established in 1986 and is the smallest of the three Sydney metropolitan dioceses. The identity of the Diocese of Broken Bay and its expression in the diocesan school system were expressed most fully in the leadership of its second bishop, David Walker, from 1996 to 2013. However, its development and sustainability benefits from the diocese's young age and its compact size in comparison to large metropolitan or sparsely populated rural dioceses. These attributes enabled the development and implanting of a shared common purpose, symbolism and 'vocabulary'. Part of this imagination originated with the founding bishop, Patrick Murphy.

Broken Bay is the only Australian diocese named after a geographical feature rather than a city or town, a characteristic positively exploited from the beginning in the building of its identity. The body of water known as

'Broken Bay' literally bisects the diocese's land area and is central to its self-understanding. The Barrenjoey Lighthouse at its southern entrance sheds its light across the bay, symbolising *Lumen Christi* (the Light of Christ) adopted as the diocesan motto in 1986. The original diocesan symbol was a simplified monochrome image of Barrenjoey Lighthouse, later expressed in the current colourful logo. The logo of the Catholic Schools Office and the Community of Catholic Schools has been illustrated continuously by variations of a lighthouse shedding light and has been employed in the system's nomenclature for various projects. The ownership, sustainability and longevity of symbols are key aspects of building identity.

In 2013 there were 24,924 students in Catholic schools in Broken Bay in 43 systemic schools and nine religious institute-owned schools. Systemic schools are the principal but not sole focus of this chapter, and they educate 97% of the primary students in Catholic schools (11,767) but only 46% of the secondary Catholic school students (5,883). These schools have a high rate of Catholic enrolments: in 2013, 88% of primary and 80% of secondary students were Catholic, giving an overall figure of 85%, compared to 71% nationally.[1]

BISHOP DAVID WALKER'S VISION FOR THE DIOCESE

Bishop David Walker's entire priestly and episcopal ministry is characterised by a fruitful concentration on Catholic spirituality and formation through his personal holiness, responsiveness to the Second Vatican Council, and his giftedness as a teacher. The diocesan website explains his pastoral drive in this way:

> *Bishop Walker is committed to promoting a truly Australian spirituality, fostering theological and spiritual education through an experiential understanding of the personal faith journey.*
>
> *From the beginning Bishop David recognised the way forward for the Church depended on all believers being willing to work together, responding to the opportunities and responsibilities of Christian leadership. He has brought to the Diocese a continued commitment to faith renewal and has invited all to engage in 'grassroots' ownership, fostering greater participation and collaboration in shaping parish and diocesan life.*[2]

---

1 Catholic Schools Office *Annual Report 2013*, 'Schools' at http://www.csodbb.catholic.edu.au/ under 'About Us'; National Catholic Education Commission, *Australian Catholic Schools 2012*, http://www.ncec.catholic.edu.au/
2 http://www.dbb.org.au/ under 'Bishop Walker'.

Over 17 years, Bishop Walker – who is always is affectionately known as Bishop David within his school system and beyond – planted, cultivated, watered and sustained a shared Catholic language and spirituality of discipleship of Jesus in the diocese and especially in the Catholic school system. This distinctiveness is even readily detected by those outside the diocese. What follows first is a narrative and interpretation of the bishop's place in this development, which the writer humbly hopes does justice to his thinking. The second essential ingredient is the critical strategic collaboration of Catholic system and school leaders that grounds and inculturates this developing Catholic school 'personality'.

Bishop David directed his thirst for formation and his love of teaching towards the purposeful achievement of his 'preferred future'. In his teaching he regularly displayed an image of the downriver confluence of two arms of a river (the 'past' and the 'present') coming together in the turmoil and creative tension of the 'now'. He was willing to work within this creative tension, truthfully naming the current reality and striving to raise it towards a shared ecclesiological vision.

In 1999 he led the development of a Diocesan Mission Statement:

> *We the Catholic Church of Broken Bay are, through Baptism, a community of disciples of Jesus. Under the guidance of the Holy Spirit, we are committed to work together to extend the Kingdom of God.*[3]

This wording is suggestive of Avery (later Cardinal) Dulles and his classic work, *Models of the Church*. At first Dulles outlined five ecclesiological models. His position was that one of the models might be a preferred starting point, but that all models need each other in order to produce a balanced ecclesiology. In a later edition Dulles added a sixth, seemingly preferred model – a synthesis: the Church as 'community of disciples'.[4] Bishop David's teaching employed many characteristics of this model even though he does not attribute his thinking to Dulles alone. The model focuses on Jesus and the community that follows him. It is deeply scriptural. The expression 'community of disciples' is found in Acts 6:2 where *communio* and *missio* are united. The model also accentuates the place of the local Church. Furthermore, when the language quickly and seamlessly extended to Catholic schools, it was a perfect image for Catholic education, for disciples are 'students' (*discipuli*) of Jesus and the Church is imaged as a school of disciples or 'learners'.

---

3 This text is by enlarged by seven commitments highlighted by verbs that provide a sense of definite action.
4 Avery Dulles, *Models of the Church*. 2nd ed. (New York: Doubleday Image Books, 1987).

For Bishop David, discipleship radically focuses on relationship with Jesus, something he emphasised more and more as his episcopate advanced. At his retirement he wrote that the 'highlight of my ministry as bishop has been to share the Gospel with you, the people of the Diocese, and to help you grow in your faith relationship with Jesus'.[5] In an almost mystical manner, he developed a template for the Christian life as a three-layered circle. The inner core is Mystery, one's personal involvement in the Mystery of Jesus. This is surrounded by the middle layer, Communion, sharing the Mystery of Jesus together. Nourished by both of these, the outer layer is Mission, sharing the Mystery of Jesus with others. He often distinguished Communion from community; one might rightly suggest that if the Diocesan Mission Statement had been developed at the end of his Broken Bay ministry, the term 'communion of disciples' might have been employed.

The bishop's mission thinking shaped the diocesan strategic directions for the work of the parishes, agencies and schools. The expression 'working together' in the Diocesan Mission Statement is very intentional. There was significant concentration on collaborative ministry and the involvement of lay people, especially women. A focus on strategic planning is evident in the diocesan pastoral plan *Going Forward Together* (2001–2005) and the vision and strategic directions for 2006–2010, *Going Forward Together: Pastoral Care for Evangelisation*. In the latter he stated that 'the previous pastoral plan was focused around collaboration, the living out of communion in Jesus we share. Now we must direct this collaboration to a pastoral care that has mission as its focus'.[6] At the same time he set up The Broken Bay Institute, which has made significant contributions to formation in and far beyond the diocese. His deep praying of the Scriptures, 'listening with the ear of the heart', led a national discovery of *lectio divina*. The strategic crown was the Diocesan Synod in 2011–2012, 'Go make disciples'. Its outcomes are expressed in a matrix of 'serving as disciples' and 'leading as disciples' in our 'way of being' and our 'way of doing'.[7] All these strategies can be interpreted in light of the template – personal relationship with Jesus, communion and mission.

THE PURPOSE OF CATHOLIC SCHOOLS

Bishop David used gatherings of Catholic school leaders (generally clergy/principals meetings and Religious Education Coordinators' days) as a prime forum for the articulation of his vision for the diocese and the schools. In 1999 he commenced what became a refrain in his characteristic PowerPoint

---

5   http://www.dbb.org.au/ under 'Bishop Walker'.
6   Diocese of Broken Bay, *Going Forward Together: Pastoral Care for Evangelisation 2006–2010* (2006), 2.
7   http://www.dbb.org.au/synod/

presentations: 'The fundamental difference between religious and other forms of education is that its aim is not simply intellectual assent to religious truth, but also the commitment of one's whole person to the person of Jesus Christ'. Reflecting on his establishment of a renewed enrolment policy in 2001, the bishop introduced the term 'Catholic discipleship' in 2002 as the principal goal of Catholic schools. The Diocesan Schools Board went on to use this to establish a statement of purpose:

> *Catholic schools in the Diocese of Broken Bay exist to educate and form students in Catholic discipleship: offering them experiences of following Jesus as members of the Catholic community.*

Bishop David consistently explained what 'being Catholic' means. While the words sometimes varied slightly, the most common description across 15 years was that:

> Being Catholic is
> - *a personal and communal response,*
> - *to the love which God has manifested in Jesus,*
> - *as it is perceived, proclaimed and lived by the Catholic Community,*
> - *in the light of its scriptural and historical traditions and its contemporary interpretation of them.*

These words demonstrate a contemporary understanding of the way the adjective 'Catholic' augments 'discipleship'.

Bishop David emphasised a traditional understanding of the dynamic interplay of intellect, will and behaviour, suggesting that the three need to exist in harmony. Each must build on the other so that Christian maturity is a creative harmony of what I think or perceive (intellect), how I choose (will) and what I do (behaviour). Bishop David had great reservations about any learning that focused on the cognitive alone, which was why he was suspicious of overemphasis on doctrinal propositions at the expense of the affective and is the reason why he eschewed knowledge-based standardised testing in Religious Education. His focus on harmony of intellect, will and behaviour is evident in his construction of the key concepts of Catholic Discipleship, Catholic Worldview and Catholic Character.

The core concept of discipleship can only be correctly understood as the harmony of all three. A 'student' of Jesus, one formed in Catholic discipleship, has a relationship with Jesus, contributes to communion and is obligated to mission. Of all three faculties, discipleship is oriented the most to behaviour. The disciple's 'way of being' of necessity leads to a 'way of doing'.

Another key concept originated as a Catholic school system strategic project to clarify how to make a Catholic worldview explicit in the curriculum. Bishop David saw the Catholic worldview as 'a comprehensive perception of the universe, revealed to us in Jesus, that provides insights into the meaning of life and how to live it'. It is 'experiencing life through the eyes of our Catholic faith'. His ten theological statements of the Catholic worldview were published in his K–12 Religious Education Curriculum promulgated in 2004. They certainly represent the interplay of intellect, will and behaviour, but the genre principally is an expression of the intellect.

Bishop David also introduced the concept of 'Catholic character', positively evangelising the behavioural framework of Thomas Lickona.[8] The harmony is clear in his definition of Catholic character as 'understanding, being committed to, and acting out of our relationship with Jesus'. Nonetheless, ultimately it is more reliant on the will, for it is about choosing to grow as a disciple of Jesus.

Bishop David's leadership was visionary and imbued with spiritual ideals somewhat removed from the everyday realities of Catholic schooling. However, his personal presence, humility and apparent effortlessness with which he taught generally captured the hearts and minds of his hearers within Catholic schools. Over 17 years, he led his week-long Ministry for Teachers courses some 40 times, the equivalent of a whole school year. Some 950 teachers enjoyed the program, roughly equivalent to the fulltime classroom teaching staff of the systemic school system today. This strategy was intentional, strategic and effective. The 'big idea' was received. It is little wonder that he had no greater supporters than his system and school leaders and teachers throughout his ministry. They are the other half of the story, for many sought to realise the practical application of this audacious vision for education and formation in Catholic discipleship, and many continue to do so. If it is to endure, they will be key players, and there is some evidence that this diocesan school 'personality' can be sustained.

SCHOOL SYSTEM COLLABORATION

The Catholic school system strategic plan for 1998–2001, *Shaping Our Future,* identified its first priority area as Catholic Life and Mission. The bishop's hand was clearly evident in the four goals within the priority:
- To collaborate with the Diocese of Broken Bay in developing with all stakeholders shared understandings on the nature of being Catholic today and on contemporary ways of proclaiming Catholic Life and Mission.

---

8   http://www.mtsm.org/pdf/What%20is%20Effective%20Character%20Education.pdf

- To develop practices which ensure that all Catholic schools are active partners in the life and mission of local Catholic communities.
- To develop practices and processes in schools which support the formation of students in the Catholic faith and the living out of the responsibilities of that faith.
- To review and revise school policies and practices in order that all students enjoy an experience of school which is distinctly Catholic in the context of contemporary society.

The Mission Services team was created in 1999 in a restructured Catholic Schools Office (CSO). It was a deliberate effort to expand on the term 'Religious Education' and to connect the school system to the mission of the diocese and wider Church in order to expedite the Catholic Life and Mission priority area. The team's leader offered to the bishop, clergy and principals an understanding of mission through a rudimentary triangular diagram which placed Jesus and his establishment of the Reign of God at the centre and Proclamation and Dialogue, Inculturation, and Local Partnerships at the vertices. The language of mission, even if it was not widely understood at the outset, remains a consistent part of educational discourse in Broken Bay and has been expressed in a number of ways.

In a substantial external review of the CSO in 2008–2009, the system's self-review documentation is a record of school leaders 'doing theology'. It argued that leadership 'has cultivated mission expressed in a range of partnerships', that there is a 'congruence in mission' among the schools and the diocese, and that there had been 'a realignment of mission in schools' in collaborative response to the Bishop's leadership. From the time Bishop David started to enunciate his hopes and expectations, the CSO leadership team embraced them readily. To some extent the responses show a balance of mission thinking, strategic thinking and operational thinking at system level and at local school level.[9] Some of the responses were:

- The school system strategic plan took its name from the diocesan plan *Catholic Schools Going Forward Together 2002–2006* and aligned its categories to it. It was the first publication of the Statement of Purpose of the Catholic Schools, which has appeared in every annual plan since that time. The first priority was that by the end of 2006 'we will have strengthened a shared understanding of the central purpose of schools as centres of formation of our students in Catholic Discipleship'. Particular strategies were developed and evaluated for each year of the plan;

---

9 The interdependence of these modes of thinking is explained in Jim and Therese D'Orsa, *Leading for Mission: Integrating Life, Culture and Faith in Catholic Education* (Mulgrave: Vaughan Publishing, 2013), 247–248.

- The Mission Services team prepared and delivered staff development sessions on the scriptural underpinnings and practice of Catholic Discipleship in 90% of schools in 2003 and 2004;
- The 'Foundations' section of the K–12 Religious Education Curriculum is a treatise on Catholic Discipleship and includes the statement on Catholic Worldview;
- The Religious Education syllabus is structured in the same way as the Board of Studies NSW syllabus was at the time. However, each outcome and associated content area was supplemented by an additional feature, a Discipleship Challenge. Examples of Discipleship Challenges are: 'students are challenged to reach out to others in love as Jesus did' in upper primary, and students 'are challenged to identify with the community of disciples of the Diocese of Broken Bay' in senior secondary. The modules that support the syllabus expand on the ways these Discipleship Challenges can be realised;
- In response to the bishop's desire for a faith formation program for all adults in the diocese, the CSO offered the bishop the services of a Mission Services Education Officer to develop it. The modules addressed four statements from the Catholic Worldview and most school staff participated in the programs through staff spirituality days presented by Mission Services staff from 2006 to 2008.[10] A separate 90-minute professional learning package that synthesised the Catholic Worldview was used widely in schools in 2006–2007;
- The partnership with The Broken Bay Institute enabled the school system to advance the bishop's theological formation agenda. The CSO has fully funded hundreds of teachers to formal postgraduate qualifications in theology, generally at Master's level;
- *Catholic Schools Going Forward Together 2007–2010* also was aligned to the diocese and had as its first priority, 'Catholic life, evangelisation and pastoral care', aiming to 'build communities of faith in our schools and parishes in the context of the Diocesan vision and pastoral directions';
- The system's *Framework for Sustainable Leadership* featured the key diocesan terminology as the envelope of its diagrammatic synthesis and identified a set of leaders' 'mission capabilities', the first of which was 'forming a community of disciples';
- More schools explicitly used the language of Catholic discipleship when they reviewed their Mission Statements, and School Review accountability processes placed emphasis on the strategic and operational expressions of mission and discipleship;

---

10   Unfortunately, these modules were never used outside the school system.

- The habit of collaboration of the CSO and schools with wider diocesan agencies intensified. The Special Religious Education Curriculum for government schools came to mirror the Catholic school curriculum and participation in diocesan youth ministry, diocesan commissions, advisory councils and working parties increased;
- The ministry of the secondary school Youth Ministry Coordinators has assisted the congruence of the schools' mission with that of the diocese. They are school-based specialist teachers with theological qualifications with a youth ministry allocation of 0.6 – 0.4 FTE (full time equivalent), depending on school size. They facilitate a range of local and diocesan faith development activities in order to assist students – to use the words of Bishop David – 'to move towards a mature, contemporary living out of their faith'. The Bishop's desire for groups of students to commit to a 'mission rite' in secondary schools was implemented by the youth ministry coordinators, but there was limited success in this area. The most effective application was a program in one college called 'disciples on mission'.

One response is worthy of more detailed analysis as it was an application of contextualised local theology that brought some of the more lofty language of Catholic discipleship and worldview into direct interaction with realities of staff and parents. Initiated in the context of the Australian Values Project, the CSO commissioned Fraynework Multimedia to develop artistic prints of the Purpose of Catholic Schools and of the Catholic Worldview, which became display banners which are still prominent in every school. A CD-ROM resource called *Our Values Our Mission* supported staff professional learning and Values Forums in schools. These were built around interactive discourse on the Purpose of Schools, Catholic Worldview, the Pastoral Letter of the Bishops of NSW and the ACT (*Catholic Schools at a Crossroads* 2007) and the school's Mission, Vision and Values Statements and enrolment processes. As an example of 'grassroots theology', the whole process assisted in critical reflection on what it means to be a Catholic educator in this place at this time. The external CSO Review Report (2009) observed that:

> By international standards this initiative is a significant contribution to discussions about "the Catholic Curriculum" and "Catholic Identity". It is the first attempt by a diocese to deal with Catholic identity within the framework of a contextualised local theology.[11]

---

11 The CSO review report is unpublished. *Our Values Our Mission* (Catholic Schools Office, 2008) is available from the Catholic Schools Office, Broken Bay.

The same report noted that 'Broken Bay is widely acknowledged as being at the cutting edge of mission in a diocesan context in Australia. The intention to bring coherence to the many arms of diocesan mission seems exemplary'. That review included a CSO Staff Engagement Survey that demonstrated a very high level of CSO staff awareness and understanding of mission. The five major mission-oriented questions were the five highest scoring items in the whole survey, all scoring at or near the maximum on the scale. The highest two were awareness of the Statement of Purpose of Catholic Schools and the assertion by staff that they understood it. Likewise, a study of the spirituality of teachers in 12 primary schools and three secondary schools was conducted by the Christian Research Association in 2009. A total of 228 teachers completed a survey and 60 teachers were personally interviewed. Some survey and interview questions specifically addressed Catholic Discipleship and Worldview and almost all respondents were aware of them, with the vast majority supporting them, although some expressed caveats about the propositional nature of the statements within the Catholic Worldview.[12]

The impetus was reshaped and renewed after the external review. A focus on 'Catholic School Improvement' was initiated in 2010 led by the Assistant Directors for Mission and for School Improvement. The school system already had some familiarity with the paradigm that 'mission' is what God does; hence the phrases 'God's Mission' and 'the Mission has a Church'. These were magnified in the understanding of Catholic School Improvement as a dynamic interplay between 'mission-in-context' and the leading of learning. The terminology owes some debt to the thinking of Jim and Therese D'Orsa.[13] Schools in Broken Bay operate in the context of secularising and pluralising forces. 'Mission-in-context' is mission that befriends Catholic tradition and befriends the context, or more properly, the many contexts in which it operates. 'Befriending the context' must never involve surrender to worldviews contrary to the Gospel; rather it is a willingness to engage the Catholic Worldview with realities as they are, to be intentional and open to dialogue and engagement with the actual situations of students, families, parents, teachers and the local Church.[14]

---

12 Philip Hughes, Stephen Reid and Peter Bentley, *Spirituality of Teachers in Twelve Schools in the Broken Bay Diocese* (Report for the CSO by the Christian Research Association, 2010) 21–27.
13 Their thinking had been expressed in programs presented in Broken Bay in 2006 and 2009 and can be found throughout Jim and Therese D'Orsa, *Explorers, Guides and Meaning Makers: Mission Theology for Catholic Educators*, (Mulgrave: Garratt Publishing, 2010).
14 This thinking and further examples are developed in John McGrath, 'Befriending Context and Tradition: Evangelisation in Catholic Schools', *The Australasian Catholic Record* 89:2 (2012), 283–298.

The journey continues. A new initiative broadens the reach of formation in discipleship to parents. Using an invitational and dialogical approach, Mission Services personnel have conducted morning parent faith formation sessions in schools across the diocese. The discipleship focus has been consolidated by the introduction of the Discipleship Response for Year 6 students in 2011. With most other NSW dioceses consolidating Religious Education Tests, generally in Year 6, it was decided that all Year 6 students would write a letter to Bishop David or use creative expressions to state how they are disciples of Jesus or how a Year 6 student can live as one. The bishop valued these expressions, which were systematically analysed by the CSO into a broad report for each school to use as data in improving their focus on discipleship. In 2013 the Bishop David Walker Student Religious Art Prize was instituted to provide another possibility for creative expression. The inaugural subject for all entries was discipleship. Responding to an emerging practice, in 2013 the Diocesan Schools Board decided that the Statement of Purpose of Catholic Schools ('education and formation in Catholic discipleship') would become the introductory statement for each school's Mission Statement. Four schools and the CSO staff have participated in the *National Enhancing Catholic School Identity Project* with the Catholic University of Leuven. Mission-in-context has affinity with the project's preferred theological and pedagogical options for the way a Catholic school shapes its Catholic identity in a pluralised, secularised context, namely by way of 'recontextualisation' in a 'dialogue school'. Assessment of the extent to which these operate in Broken Bay can provide a deeper understanding of the mission context and lead to strategies for deeper engagement.

SUSTAINING MISSIONARY DISCIPLESHIP

There is no suggestion in this account that Broken Bay schools and their students and staff are somehow better than others in the areas of mission and discipleship. Nonetheless, the account demonstrates that there is a defining spiritual element that can be seen as a renewed way of living the Gospel. A possible outcome that had to be addressed was whether it could be sustained after Bishop David's retirement.

Fortuitously in the same month that the bishop retired, Pope Francis issued his apostolic exhortation, *Evangelii Gaudium*. The Church, and indeed the wider world, continue to be entranced by what he does and what he says, and the exhortation has become a catalyst for sustaining the mission. System leaders extended their mission thinking into a strategic orientation for the years 2014–2016 called 'God's Mission: the Joy of the Gospel'. It is expressed in the following way:

> *'God's Mission: the Joy of the Gospel' aims is to ensure that our schools more consciously realise that missionary discipleship is the heartbeat of all our endeavours. This is not an 'additional project'; rather it is a renewing lens through which we look at everything we do. As disciples of Jesus we are called to proclaim the Joy of the Gospel of Jesus.*[15]

The three-year orientation focuses on laying the foundation with school leaders in 2014, building staff mission capabilities in the middle year and focusing on students and parents in the next year. The Pope's statement that 'in virtue of their baptism, all the members of the People of God have become missionary disciples (cf. Matt 28:19)'[16] is particularly pertinent. Through the previous 15 years the terms 'mission' and 'discipleship' have been readily associated but never in the Pope's apposite phrasing, 'missionary discipleship'. There was no need for persuasion to introduce it to Broken Bay schools as it is a more complete way of naming the spiritual element that has developed in the school system.

The narrative above is not a mere recitation of happenings, but outlines a strategic response that enabled the 'reception' of the bishop's mission thinking. What is needed to cultivate such a seed? Firstly there is coherent teaching and lived example that a critical mass of leaders and teachers find meaningful and that is translatable for students and parents. Next it needs a strategic system response built around contextualised mission thinking that is strong and consistent, but is not legislated or enforced. It involves constancy and coherence in intentionality, language, symbolism, action and evaluation, along with the 'mission agility' to adapt to changing circumstances. Features such as these have resulted in what can be called a distinctive spiritual identity and a renewed way of living the Gospel in the Catholic school system of the Diocese of Broken Bay.

---

15   http://www.godsmissionjoyofthegospel.dbbcso.org/
16   Pope Francis, *Evangelii Gaudium* (2013), #120.

Anita Carter

Anita Carter has worked continuously as a Religious Education teacher and school counsellor in Catholic colleges since 1979. She has been a leader in Student Wellbeing at both Nazareth college, Noble Park, and St Peter's college, Cranbourne, where she currently holds the position of Head of the Wellbeing Team. Anita has post-graduate qualifications in both Psychology and Theology, which facilitate her role in the growth of both the spirituality and the mental health of young people. She believes school leadership is both a gift of the Spirit and an art: that in a Catholic school, the true leader should seek to touch the soul of the community.

16

THE CHARISM OF ST PETER'S – WHAT'S IN A NAME?

...he said to Simon, 'Put out into the deep water and let down your nets for a catch' (Lk 5:4–5).

Anita Carter

In an earlier chapter, charism has been described as that which sits behind the 'passion' and 'fire' that drives what happens in a Catholic school community. One learns about charism and its impact from the community's narrative, particularly as this relates to the founder. While this is clearly true of the founders of religious congregations, these are not the only gifted individuals to inspire teachers in Catholic schools. Nor is charism, at least in the sense outlined above, confined to schools associated directly or indirectly with a congregational tradition.

Every school, each in its own way, provides a unique witness to how the Gospel can be lived in its particular social and cultural context. The action of God's Spirit is not confined to particular settings. The fire and passion God inspires can be found in all school settings. The problem is often that people do not have a great consciousness that this is the case. Catholic schools of all sorts evidence each day the 'fire' and 'passion' of God at work in their communities.

We discover this, however, only if we are in contact with the narrative of the community and develop some realisation of how God is at work in the community. It requires a certain level of spiritual maturity and effort on the part of leaders to bring to consciousness what is implicit in the daily work of teachers and support staff in Catholic schools.

Congregations are more adept at this because they have a corporate story to tell, often hundreds of years in the making, and are canonised by the Church. A local regional school has to create its own story and within this its own mythology of living the Gospel if it is to develop a unique culture, one that is recognisably Catholic, and one that speaks to young people about how the Gospel can be lived out in their lives. In this chapter we look at an example of how this can happen. Our beginning point is the narrative of the St Peter's College community.

In order to write about what has been created at and embedded in St Peter's Catholic Regional College, Cranbourne, it was necessary to catch up with a number of the 'pioneers' from those early days when a small school staff collected around its charismatic first principal, Terry Feely.[1]

Terry was only 37 years old when he was appointed to his first principalship at St Peter's. He had originally come from Glasgow in Scotland and the Catholic faith as it was lived in the Celtic lands was very dear to him. He was a man who understood what it meant to be living on, as he would say, 'the margins'. He recalled sacred places from Scotland and Ireland where Catholic communities clung to hillsides and clifftops battered by fierce north winds and high seas and withstood foreign invasion and persecution on behalf of their faith. This was all very real to him not the least because of his facility with Celtic poetry, music and spirituality.

'Put out into the deep water and let down your nets for a catch'. These words of Jesus to Peter resounded often in Terry's heart and mind. He had launched into the deep and the unknown in his own life by migrating to Australia and knew what it was like to feel marginalised by geography and history.

As we have been able to put the narrative together, the beginnings of the spirituality that underpins life at St Peter's comes, to a very large extent, from the mind, heart and spiritual understanding of its first principal. He would repeat the words above to the fledgling staff. This text from the Gospel inspired his search for new teachers and leaders. He was on the lookout for those who were not afraid to take risks, who were not afraid to face the unknown and who were prepared to work with him to build a spiritual tradition in a place where he saw both *a human need and a genuine evangelical opportunity*. That place was the outlying, semi-rural and rapidly growing community of Cranbourne, Victoria. Our story begins exactly 20 years ago.

THE CHARISM OF PETER

The life and times of Simon, a simple fisherman living in an outpost of the Roman empire, were tipped upside down when Jesus invited him personally to be part of his mission. He was called on subsequently to lead the early faith community. It is almost impossible for us today to grasp the challenge

---

[1] Mr Feely was principal of St Peter's College from its foundation in 1994 until 2009 when he retired due to ill health. He died suddenly two years later.

this implied in his own time. He really did face the unknown and overcame a multitude of challenges to build what have proved to be lasting faith communities. The task required both faith and a commitment to service.

Terry Feely was intensely inspired by the story and charism of the simple fisherman Simon, who *became* St Peter. The unique disciple, Simon, whom Christ transformed into 'petros' – became in time the rock upon which Jesus would build the Church. Scripture helps us map out the character of Peter:

- Peter was called and responded: 'Follow me … Immediately they left their nets and followed him' (Matt. 4:19–21);
- Peter experienced Jesus' earthly mission from the beginning and remained resolutely *with Christ* through the trials and moments of doubt during his public ministry;
- Peter was the first apostle to profess his *faith* unequivocally: 'You are the Messiah, the Son of the Living God' (Matt. 16:16–17);
- Peter was not perfect. He *fled when the final crisis unfolded, denied* he knew Jesus when challenged, but soon came to regret his lack of courage (Matt. 26:69–75);
- *Recognising strength in a leader who was aware of his own vulnerability,* Jesus commissioned Peter to lead his 'flock': 'Feed my lambs … Tend my sheep … Feed my sheep' (John 21:15–18).

A charism is widely considered to be a gift of the Holy Spirit, freely bestowed on a person and freely used for the good of the people of God. We are told that St Peter was able to communicate powerfully with people from all sorts of countries and cultures through the power of the Holy Spirit… and that when he spoke, people were 'cut to the heart' (Acts 2:5–38).

CREATING A SCHOOL SPIRITUALITY FROM SCRATCH

Two Irish Catholic educators on opposite sides of the Atlantic set the scene for what has happened at St Peter's since 1994. Based at Boston College, Thomas Groome writes:

> *Like never before, the future of Irish education and particularly of what is done by the designation 'Catholic', depends on the spirituality of its educators – 'what the heart is and what it feels'.*[2]

---

[2] Thomas Groome, 'Forging in the Smithy of the Teacher's Soul: The Best Hope for Irish Education', in Ned Prendergast and Luke Monahan (eds), *Reimagining the Catholic School* (Dublin: Veritas, 2003), 35.

Developing this theme, Ned Prendergast, senior Catholic educator based at Maynooth College in Dublin, comments:

> Schools are living, breathing organisms which have a life of their own... the life force of a Catholic School is ... its ethos. ... The ethos is created by the way the members of the school community interact with each other on a daily basis, the heroes admired by the community, the icons which populate the spaces in the school and the activities to which the school gives priority.[3]

To this list we would add the *power of narrative* in creating a Catholic school's ethos, spirituality and culture.

As a school leader and very proud Celt, Terry well understood the importance of a unique spiritual story and how this could be used to inspire, motivate and shape a new educational and faith community in a unique time and culture. The landscape of Cranbourne in the early 1990s was essentially secular (only one church in the whole town) and both geographically and culturally isolated. Terry often lamented that Cranbourne did not have *even one* bookshop!

How then, Terry asked, do you 'tell the story' and give it meaning in this particular community? He asked 'what did Peter do?' His answer was that Peter started with people and built spiritual communities around Jerusalem by communicating Jesus' message and modelling what today we call 'servant leadership'. In this way Peter took up Jesus' challenge that he and his brother Andrew 'be fishers of men'.

Terry intentionally followed this pattern in moulding his small band of school leaders, all of whom came to see that both Jesus' mission and education shared a common element – to *transform* people for the better by creating a community. This is the concept these early leaders remember being reiterated at board meetings and leadership team briefings. For them Terry's strategy was 'highly intentional'. The fire and passion of the leader became the fire and passion of the staff, not by accident but by intention. Charism for the first leaders of the College was experienced as a shared reality. Terry was seen as the firelighter with his passion being communicated to others. His fire became in time their fire.

In 1963, the Catholic archbishop of Melbourne, Justin Simonds, conscious of the rapid growth in the outer suburbs of Melbourne, announced that a new model of provision was necessary if the growing population was to have access to a Catholic education. Religious congregations that, until then, had been responsible for Catholic Secondary education, could no longer meet the increasing demand for schools. Consequently, groups of parishes

---

3 Ned Prendergast, *What Makes a School Catholic?* Available at *www.schoolethos.ie/webfm_send/941*

were called upon to build *regional* colleges for their young parishioners. The Diocese of Sale, which includes a large proportion of the growth area of outer Melbourne, similarly adopted the model of regional provision of secondary schooling.

In 1994, the inaugural College Board, together with the parish priest of St Agatha's Cranbourne, Fr Herman Hengel, and the newly appointed principal, set out 'into the deep', in earnest Fr Hengel, remembers remarking to the board in its early discussions: 'It's a pity that we have no (religious) congregation upon which to base our spirituality and traditions.' Starting a spirituality 'from scratch', he felt at that time, came down to 'the spiritual understanding, mental strength and capacity for firm decision-making of the principal'.

The board was clear that the College needed a saint's name and they also wanted to pay tribute to the former parish priest of St Agatha's, Fr McGuigan, who with Monsignor Gallagher, parish priest of Berwick, had established the first campus to provide Catholic secondary education for Catholic families at the western end of the diocese. Discussion then narrowed to his Christian names – *James* and *Peter*. According to Fr Hengel, Terry advocated for Peter. In his view, Peter was more of a character: '*he cried; denied, was lost, and was found*'. Fr Hengel felt that Terry believed that choosing Peter opened up a great set of connections with which he could work. It was thus collectively agreed by the inaugural Board that both the *story of Peter and the person of Peter* were something that should be continually and actively made spiritually relevant to the students, staff and wider community.

From the saint's life came the College's vision and the motto – '*Be Not Afraid*'. Importantly, Peter Houlahan[4], a pioneer staff member and later Curriculum Coordinator at the College, recalled Terry Feely insisting the motto be in English, unlike many Catholic schools which traditionally used Latin mottos. He believes Terry had an innate understanding that the people of Cranbourne had to be able to 'be caught in the net' through a language, symbol, and song that *were strongly Catholic, yet culturally accessible*. As a Celt, Terry understood the sway music, images and symbols held over people and wished to put them to good effect in building the new school community.

The *School Song* became the hymn 'Be not afraid' – not only accessible for its message of hope, but also because it was widely sung in churches around Melbourne and hence well known. Despite this, Peter recalls that getting the students to sing it with enthusiasm was an uphill battle. However, it was Terry's unambiguous insistence with both students and staff that the song be

---

4 Current principal of Marist–Sion College, Warragul.

sung *with frequency and with gusto* that helped inspire an energy and spirit that can now be felt whenever 'Be not afraid' rings out at the school.

The *College Crest* is also symbol-rich: Peter, the martyr (burgundy/red), the storms of life (grey), the Keys of the Kingdom given Peter as leader (gold). The Crest visually represents the Petrine story and spirituality of the school community.

When it came to creating symbols that underpinnned the spiritual ethos and traditions of the school, the principal led from the front. As he often used to repeat to school leaders, 'We all have to get to know St Peter very well!'

HOW SCHOOL LEADERSHIP AND SCHOOL SPIRITUALITY INTERSECT

Within any Christian cultural tradition '*the leader is the holder of the narrative, and carries responsibility to discern the action of God's spirit in the life of the community as it continues the mission of Jesus*'.[5] The experience of St Peter's College illustrates the critical role leadership plays in the development of the spiritual narrative of a school, particularly in its early days. One way to achieve this is if the founding principal can interpret school life through the story of its patron saint and foster the witness to faith this contains by co-opting the gifts that a variety of people bring to the school community. Lacking the spiritual base provided by a religious congregation, with its attendant traditions, culture and resources in spiritual formation, the principal of Regional College must be able to *spiritually animate* others. This is a major challenge.

According to Mark Murphy[6], St Peter's first Senior School Coordinator, the principal must, from the start, be able to interpret the story of the community and reveal for that community its relevance. He was able to personally model the *charism* of St Peter. Mark recalls that Terry, as founding principal was 'thoughtful and interesting; he would nudge your conscience in the light of our ethos… ask you to reflect.' He then went on to say that Terry had a strong background in theology and this gave the community a sense of leadership that was both authoritative and authentic. Further to this, he believes the principal surrounded himself with, and was indeed surrounded by, strong, questioning school leaders, parish priests and leaders at the diocesan Catholic Education Office.

To get the collective and cooperative 'buy in' of these people, Mr Feely had to think and lead theologically. He choose to interpret the mission of

---

5 James and Therese D'Orsa, *Leading for Mission* (Mulgrave:Vaughan Publishing, 2013), 82.
6 Currently principal at Marcellin College Bulleen.

St Peter's College in a way that was not parochial but was part of the story of the diocese and the global Church. And in this, Mark recalls, key people believed Terry succeeded admirably.[7]

SIGNS, SYMBOLS AND TRADITIONS – SPIRITUALITY EMBEDDED

'A feature of life on a frontier is that there are no roads or bridges'.[8] Terry Feely had a sense, possibly influenced by his strong Celtic sense of place, that in our age, spiritual markers needed to be created rather than found. Such markers needed to be '*physical touchstones*' that people could visit, pass and immerse themselves in, which would reflect the spirituality of the school. He understood and *imagined* ways in which people could traverse the landscape of the College and be touched by the spirit of Christ, through a series of objects that reflected a *Petrine* spirituality.

A *Prayer and Memorial Garden* was commissioned in 1996, with a centrepiece being a large piece of rough–hewn granite. The memorial 'Rock' would stand forever, as did the old stones which emerged out of the Celtic landscapes that he remembered. On this large Rock at St Peter's would be the names of students who had died, yet who would remain forever a part of the school. The *School Magazine*, a chronicle of the daily life and achievements of the *living community*, would also be called '*The Rock*'.

The first commissioned religious artwork, a tapestry to hang in the school library (the most central building at the time), was a representation of Peter coming to Christ, walking on the Sea of Galilee. Terry's vision was that this first commissioned piece of religious art would be a clear statement of Peter's faith at its strongest and its weakest. He hoped that students, would make a connection to their own times of strength and weakness, to see that Christ would be there for them 'through it all'.

In listening to the memories of the pioneer staff, it becomes clear that Terry Feely's strategy in creating a school spirituality was based on what is known in Catholic circles as 'pastoral' or 'grassroots' theology. The essence of this is the *see, judge, act, review model* whereby the leader 'learns theology, by doing it'.[9] The principal led key members of the leadership team – the deputy principal, the religious education, curriculum and year level leaders, and indeed the student and parent bodies – via this quintessentially

---

[7] Mr Feely served for many years as Chair of the Diocesan Secondary principals Association and in 2006 personally prepared and led a pilgrimage of Catholic educators from the diocese entitled *In the Steps of St Columba*, which connected participants to spiritual roots in Ireland and Scotland of many Catholics in the Sale Diocese.
[8] Jim and Therese D'Orsa, *Explorers Guides and Meaning-makers: Mission Theology for Catholic Educators* (Melbourne: Vaughan Publishing, 2010), 7.
[9] ibid, 237ff.

'grassroots' theology. It became both effective and instructive, because according to these pioneer staff, it was easily understood as responsive to the needs of the community and was readily interpreted in spiritual terms.

The *School Crest Competition* was emblematic of this style of theology. The principal launched the project by speaking to the whole student, parent and staff community 'talking up' the story of Peter's faith journey and highlighting the possible symbols which could reflect the essence of a Petrine spirituality. As it turned out, the selection committee chose the crest that Terry himself had entered, unaware that it was his. However, Mr Feely never 'let on' that the winning entry was his. What mattered for him was that the community had engaged in the process, and were therefore involved in efforts to make sense of what the *Petrine* faith experience was all about. Peter Houlahan believes a key feature of this type of leadership was its persistent, intentional and ongoing effort to '*engender widespread thought and engagement with the spirituality of St Peter*'. This was literally the 'pick and shovel' work of building a spirituality.

Julie-Ann Williams, the first Religious Education Leader of the College, recalls the importance placed on the *relational* nature of the school community that was being built. Peter's journey with Christ was nothing if not relational. Christ knew his disciple well and did not give up on him when the going got tough. In those early days, the principal and those in leadership positions intentionally built relationships with the families and the staff. She recalls:

> ...*the spirituality of this campus was born on the values of hard work, a dogged determination to build a flexibility and a sense that 'we are all in this together'. Those early students were...seen as and repeatedly told they were ...all contributors to the school's spirituality. When they graduated... they knew they had experienced and were proud of, their unique, shared educational journey.*

The Year 12 retreats were critical for inculcating the spiritual value of *servant leadership* among the students. The principal insisted the retreats be an experience of relationship between staff and students and staff and school leaders. His view was that by being 'in genuine relationship' with one another on these retreats, students and staff would want to become servant leaders. As Terry explained to the Year 12 group, Christ had already proven this through his relationship with the apostles. For Christ, and thus for Terry, *relationships come first*. the servant leadership of the staff and students would then follow, and, according to Julie-Ann, it did. She notes:

> We (the pioneer staff and retreat leaders) espoused that all of the Year 12's were leaders in the St Peter's community. The net was cast on all of them! By the end of the Leadership Retreat, all of the students had come to a new understanding of the central figure of the Cross and what it meant to them as individuals and the significance of the cross and the net, to this Catholic community.

In order to enhance staff spirituality, and in particular their understanding of the Petrine way of carrying out Christ's mission, the principal provided staff with opportunities to experience the Petrine story first-hand. 'Terry had a way of tapping someone on the shoulder and offering them the chance to participate in a unique program, supported by the College.'

In this way, Julie-Ann went to the Holy Land. The principal asked her in return to bring back something that could be placed in the College as a permanent reminder of the origins of Peter and as a symbol of what Peter represented spiritually. She returned with a beautiful prayer shawl. However, she also did something that was a little more impulsive. While standing on the shores of the Sea of Galilee near St Peter's Monastery, she scooped up some rocks from the shore. On her return, she sheepishly emptied her 'stolen' symbols onto Terry's desk. He loved them and there is now a small shrine in the prayer room to St Peter, featuring actual Galilean rocks, for the students and staff to connect with.

Other staff were similarly 'tapped on the shoulder'. Several staff members, similarly charged, went to Rome, following *'in the footsteps of St Peter'*. They returned with framed images of Michaelangelo's *Pietà*, tapestries of St Peter's and original Jewish Prayer Scrolls from Jerusalem. These all adorn various areas of the school, with explanatory inscriptions.

The beautiful and original chapel is another significant element of Terry's intentional practice of *'grassroots theology'*. When the tiny church of St Peter at Tooradin, not far from Cranbourne in the Diocese of Sale, came up for sale, Terry and the parish priest, with the full support of the College Board, bought the building and had it moved onsite at Cranbourne. Terry's vision was that its renovation be a *student-staff theological project*. The aim was to completely renovate and refurbish the structure to its original mission-church glory. The original stained glass window of Peter receiving the keys to the kingdom was to be its centrepiece. 'The Chapel' is a tangible link with the past Catholic narrative of the diocese and a present-day symbol of our Catholic practice. Perhaps, just as importantly to all those who laboured restoring it as a place of worship at St Peter's College, it will remain a life-long memory and spiritual lesson.

The first deputy principal at St Peter's, Regina Rowan, remembers Terry's own spirituality being influenced by key beliefs that spirituality in a

Catholic Regional College should be practical… but it should also be based on a solid foundation of knowledge, rigorous debate and reflection leading to conviction. The school community needed to recognise that the power of God works through human beings and so they are often called on to mediate the redemptive healing power of God. Finally, Catholic education demands of all teachers that they love young people and respect their right to a transformative education.

In consequence, Terry purposefully employed people in the Religious Education area who had a passion for some aspect of the Church's mission, and they were then given 'permission' to develop that passion. These particular 'passions' were often given spiritual expression at a grassroots level in social justice initiatives such as working on the city soup vans, St Vincent de Paul fundraisers, Red Cross drives and so on. She believes Terry showed good judgement in making appointments – as each new REC came into the school, it seemed 'ready for that person', and so the next incarnation of the spirituality of the school unfolded. Equally, the role of the first canonical administrator, Fr Herman Hengel, cannot be underestimated. Regina recalls that:

> *Without (Fr Hengel's) complete commitment to the school and his unwavering partnership with the principal, much would not have developed. His presence in the school grounds, at school functions, his preparedness to come to us for anything we wanted of him as our pastor, was also crucial in establishing our difference from other local schools and providing us with a very concrete and real presence of the Church on earth.*

The early leaders of the College indicated unanimously that the emerging school spirituality reflected the principal's absolute belief in 'casting the net wide' as far as staff were concerned. The school was staffed with a mind to diversity and talent. It had to be a community that could animate the students with a message of inclusion and redemption. The community would thus be staffed with a range of talented people who could variously respond to the needs of the students.

GOD'S CREATIVE SPIRIT IS REFLECTED IN CREATIVE ACTION

> *Now, there are varieties of gifts, but the same Spirit; and there are varieties of services, but the same Lord* (1 Cor 12: 4–6).

To look at how best to meets the needs of students, the principal asked the question: What unique gifts do people bring to this community and how can we put them to use? He did this with the clear intent that the faculty not only showcase and develop the gifts of the students, but that this should be seen as a spiritual task, part of the Catholic mission to educate the whole person. He asked staff to find/develop/invent creative vehicles that responded to the educational and spiritual needs of the students and which would showcase their unique potential. As a result, St Peter's College *did not* choose creative vessels and try to fit the child within them, but rather consciously started with the specific gifts of the students and created opportunities from there.

As a direct consequence, Terry asked his first Head of Creative Arts to create completely new works for school musicals that *highlighted the Catholic message and the spirituality of those involved in these creative enterprises.* Students, staff and parents would not only be part of the creation and production of musicals and plays, but importantly the '*Production*' would leave them and their audiences with spiritual messages that would stay with them for life. With later appointments of staff to positions in the Department of Visual Arts, the establishment of the *Principal's Prize for Art* not only recognised artistic excellence for its own sake, but also was in sympathy with the shared belief among staff that 'art elevates people in a spiritual sense'.

Each of these staff members was taken into the principal's confidence and vividly remembers being *individually commissioned* to interpret this vision, within their respective creative fields. From the words of the school motto 'Be Not Afraid' came the title of the original school musical production *For Art's Sake*, which had as its underlying theme: '*Be Yourself... believe in who you can be.*'

Messages of hope and faith rang out on stages and were illustrated on canvasses for many years to come. The Creative Arts at St Peter's College have left a tangible visual, written and musical record of the school's values and spiritual ethos, on paper, on canvas and in original musical recordings. None of this was *ever unintentional*. In considering all of the above, the early College leaders were fully engaged in 'leading for mission' and had a clear sense of the spiritual values they wished to make clear and alive at St Peter's.

TO THE PRESENT DAY

'And I tell you, you are Peter and on this rock, I will build my church'
(Matt 16:18)

Both the cultural and social contexts of St Peter's College have changed, indeed they has been transformed in recent years. We have grown from a College representing four or five nationalities to one whose students are, at the time of writing, now drawn from 37 ethnic backgrounds. However, *spiritual continuity and growth* continues. In taking up the challenge of his new role, the current principal, Tim Hogan, readily acknowledges that 'without a religious congregation supporting and guiding you, making spiritual traditions stick, can be difficult. However, it can clearly be done.'

The Sale Diocese's *School Renewal* process has proved an important resource in allowing the College to focus on its unique story and develop strategies that allow us to evoke the story and example of St Peter. A by-product of the process is the beautiful sculpture of St Peter by Bart Sanciolo (2012) that now stands at the College entrance. The design process, which involved people from the Creative Arts and Religious Education faculties, began with the *school tradition in mind*. In commissioning the project, the principal and the school board asked the group to bring together their ideas on how the symbolism and imagery of the sculpture could make the tradition of the school real to the present generation of students. In particular, they were asked to find ways to show the nexus between the faith journey of our patron Peter and the spiritual journey of the College itself. These things were seen as critical in creating a permanent reminder of who we are as a faith community at St Peter's.

The decision in 2011 to introduce an *annual spiritual theme into College life* represents another conscious decision by the College leadership team to relate the mission, ethos and community consciousness to Peter. The three *Petrine*-related themes developed to date have been: '*Command Us To Come, Lord*' – 2012; '*You Are Peter…*' – 2013; and '*How Many Times Must I Forgive?*' – 2014. These are only some examples of how we try year on year to stoke the 'fire' implicit in our charism.

CONSCIOUSLY SUSTAINING AND DEVELOPING OUR SCHOOL SPIRITUALITY

As with any successful organisation, history teaches us that there must be a balance of continuity and change – these are the elements that help human communities remain both secure and vital.

We have been blessed that the College has been able to both lay down some key traditions and yet is able to be consciously aware of the need to be flexible so that the spiritual and educational needs of our students are being met in challenging times. In the words of James Roberts, Deputy principal and Head of the new Cranbourne East Campus:

> *I think a key feature of what we do here at St Peter's is our constant evaluation of what we do and why we do it … Being prepared to alter/ change to suit the needs of the community as St Peter himself did … I think this is one of the great hidden legacies of Terry Feely.*

Tim Hogan, formerly a Deputy at the College in its formative stage, has been part of the history of the College for more than half its life. He well understands its past. A key goal of his principalship is 'making Catholic traditions contextually relevant'.

Tim believes that while it is encouraging to see signs of our spirituality adjusting to the evolving needs of the community, he believes the principal is also a key conduit for transmitting special spiritual traditions embedded by the first principal. Hence he continues to 'walk the students in the footsteps of Peter', by continuing the *principal's Chapel Tour* with each Year 7 class. He takes the students on a walk and talk – he explains the school chapel's link to St Peter, the stained glass window above the altar and the symbols of the keys and the motto and finally the links to their Year 7 curriculum where the story of Peter is studied and told. This is always conducted just before Easter – where Peter's faith wavered and was forgiven by Christ.

OUR LIVED EXPERIENCE THUS FAR ... AND OUR FUTURE CHALLENGES

'You know, Peter was so human ... Anita.' (Terry Feely, 1998).

What is a Catholic school named *St Peter's*, if it is not a place where humanity meets and recognises Jesus as God? As part of the *Enhancing Catholic School Identity Project* completed in 2013 at our school, some challenging questions have emerged given our relatively rapid transition to a pluralist community, i.e., one which is noted as having a wide range of ethnic, cultural and religious diversity amongst its student, parent and staff body. Some of these questions will require a structured dialogue around bringing our culture, human experience and our religious tradition into synchronicity. Again, however, this is at the core of the 'grassroots theology' that has characterised the leadership of our school from its beginnings right through until today. Some of the key questions going forward for our spiritual community include:

- While the study shows that we have active support for our Catholic Identity and Spirituality from the adults, how do we continue to promote an 'engaged awareness' among the students?
- In a historical era and cultural milieu in which 'growing closer to God' is a declining notion of importance in Australia, how do we, as a Catholic Regional College, make it of real importance in the lives of our students?

- If prayer is an essential way of encounter with God in our tradition, how can we, at St Peter's, promote individual and communal prayer lives which will help enhance the spirituality of the school and the individuals within it?

Our story to date contains some important lessons that can help us address these challenges:
- Intentional, faith-driven and focused leadership *can animate* the spirituality of the College and energise key individuals, teams and generations of students to work together to build meaningful and lasting spiritual traditions;
- School leaders, and particularly the principal, in such a diverse Regional College need to be consciously aware that *spirituality cannot and should not be confined to the Religious Education Department* or even the obvious religious rituals and symbols around the school. Catholic spirituality seeks out and draws upon the gifts people bring to a variety of areas and, only when this is recognised, can it be transformational for the individual and the community;
- Students and staff must find the *school spirituality accessible on a number of levels* and by a number of means: visual, symbolic, ritualistic, story, song and through structural forms both natural and man-made;
- We, as a Regional College community, have found that if a College bases its spirituality around a real and relevant model of spirituality such as St Peter, the spirituality of that community has the capacity to reach across the generations and cultures, and thus can be successfully continued and maintained. Peter's special charism has given animus to our community because, as our members attest, it speaks to and connects with commonly shared human experience when it comes to the spiritual faith journey: *being called, being unsure, being challenged and being forgiven by a loving God*;
- School communities inevitably experience changes in leadership and changes in the cultural and religious diversity of their communities in Australia. The Regional College must respond to its immediate community's needs. However, as a *Catholic* Regional College, it must embed its practices in spiritual traditions which are authentic to Christ's mission, so that students know that they are part of an authentic experience which, if they allow it, will transform them and anchor them in Christ.

Every faith community has a charism. However not all realise that this is the case and, failing this, the fire of charism can die. To flame up and continue to inspire, charism needs both *firelighters* and *stokers*. St Peter's was fortunate in having a leader who interpreted his role as that of firelighter and who had the capacity to pass the flame onto others who, as I hope this chapter shows, are intent on keeping the fire not only alive, but burning bright. We hope our experience, recounted above, may prove helpful to other similar colleges and schools.

17

EPILOGUE – REBUILDING SPIRITUAL CAPITAL

Jim and Therese D'Orsa

Most of the preceding chapters tell a story of how a range of school communities currently endeavor to build the spiritual capital needed to preserve their Catholic identity and thus the authenticity of their mission. The narratives reflect the fact that Catholic education in this country has moved through four discernable periods. It says something about the speed of change in recent decades that three of the four periods have been or are being experienced within the lifetime of contributors to this volume. The distinctiveness of the periods in terms of context, challenges and sources of spiritual capital is important. It is to the last of these periods, and to the importance of creating and sustaining the spiritual capital on which communities draw to enliven and authenticate their efforts in mission, that this volume has been addressed.

The first period of Catholic education was from about 1820 to 1870.[1] It was an enterprise built on the spiritual capital of pioneering priests who employed lay teachers to establish small schools to bring religious instruction and basic general education to children of Catholic families.[2] A collection of small, scattered schools for Catholics grew up throughout the colonies. Often these schools were short-lived, dependent as they were on the commitment of the priests, unreliable funding sources, and the availability of suitable teachers.

The second period was from about 1870 to 1970. During this period, Catholic education was established on the spiritual capital built up by religious congregations, both those which were 'home-grown' and those from overseas. These congregations invested heavily in the spiritual

---

1 The dates here are approximate. They vary slightly from state to state reflecting the political atmosphere of the times in the different states.
2 Even in this first period these Catholic schools included children whose parents were not Catholic.

formation of their members. They also brought stability and organisation to Catholic education, even as governments withdrew public funds from Catholic schools. Their dedicated work in this second period came to define Catholic education as it was known to generations of Australians.

From 1970 to approximately 2000, religious began to hand over responsibility, firstly for teaching and later for management and leadership, to lay people. During this period some of the lay people accessed spiritual formation and engaged in religious studies, as a result both of their own initiative, and of opportunities created by dioceses and congregations. However, the period generally saw an undue dependence on the diminishing capital of the religious congregations and of former religious. The net result was a serious diminishment in the spiritual capital needed to ensure the long-term future of Catholic education. Catholic Education Offices certainly played an excellent role in putting management and leadership frameworks in place during this time, and their work enabled Catholic education to survive. However, it is now obvious that attention to and resourcing of the development of spiritual capital by both dioceses and congregations was seriously below the level of what was needed to create a viable or sustainable future for authentic Catholic education.

From approximately the year 2000 onwards, Catholic educational leaders came to see more clearly that, without massive investment of time and resources into the spiritual development of personnel, both teachers and leaders, Catholic education would lose its Catholic identity, and as this happened its mission would be compromised. The situation has not been helped by the near collapse of the parish-based Catholicism experienced in the second era of Catholic education, and a series of leadership crises besetting the Church, which serve to highlight the need to rebuild spiritual capital. It is the internal Church context, as well as the speed of the impact of globalisation and pluralisation in the broader context, which define this, the fourth, period of Catholic education. The present is a time of veritably *refounding school and parish communities*, as a number of writers have named the challenge.

An analysis of the context in which Catholic schools presently function is vital to this work of refounding, and has been made at some length in other volumes of this series.[3] The point of this volume is to acknowledge the efforts of the committed leaders from within Catholic education who are grasping the formational challenges central to this task.

---

3   E.g. Jim and Therese D'Orsa, *Explorers, Guides and Meaning-makers: Mission Theology for Catholic Educators* (Mulgrave: Garratt Publishing, 2009), and Jim and Therese D'Orsa, *Catholic Curriculum: A Mission to the Heart of Young People* (Mulgrave: Garratt Publishing, 2012).

The dominant wisdom of the contemporary context, impacted upon by powerful postmodern philosophies, is that the only human experience worth having is that of the ever-changing present. For young people, it may seem that life has to be reinvented in every era. The experience of being very much alone, despite instantaneous connection with the rest of the world, is one which faces not only young people but also their parents and teachers. This stands in contrast to seeing oneself as part of a community whose identity is anchored by a valued narrative.

The initiatives described here outline at a point in time the scope of certain significant endeavors to rebuild the spiritual capital needed to sustain identifiably Catholic school communities. These efforts build, one way or another, on the spiritual traditions that are a vital element in our Catholic heritage. They do this by looking back, since they depend on a narrative based in a particular human experience of living the Gospel. This looking back is not self-indulgent nostalgia. It reveals how those who have preceded us have risen to the challenges presented as circumstances have changed, particularly for those at the margins. At the same time, the initiatives take us forward to an unfolding future, fraught with uncertainty. In a sense they chart what God's Spirit has done and point to the possibilities of what God's Spirit can accomplish.

All contributions highlight the fact that *God's Spirit is found in community, since it is the faith community that is the holder of spiritual capital*. Building a sense of community, one that enables people to come together to share a common purpose and take ownership of a common story, is now a vital task in Catholic school leadership at all levels. It is of the nature of narrative that it must be reinterpreted in new circumstances. In this sense, narrative is more than story. It is interpreted story. *The issue is whether this interpretation is to be adequate or not.* Without appropriate efforts in terms of understanding and formation, generous efforts will falter. The accounts in the previous chapters highlight the fact that planning and executing a formation program is hard work requiring persistence, trialing of new approaches, networking, and learning from mistakes. There is no guidebook at present.

In the final analysis, it is only through participating in the life of a community that teachers find 'a story to enter, a language to speak, a group to belong to, a way to pray, a work to undertake, and a face of God to see' (i.e., that they come to personally experience God's action within their human history). This message about the vital role of community is counter-cultural in our contemporary world.

The Catholic school today remains one of the few settings in which students can encounter the experience of community, and so it is a base on which a future Church committed to God's mission can be built.

This book charts some of the ways in which this is already occurring – these are important signs of new life. It does not pretend to offer a comprehensive account, as the fact that it has actually taken life has depended on the generous efforts of a 'coalition of the willing and available'. Its specific focus is how spiritual capital is being rebuilt within some systems, providing important lessons for all systems.

Furthermore, the initiatives described here do not claim to cover all that is necessary if the refounding process is to bear fruit. Obviously, for example, deep consideration of the curriculum and pedagogy of Catholic schools must complement that of formation for mission. Catholic education involves what the late Pope John Paul II called 'an ecology of human growth' that holds in tension, pedagogy, curriculum and the experience of community.[4] What is clear from all the accounts collected here is the role that being part of a community has played and is playing in preserving the Catholic identity of Catholic schools. In some cases this involves the creating of new forms of community, as religious hand on responsibility to lay people for schools they once controlled.

The accounts here also highlight how spiritual capital was developed in the different periods of Catholic education. It happened as charismatic leaders made the connections needed to open up new ways of living the Gospel. In many cases these have now been transformed to meet new challenges. As such, the initiatives featured here are substantial and impressive, and in themselves constitute a gift to contemporary Catholic education. They remind us that God's Spirit continues in every age to create life anew, moving among human communities in unexpected and very powerful ways.

---

4 Pope John Paul II, Address to the President of the Republic of Malawi, 14 December 2000.

INDEX

agapic love 196
Agathon, Brother 155
Aquinas, Saint Thomas 111
Arbuckle, Gerald 90
Athanasius, Saint 14
Augustine, Saint 14
Augustinians of the Assumption 62
Australian Catholic Bishops conference 199
Australian Values Project 215

baptism 19, 43, 57
Basil, Saint 14
Benedictines 68, 149
Bernard, Saint 17
Bevans, S. 74
bishops, teaching 14
Book of Glory 50, 52–3
Book of Signs 50–2, 57
Bosco, Don (Saint John) 63, 95–105
Bourdieu, P. 117
Broken Bay diocese 6
  lighthouse logo 208
  mission and discipleship 217–18
  Mission Statement 209, 210
  vision for 178, 207, 208–10
Broken Bay Institute 11, 210, 214
brotherhoods
  charism of 156
  concept of 149–50
  'missionary outreach' 155–6
  'philosophes' attack 154–5
  shared with laity 158, 159–60
  syllabary 152
  teacher training 155
  teaching 26–7, 149, 150–3, 156, 157
Bruner, Jerome 200
Buber, Martin 165–6

care for the earth 58
Carroll, Archbishop James 25
Carter, Anita 178, 219, 221–35
Cassian, Saint John 194–5

catechesis 199–200
Catechism of the Catholic Church 17, 202–3
cathedral schools 14
'Catholic character' 212
Catholic Church
  academic and political elite 25
  Anglo-Irish model 26
  'being a Catholic' 25, 26, 30, 211
  Catechism of the Catholic Church 17, 202–3
  leadership criticised 23
  Mass attendance 27
  migrant influences 26–7
  People of God 90
  a political force 27
  Vatican II changes 28–31
  worldview 212
'Catholic discipleship' 211
Catholic Education Office, Lismore 30, 31, 111, 175, 178–9, 184, 185, 187, 188, 238
Catholic Schools Office 184, 208, 213–17
Catholic Social Thought 118
Catholic Young Men's Society 26
Champagnat, Saint Marcellin 6, 136, 138, 139, 156
charism 2
  Australian congregations 63
  of brotherhood 156–7
  concept 4, 6, 9, 29, 32, 62, 63, 68, 84–5, 89, 111–13, 156, 161, 165–6, 221, 223
  in education 31, 32, 77, 112–14
  of founders 4, 29, 63, 111–12, 156, 159
  international movements 63
  of Mary MacKillop 86–90
  promoting 62, 116
  sharing 159–60
  in today's context 4, 87–8
'charismatic circularity' 77
Charter for Catholic Schools in the

Edmund Rice Tradition 125–8
Chautard OCSO, Dom Jean-Baptiste 16–17
Chavez SDB, Fr Pascual 95–8, 105
children
    meditation 197–201, 203
    see also schools
Children of Mary 26
Chittister, Joan 85
Christian Brothers
    advocacy 131
    characteristics 27, 125–6
    culture 126
    Identity Leaders 129
    national network 130
    Oceania Province 128
    schools 63, 125, 155
    School Renewal 129
    spiritual foundations 124
    see also Edmund Rice Education Australia
Christian heritage 2
Christian life 15–17, 25–6, 63
    interior and exterior 19, 20, 26
Christian meditation 193–9
church, definition of 90
Clement of Alexandria, Saint 14
Congregation for Catholic Education 77
congregational identity 62–3
contemplative prayer 202
conversatio 68
cultural capital 117
cultures, evangelising 58

de Bonifacio, Juan 168
de La Chalotais 154
de La Salle, Saint Jean-Baptiste, 149, 150, 152, 153, 155, 156–7, 160
De La Salle Brothers 63, 160
    'brotherhood' 149–50, 151, 156–8, 161
    critics of 154–5
    lay staff 157
    missionary outreach 155–6
    'Reflection' 153
    residential programs 158–9
    schools 27, 150–3, 155
    teacher training 155
    Vita Consecrata 158
    women teachers 158
deacons 13
Decree on the Adaptation and Renewal of Religious Life 156

Desert Fathers 14, 149, 195, 196
de-traditionalisation 24
dialogue 54, 55
discipleship 2, 6, 44, 178, 211
Dodds, Sister Elizabeth 84
Dominicans 14
Dulles, Cardinal Avery 209

Eckhart, Meister 195–6
Edmund Rice Education Australia (EREA)
    associate schools 125
    Charter 125–7, 129
    established 123–4
    Flexible Learning Centres 122, 125
    governance 125–6, 132
    mission 121, 123, 124, 131–2
    national network 130
    schools 121, 122–32
    staff 126
    Touchstones 126–31
Edmund Rice International 131
education
    Australian blueprint 69
    and Catholic identity 23–4, 25, 69–70, 71, 74, 240
    charism 31, 32, 77, 112–14
    'Christian values' 31–3
    contemporary context 238–9
    decline of religious in 18, 71
    experience of community 239–40
    and faith 14–16
    formation programs 75–6
    inner life for teachers 178
    lay teachers 18–19
    and Masonic influences 25
    and migrants 27
    mission in 39
    periods of 237–8
    purpose 210–12
    Shaping Our Future 212–13
    and spiritual development 238
    and Vatican II 27, 28, 30–1, 75–6
    see also religious congregations; schools
Enhancing Catholic School Identity Project 233
EREA Youth+ 122
Eucharist 57
evangelisation 42, 53–5, 199

Index

faith maps 63
Feely, Terry
  background 222
  'grassroots theology' 227–8, 229, 233
  principal, Saint Peter's 178–9, 223–33
  social justice initiatives 230
Flexible Learning Centres 125
Francis, Pope 33, 169, 217, 218
Francis de Sales, Saint 100
Franciscans 62–3
Freeman OSB, Father Laurence 195, 197, 200, 201, 202

Gallagher, Monsignor 225
General Directory of Catechesis 199
Geoghegan, Bishop 81–2
Gerson, John 15
Gibbons, Mother Scholastica 67
Good Samaritan Education 72–6
Good Samaritan parable 67–8
Gospel of Saint John 35, 39–59
Graham, John 178, 181, 183–90
Gregory of Nazianzus, Saint 14
Gregory of Nyssa, Saint 14
Griffiths, Father Bede 196
Groome, Thomas 223

Hengel, Father Herman 225, 230
Hogan, Tim 232, 233
Holy Spirit 58–9 see also Paraclete
Houlahan, Peter 225, 228

Ignatian charism and mission 32, 165–7
Ignatian education 166, 169–73
Ignatius of Antioch, Saint 201
Ignatius of Loyola, Saint
  Spiritual Exercises 168, 169, 171, 173, 185–6, 188–90
Ignatian Pedagogy 173
Imitation of Christ 17
inner life 15–20
  case studies 177–238
inter-religious dialogue 58

Jesuit education 27, 63
  Australian Province 175
  Coordinators 174
  curriculum 169
  Jesuit Partner Schools 175
  Ratio Studiorum 168–9
  schools 167–8, 175

spiritual tradition 6, 167–73, 178–90
The Characteristics of Jesuit Education 169–73
The Ignatian Ethos and Identity Review 173–4
John the Baptist, Saint 46
John of the Cross, Saint 195–6
John Paul II, Pope 49, 240
Josephite Sisters schools 27, 61, 82–3

Keating, Thomas 196
Kingdom of God 49–50
'Kingdom spaces' 2, 4
Kolvenbach SJ, Father 167

Lallemont SJ, Fr Louis 17
Launch into the Deep – Policy Framework for Religious and Spiritual Formation in the Apostolate of Catholic Education 188
lay movements 19–20, 62–3
leadership 33, 61, 178
lectio divina 11, 20
Legion of Mary 26
Lickona, Thomas 212
Lismore Parish schools 6, 183, 188–90
  Spirituality Days 184–5, 186–7
logos 50
Loyola Institute 188
Luke, Saint 40, 44, 45, 48, 50, 176
  Gospel of 40, 45, 50

McAuley, Catherine 109–18
McGuigan, Father 225
MacKillop, Saint Mary 6, 61, 82
  charism 86–9, 90
Main OSB, Father John 6, 194, 195, 196, 197–8, 202
Mannix, Archbishop Daniel 25
mantras 195
Maréchal AA, Fr Claude 9, 62, 68, 166
Marist Brothers 63
  alignment with mission 136–7
  canonical legitimacy 141
  Constitution of the Marist Brothers 136
  current directions 139–41
  and education 27, 138–9, 140
  'Marian way' 138
  spiritual foundations 138–9

243

strategic priorities 146
Marist College, Bendigo (case study) 141–6
Mark, Saint 42, 44, 45, 48, 50
   Gospel of 40, 50
Matthew, Saint 42
   Gospel of 39–40, 44, 45, 50
Mary MacKillop College 83
Mass
   attendances 26
   Vatican II changes 28
meditation 193
   for children 197, 198–9, 200–1, 203
   origin and practice 194–7
   silent 202–3
   teaching 197–9
   World Community for 197
Merton, Thomas 196
ministry with passion 176
'miracles' 51–2
mission
   commitment to 44
   in education 39
   focus Post-Vatican II 74
   global context 42–3
   Gospel of Saint John 39–59
   John Paul II on 49
   meaning 41–2, 44, 90
   modes of 54, 56–9
   post-resurrection 39–59
mission statement 41
mission-in-context 216
missional leaders 39, 47, 48
missionary discipleship 217–18
Models of the Church 209
Modern Devotion movement 15
monasteries 14, 19
monastic tradition 14
Mt Sion School 123
Murphy, Mark 226
Murphy, Bishop Patrick 81, 207

Newman, Cardinal 114
Nicodemus, Saint 50, 51, 57
Nicolás SJ, Adolfo 167, 173

O'Hea, Eileen 194
O'Leary, Daniel 200
O'Malley SJ, John 168
Origen 14
Ormerod, Neil 159–60

Paraclete, role of 35
participatory knowing 196–7
Passover 57
Paul, Saint 16, 17, 111, 195
Paul III, Pope 167–8
peace 58
Pell, Cardinal George 72
Peter, Saint 222–3, 228
philosophes 154
pluralism 42
Polding OSB, John Bede 67, 69, 72
Porter, Adrian 175–6
post-resurrection commissions 39–59
prayer
   contemplative 193–4
   experiencing 39–59
   silence in 202
Prendergast, Ned 224
Preventive System 99
proclamation 54
public school system 69

Ratio Studiorum 168–9
reconciliation 57
'refounding' Catholic institutions 118
religious congregations 3–4
   and education 15, 28–9, 62
resurrection 48, 58
Rice, Blessed Edmund 121, 122–4, 125, 126, 127, 130, 156
Roberts, James 232–3
Roche, Sister Maurice 83–4
Rolheiser, Father Ron 166
Rowan, Regina 229–30

Saint Ignatius College, Geelong 175
Saint Peter's Catholic Regional College, Cranbourne
   chapel 229
   charism 224, 226
   creative arts 231
   crest 226, 228
   ethnic backgrounds 232
   Feely's leadership 6, 178–9, 222–33
   the future 233–4
   'grassroots' theology 227–8, 229, 233
   Hogan as principal 232, 233
   lessons from the past 234–5
   meeting students' needs 230–1
   mission 226–7
   name 225
   retreats 228–9

spirituality 6, 178–9, 222, 223–30, 232
symbols/traditions 226, 227, 228, 232
vision, motto, song 225–6, 231, 233–5
visual arts 231
Salesians of Don Bosco 63
  charism 96, 97–8, 101–2
  school charter 27, 102–4, 105
Samaritans in the Bible 46, 58
Sanders, Susan 112
Sardello, Robert 202–3
Schneiders, Sandra 41
School of Alexandria 14
schools
  cathedral 14
  co-educational 157
  constraints 32
  creating life chances 25
  earliest 14–15
  'educational communities' 31
  foundation 69–70
  government funding 27–8
  impact of migrants 27
  purpose 210–112
  staffing 27
schools, faith and ethos 18
  'apostolic effectiveness' 31
  attracting vocations 71
  'Catholic identity' 23–4
  charism 32
  'inner life' case studies 177–238
  meditation 194–9
  mission 2, 4–5, 30, 31, 32, 33, 157–61
  name and symbols 32
  Religious Education 30
  and spiritual journey 23–4, 179
  spiritual traditions 2, 3, 4–5, 63, 74
  spirituality decline 71
Schools of Spirituality 185
secularisation 24
secularism 24
servant leadership 224, 228
Shaping Our Future 212–13
Sheil, Bishop 82
silence 194, 202–3
Simonds, Archbishop Justin 224
Sisters of the Good Samaritan
  charism 63, 68–9
  and education 27, 65, 70–7
  foundation 67, 72
  governance review 72

identity and mission 69, 74
lay teachers 70
Mission Teams 76
spiritual tradition 67, 75, 77, 118
vision statement 68
world network 69, 70
Sisters of Mercy 63
  in Australia 110–11
  charism 112, 113–16
  founded 109–10
  House of Mercy refuge 110
  schools 27, 109, 110–11, 113–16
  spiritual capital 116–18
  spread 110, 113–14
Sisters of Saint Joseph 63
  lay teachers 84
  schools 27, 61, 82–3
  spiritual tradition 81–91
social justice 57–8
South Australia
  missions 81–2
  Sisters of Saint Joseph 61, 63, 81–91
Special Religious Education Curriculum 214
spiritual capital 116–18
Spiritual Exercises 169, 171, 173, 185–6, 188, 190
spiritual journey 33, 178
spiritual traditions 1–2, 63, 64
spirituality 2, 89
  without religion 33
Spirituality Days 184–5, 186–7
student meditation 193–9
Suenens, Cardinal 84

teachers 200
  bishops 14
  brotherhoods 26–7, 149, 150–3, 156, 157
  lay 18–19
  retreats 185–6, 187–8
  sense of vocation 183, 187
  and Spiritual Exercises 185–6, 187, 188, 190
Tenison-Woods, Father Julian 82
Teresa of Avila, Saint 195–6
The Characteristics of Jesuit Education 169–73
The Cloud of Unknowing 196
The Conduct of Christian Schools 150–1, 155
The Ignatian Ethos and Identity Review 173–4

The Twelve Virtues of a Good Master 155
theological reflection for mission 48–9
Townsville diocese 193–4, 197–8
trade unions 30
tradition 85
   message from 13–20
   nature of 61–3
Treacy, Brother Ambrose 123–4

universities 14, 114

Vatican II 19–20, 27, 28, 29–31, 33, 71, 75–6, 84, 90, 112, 125, 156, 196, 207

Walker, Bishop Emeritus David 11, 25–6, 27, 33, 178, 206–13, 215, 217–18
Wiesel, Elie 167
Williams, Julie-Ann 228–9
Williams, Rowan, Archbishop of Canterbury 203
'works of charity' 29
World Community for Christian Meditation 197

Xavier College, Melbourne 175

Yamaguchi, Bishop of Nagasaki 70
Young Christian Students 26
Young Christian Workers 26

CPSIA information can be obtained
at www.ICGtesting.com
Printed in the USA
LVOW13s1522270218
568050LV00028B/1227/P